LUFTWAFFE OVER
AMERICA

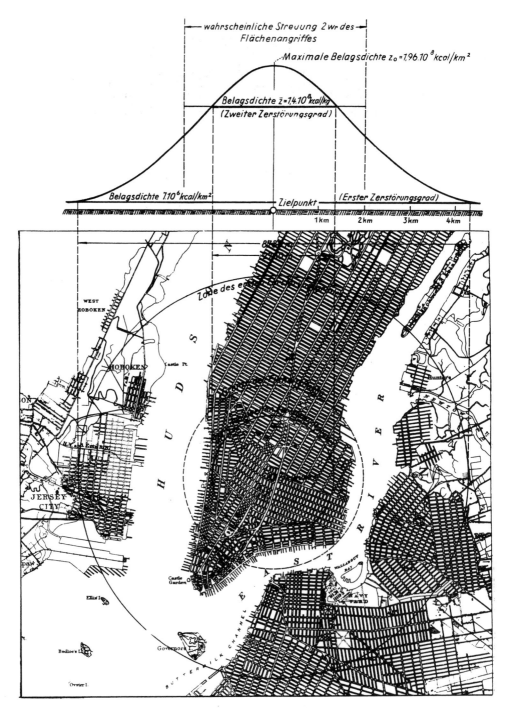

Calculated effect of a bomb dropped on the centre of Manhattan from a
rocket bomber in the stratosphere.

LUFTWAFFE OVER
AMERICA

The Secret Plans to Bomb
the United States in World War II

Manfred Griehl

Translated by Geoffrey Brooks

FRONTLINE BOOKS

Luftwaffe over America
The Secret Plans to Bomb the United States in World War II

A Greenhill Book
First published in 2004 by Greenhill Books, Lionel Leventhal Limited
www.greenhillbooks.com

This paperback edition published in 2016 by

Frontline Books
an imprint of Pen & Sword Books Ltd,
47 Church Street, Barnsley, S. Yorkshire, S70 2AS
For more information on our books, please visit
www.frontline-books.com,
email info@frontline-books.com
or write to us at the above address.

Text © Manfred Griehl, 2004
Translation © Lionel Leventhal, 2004

ISBN: 978-1-84832-842-6

CIP data records for this title are available from the British Library

Typeset and edited by Donald Sommerville

Printed and bound by CPI Group (UK) Ltd, Croydon, CR0 4YY

Contents

Photographs

Photographs

Diagrams

Diagrams

'The most intriguing point for the historian is that where history and legend meet'
Goethe

Prussian Dreams of Conquering the New World

From a quite early stage there existed, at least hypothetically, a threat to the United States of America:

> The German High Seas Fleet, followed by an armada of colliers and troop transports, each tightly packed with tens of thousands of grenadiers, heads for the eastern shores of the USA. Perfectly trained, a perfect example of European military planning, the Kaiser had despatched his Fleet against the motherland of democracy.
>
> The US Navy put to sea but suffered a devastating defeat off Norfolk, Virginia. Admiral George Dewey lacked the ability of his German counterpart, von Tirpitz, and so lost the battle.
>
> German occupation troops came ashore at Cape Cod and set off for Boston while battleships and battle-cruisers entered New York's Lower Bay, pounded the coastal batteries into submission and bombarded Manhattan. Endless salvoes from the battle fleet's 16-inch guns turned New York into a city of burning ruins. The population fled in panic.
>
> Now the USA was forced to negotiate with the German *Reich*...

During the winter of 1897, this was how naval lieutenant Eberhard von Mantey considered that an attack on the United

States would succeed. Around the turn of the century, after the Samoan Crisis, Imperial Germany thought war against the USA a strong possibility, but at the time the *Reichsmarine* lacked the necessary battle fleet.

In March 1889, von Mantey presented his second study. This bold scenario reckoned that New York would fall to three battalions of infantry and one of engineers! The invasion force would require 25 days for the Atlantic crossing. Up to 60 colliers would be attached to the naval squadron. The young lieutenant thought it could definitely be done. Secretary of State Admiral Alfred von Tirpitz concurred and ordered the plans to be drawn up. But General von Schlieffen, Chief of the General Staff, had his doubts. He thought that such an expedition would require at least 200,000 troops for any hope of success. Imperial Germany still lacked the means to achieve such purposes but ideas like these played a part in providing the impetus for a rapid expansion of the German High Seas Fleet.

In November 1903, Operational Plan III for an offensive against the United States had not diminished in importance. Wilhelm Buchsel, a close confidante of Tirpitz, had been appointed Chief of the Admiralty Staff and was given permission to prepare plans for an attack against the United States, using the assumption that the German *Reich* would be completely free from other conflicts in Europe. Buchsel's idea was to take control of the Panama Canal and use this to break down Washington's domination of the entire continent. Schlieffen was asked to calculate what would be required in terms of ground forces, but by then the Venezuela Crisis of 1904 had demonstrated that the US Navy had begun to arm.

The growing problems in Europe, with the ominous signs of a new war brewing in the 'Old World', led within a few years to an increase in naval armaments across the continent. Within a few more years, Admiral Dewey's prophecy that the next enemy of the USA would be the German *Reich* proved correct.

Besides plans for an attack by German naval forces, from

about 1917 the idea of using long-range bombers or large airships began to blossom. Airships easily had the range to drop up to 1,800 kilograms (kg) of explosives along the US eastern seaboard, but the planned bomber, with a maximum range of 8,000 kilometres (km), could not have managed the homewards leg.

The fascination for attacking the United States which had developed in the late 19th century lasted well into the 1940s. An intensive geopolitical study compiled by Department Ic VIII of the *Luftwaffe* Command Staff in 1941 under the title 'Grossraum USA' held forth:

> The many nations of Europe embrace an area of ten million square kilometres. The United States, a single nation, is almost the same size. Impose a map of the USA without its exterior possessions over one of Europe and the breadth of the USA stretches from Gibraltar to the Black Sea. The distance between the American northern and southern frontiers is as far as Stuttgart is from Aswan on the Nile. Yet this enormous area has only one and a half times the population of the Greater German *Reich* alone. The USA is only a little smaller than all Europe and has just 120 million inhabitants, while Europe has 450 million. It is therefore not difficult to see that people over there cannot grasp what we mean when we say we are a 'people without living space'. New York lies 6,500 kilometres from Europe, six and a half times the distance from London to Berlin. The distance to Japan is much greater, from San Francisco to Yokohama 8,840 kilometres, to Hong Kong 13,000 kilometres. Americans seem to have no clear under-standing of these immense distances, for otherwise they would not need to have practice air-raid blackouts in New York against German air attack.

In 1941 7 per cent of the world's population occupied 6 per cent of the world surface but controlled more than 60 per cent of the total oil resources, 56 per cent of the rubber production, turned out 78 per cent of all motor cars and 67 per cent of all lorries, and cornered between 30 per cent and 40 per cent of the world production of lead, coal, copper and zinc. American industrial production served not only its own markets but cemented its alliances by the supply of weapons and food. The Atlantic and the Pacific protected the United States against external aggression, particularly the expansionist designs of Imperial Japan or the Greater German *Reich*. Well distanced from any foreign threat and provided with all necessary raw materials, the United States could engage in an armaments programme enabling it, should the need arise, to intervene in the farthest-flung theatres of war in Asia or Europe.

The German plan to use trans-oceanic aircraft such as the six-engined Junkers (Ju) 390, Messerschmitt (Me) 264 or Tank (Ta) 400 for global air war failed because the capacity to produce such machines in great numbers, as was possible in the USA and Britain, did not exist. Not even a limited colonial enterprise could be undertaken. Yet these great plans might have become reality if it had been possible to overcome the Soviet Union by the beginning of 1943. With the seizure of Grozny and the Caucasian oilfields, the *Wehrmacht* would have had more fuel available than it knew what to do with. Victory in the East would have provided German industry with the material to mass-produce giant bomber aircraft. With a range exceeding 14,000 km, they would certainly have been the starting point for a strategic air war.

The defeat at Stalingrad, inflicted by a Soviet Army partly supplied and armed by the United States, and a *Wehrmacht* hemmed in between two fronts in a 'Europe without a roof', sealed Germany's fate.

Besides the gradual collapse of the whole infrastructure and its transport system, the lack of fuel and raw materials for the construction of aircraft and rockets became increasingly apparent from 1943 onwards. From 1944, drastic cuts followed in the huge aircraft development and production programmes, and at the end of it all the Thousand Year *Reich* caved in.

Since the reunification of Germany in 1990 the idea of

so-called 'wonder-weapons' has gained prominence in a certain branch of specialist literature. These range from guided missiles such as the V-1 flying bomb and V-2 rocket to partial further developments, such as the A9 to the multi-stage A15. The numerous concepts based on the A10 and A11 intercontinental rockets advanced little further than mathematical calculations and design sketches. The breakdown in the infrastructure from mid-1944 ensured that guided missiles of that type could not be proceeded with at the pace the exigencies of the war situation demanded.

Numerous small groups seemed to have worked in parallel in the quest for nuclear power and explosives. What level of collaboration existed between them remains uncertain. Whether, as seems possible, they were close to perfecting small explosives with great destructive effect built on the atomic principle only the still-classified files in British, French and American archives can prove. That Germany was far more advanced by the end of 1944 in armaments technology than is widely believed today is confirmed by the intensity with which Allied scientific teams rounded up German scientists and confiscated their research work. The switch to building the flying-wing jet bomber in the last year of the war, and the search for airframe surfaces and paints able to deflect radar beams, is evidence for this. From the beginning of 1945 a properly directed exploration of such possibilities had become as impossible of achievement as a programme to develop weapons of mass destruction or their carrier systems.

Chapter 1

The Path to Strategic Air War

The idea of establishing reliable air links between Europe and America interested a number of German aircraft manufacturers from about the summer of 1917, even at the height of the First World War. Supported by Deutsche Bank, the Mannesmann firm outlined an ambitious project for gigantic biplanes and triplanes for the civilian air route to the United States. Military planning for air raids against targets along the American eastern seaboard began at about the same time when, on 18 October 1917, engineer Villehad Forssmann presented his promising portfolio. All these ideas came to naught with defeat and the terms of the 1919 Treaty of Versailles. In the years following, attention focussed on plans for huge airships, but the financial and political climate of the 1920s was not conducive to the enterprise.

The principles for large bomber operations were laid out in a report entitled 'Development of Large Aircraft for Bombing Purposes' written by *Major* Helmuth Wilberg in 1926. About three years later the *Heereswaffenamt* (Army Weapons Office) mapped out in secret its criteria for bomb carriers, but it was 6 July 1933 before it announced its tactical requirements. It was thinking of a four-engined machine with a crew of eight. Armament would be two 20-mm cannon and five machine guns. Operational height would be 6,000 metres, the ceiling 7,000 metres. A top speed of 300 km/hr was wanted. Range would be about 2,000 km.

Amongst the first projects offered by German industry was

the four-engined Rohrbach large night bomber 'Gronabo', while other manufacturers supplied very progressive studies. When Hitler seized power in 1933 a whole new range of ideas came into vogue, not least the idea of a German Central African colonial region and ultimately world domination. Such plans required very long-range transport aircraft and trans-oceanic bombers for distant theatres of war overseas. Relatively early the United States was identified as the ultimate opponent in the quest for world mastery. In the unpublished version of *Mein Kampf*, Hitler made his plans for world domination explicit, and these were the fundamental ideological objectives of the Nazi Party programme.

Plans for long-range aircraft preceded Hitler's arrival on the world stage, however. In 1932, at the instigation of Willy Messerschmitt, Bayerische Flugzeugwerke (Bf) had begun a project to build an aircraft able to reach the Antipodes, and the M34 was scheduled to make a circumnavigation of the world in 1936. Lack of development potential ensured that nothing came of the design, and in any case the *Reichsluft-ministerium* (RLM – German Air Ministry) was by now more anxious to see a fast fighter (Bf 109) and a fast long-range fighter (Bf 110) for European service. All that remained of the M34 was a two-engined machine for long-range courier duty between Europe and Japan, while a new design – the Me 261 – was pet-named 'Adolfine' because the *Führer* had spoken of it in favourable terms.

The first useful prototypes to appear in the mid-1930s were the Dornier (Do) 19 and Ju 89. Both machines were under-powered, however, and the *Luftwaffe* considered them only fitted for the air transport role. All efforts by the RLM to turn out a large bomber with great range were frustrated by the lack of a suitable engine. It was evident from a mere glance at the map that in a future conflict with the USSR, targets well inside Russia, and particularly armaments factories and power plants behind the Urals, lay beyond the tactical reach of the *Luftwaffe*. The development of aircraft hull forms had out-paced engine development to such an extent that it prejudiced all ideas of a balanced long-range bomber from the outset.

The Dornier company began work at its own risk in the summer of 1933 on a four-engined bomber known as 'GB' (*Groß Bomber*) for short. On 1 July that year Design File 1173 was presented to the RLM. After positive discussions on 31 October between the firm and *Oberst* (Colonel) Wimmer, head of the RLM Technical Office, Dornier pressed ahead with the work, despite having no official order, and came up with Design File 1188 offering a four-engined bomber with several gun positions. By now the RLM had decided upon the technical and tactical criteria required and the guidelines were circulated in November to Dornier, Junkers and Rohrbach amongst others.

On 24 February 1934 Dornier received a contract to build a wooden mock-up of its design for presentation at Friedrichshafen in August that year to enable the RLM to form an impression of how the long-range bomber of the future would look. The first details of the Do 19 appeared in the Aircraft Development Programme of 8 May 1935. Three prototypes, Do 19 SV-1, SV-2 and SV-3, and a series run of nine were to be produced. The first prototype, Works No. 701, D-AGAI, was piloted by *Flugkapitän* Egon Fath for its maiden flight at Friedrichshafen-Löwenthal on 30 October 1936. The Inspection Board took possession of the aircraft on 10 January 1938 and the RLM accepted it on 26 January. By then the prototype had flown at least 80 times, spending more than 32 hours in the air. The first prototype was transferred to *Flugkommando Berlin* and served as a flight trainer for Lufthansa before the war. Allocated to transport duty with 10. *Staffel, Transportgeschwader* (TG – Transport Group) 172 on mobilisation on 5 September 1938, together with two Ju 89s, the machines saw service as auxiliaries during the Sudeten crisis. The last report mentioning Do 19 SV-1 places it at Kölleda in 1939 and notes that the RLM had listed the machine for scrap. None of the remaining Do 19s could be completed. SV-2 (Works No. 702) was due to be fitted with four BMW 132F engines but these failed to meet requirements.

SV-3 and the materials for the nine machines of the series run were scrapped. A Dornier design for a civilian machine (Do P 30), powered by four SAM 322B engines with capacity for 30 passengers but easily converted into a long-range bomber, found the RLM unenthusiastic.

Junkers had more experience in the field of multi-engined aircraft and soon led Dornier with its 1933 design for the future Ju 89. Delays in supplying the four DB 600C engines put the development behind schedule and the two prototypes were not ready at Dessau until March 1937. Two different sets of construction plans had been submitted: SV-1 was based on plan 290236/29 February 1936, (Works No. 4911, D-AFIT) and SV-2 on plan 150356/15 March 1936, (Works No. 4912, D-ALAT). *Flugkapitän* Hesselbach piloted SV-1 on its maiden flight of 11 April 1937. SV-2 under *Flugkapitän* Kindermann followed on 12 August. The aircraft were underpowered and proved a handful. Nevertheless, Kindermann achieved the distinction of breaking two world air records when he flew SV-2 to 7,200 metres with a payload of 10 tonnes, and to 9,300 metres with 5 tonnes. For commercial reasons the record was attributed to the Ju 90 which was being offered for export. The two prototypes' last flights before official proving were made from Dessau in September 1938 after which they joined Do 19 SV-1 with *Flugkommando Berlin*. Subsequently one of the two Ju 89s was at Dornier in Löwenthal for a short period while the other was used for gunnery practice and bomb testing at Roggentin airfield near Rechlin. The RLM had no further interest in the type and ready parts not required for the Ju 90 were scrapped.

One of the first conferences to consider powerful long-range bombers was held in Berlin on 3 June 1936 under the chairmanship of Roluf Lucht (RLM, Office LC II 1). Taking part were engineers Zindel (Junkers), Dr Vogt (Hamburger Flugzeugbau), Lusser (Messerschmitt), Nikolaus (Henschel) and Eichner (Heinkel). The Air Ministry was asking for a four-engined bomber with three crew ready for testing by the beginning of 1938 at the latest. The initial requirement was for an aircraft with a range of 5,000 km capable of carrying a relatively light 500-kg bomb-load. Heinkel responded with Project He P41 (later He P 1041, and later still the He 177 A-0 to A-10, the new standard bomber of the *Luftwaffe*). Six prototypes were ordered, and the full size mock-up inspected on 20 October 1938. The power plant was to be two DB 606 coupled engines, but by the beginning of 1939 four Jumo 201 or four BMW 801 coupled radials were planned instead, and for the B variant four BMW 801/80s or four Jumo 212 air-cooled engines and a wing-surface cooling system. The reason behind opting for BMW engines still under development was primarily for better handling in the event of engine failure. The other manufacturers, including Rohrbach-Werke, began with designs for a heavy four-engined short-range aircraft.

In February 1936 the RLM had asked Focke-Wulf to design a four-engined commercial aircraft with four BMW 132G radial engines. Following the submission of Offer No. 760 on 9 July, a provisional order for two prototypes was placed on 13 August. The first of these machines (Fw 200 V-1 Works No. 2000, D-ACON, later D-AERE) was provided as little more than an airframe with engines on 19 July 1937 and was first flown on 6 September by Kurt Tank and Johannes Sander. After proving trials the machine was distance-tested by Lufthansa. V-2 (D-AETA) was found less satisfactory as regards stability and had problems with the engine cowlings.

On 11 August 1938 Fw 200 V-1 caused a sensation when *Flugkapitän* Dr Alfred Henke flew the machine 6,370 km non-stop from Berlin-Staaken to New York. A planned circumnavigation of the globe (Berlin–Tokyo–San Francisco–New York–Berlin) was called off after the American entrepreneur Howard Hughes made a four-day flight of 23,500 km to the North Pole, Russia and Tokyo. The civilian career of the Fw 200 was to be of short duration, however. Lacking long-range aircraft, the RLM was soon forced to requisition four-engined commercial machines for conversion into the naval reconnaissance role.

On 23 November 1937, in company with Ernst Udet and Erhard Milch, Hitler paid a visit to Augsburg for talks with Willy Messerschmitt whom he rated highly. Hitler's *Luftwaffe*

ADC *Oberst* Nikolaus von Below observed in his memoirs that Messerschmitt said: '*Mein Führer*, I would like to show you something else here,' and led Hitler to the mock-up of a four-engined bomber. Apparently neither Udet nor Milch had foreknowledge of the new design, and both appeared taken by surprise. Hitler left Augsburg convinced that the *Luftwaffe* would soon have the strength in depth in bombers it needed for global war. Shortly afterwards, at the beginning of 1938, the RLM drew up fresh technical specifications and presented them to industry. They contained the guidelines for the future long-range bomber programme. Operational altitude was set at 5,000 metres, range 6,700 km. The bomb-load had been doubled to 1 tonne and the crew increased to four.

Messerschmitt was actually working on three long-distance bomber designs. Me P 1062, known affectionately at Augsburg as the '*Führerflugzeug*', was an aerodynamically advanced machine powered by four DB 606 engines coupled in pairs. The decision to order the first Me 261 prototypes was taken in the spring of 1938 and within twelve months the work was well advanced. At the time the Me 261 was required as a courier aircraft and lightly armed long-range bomber. For this reason intensive effort was put into designing a bomb release gear. Consideration was also given to the idea that the Me 261 could tow a Bf 109 as its escort. Experiments of this kind were the brain-child of Dr Wurster who had made a number of successful flights in his Bf 109 E-3 (Works No. 1952) whilst under tow by an He 111. The series programme of 26 April 1939 scheduled three prototypes for readiness between December 1939 and March 1940, and by September 1939 the first scale models of the Me 261 had been wind-tunnel tested by the *Deutschen Versuchsanstalt für Luftfahrt* (DVL – German Test Institute for Aviation) and the Messerschmitt firm.

Me 264/4m (project Me P 1061) was concurrent with Me P 1062, the principal difference being the arrangement of the four engines singly. The design was known scornfully as the 'banana aircraft', and on account of the more urgent work on the order books – the production of the Bf 109 and Bf 110

– received only sporadic attention between 1938 and the summer of 1940.

The third Messerschmitt project, Me P 1073A, evolved in July 1937 and was intended as a long-range anti-ship bomber for the U-boat arm which could double as a well-armed intruder over the land. By the summer of 1940 it was being seen as a useful addition to the global attack strategy.

The Minister for Aircraft Production, Ernst Udet, and the Chief of the *Luftwaffe* General Staff, Hans Jeschonnek, were both highly sceptical about mid-air refuelling for heavy bombers, and a suitable alternative was seen in six-engined flying boats for long-distance reconnaissance and bomber operations far from the *Reich*. Refuelling seaplanes from U-boats or other *Kriegsmarine* vessels at sea seemed feasible with a modest outlay. The resupply of fuel and bombs, and crew change-overs, made possible nuisance raids anywhere in the world. Two Blohm & Voss flying boats, the BV 222 and BV 238, were the only giant seaplanes to be considered for operations. Only the former saw active service. Designs offered by Heinkel and Dornier were far too heavy for the task. As was to prove the general problem, the production of any kind of heavy bomber in appreciable numbers in wartime Germany was simply not possible.

The BV 222 was originally a six-engined civilian flying boat (a four-engined version was never realised for lack of the required power plant). At the beginning of 1938, a full-size mock-up was inspected after which Blohm & Voss began work on a military version of the design. At the end of March 1939 the builders announced that the BV 222 had a cruising speed of 275 km/hr and a range of at least 7,000 km. That summer Blohm & Voss clarified the specifications for Deutsche Lufthansa which wanted the machine for its *Transozean* service. However, Blohm & Voss did not receive instructions to design the BV 238 until February 1940.

Blohm & Voss' direct competitor Dornier had sketched the outline of a civilian 40-passenger flying boat for the transatlantic route in 1939. The enormous fuselage, 5.6 metres broad and 6.5 metres high, allowed for almost every imaginable luxury. The Do P 93 project – later the Do 214 – was to have eight DB 606 engines or, failing that, eight Jumo 212s or eight DB 613Cs, each developing 4,000 horsepower (hp). Fuel load was 6,000 litres. Instead of the usual Dornier below-wing outrigger floats the fuselage was given an all-round bulge on the waterline. In July 1939 Dornier received a provisional order and began work that autumn on the huge mock-up. As an easier and less costly means of obtaining information about flying qualities, a one-fifth scale model was built. The Göppingen (Gö) 9, as it was called, performed successfully in towing trials on the water and in the AVA wind tunnel at Göttingen.

An important Focke-Wulf design derived from the type of flying boat in which Blohm & Voss specialised was a four-engined wheeled aircraft known as 'TO' (*Transozean*) for which the first studies and theoretical work began in 1937. On 11 October 1938 Focke-Wulf completed the provisional design for a civilian Europe–USA long-haul 40-seat commercial aircraft which could also be used as a long-range bomber and reconnaissance aircraft. Even against a 40-knot headwind all the way the civilian version in 1938 was expected to have a range greater than 5,600 km. The four DB 606 engines would produce a top speed of 600 km/hr. Dimensions were 35.8 metres, both hull length and wingspan, and a wing surface of 128 square metres. Take-off weight would be 42 tonnes.

The four airscrews were turned by long shafts driven by a motor installation in the centre fuselage. Beyond this lay the toilets and washrooms for the passengers. Because the location of this installation affected the centre of gravity, Dornier wanted to install a retractable nose-wheel. The RLM was altogether unimpressed and version B was replaced eventually by version F which had its four DB 606s or paired Jumo 212s in the wings for no loss in speed. The modifications involved a longer wingspan of 40 metres, the wing surface area increased to 236 square metres, take-off weight 49 tonnes and payload 3.8 tonnes. In version L the crew and passengers were accommodated in a pressurised cabin. By now the RLM had increased the required military range to

7,500 km. The extra fuel meant an increase in take-off weight to 54 tonnes, although the wing area remained unchanged. Neither this version, nor designs R and S which followed it, ever flew. The military version also went under the axe. The development of the Fw 190 fighter robbed the company of any capacity it might otherwise have had for another large project. As it was, the later Fw 300 and Ta 400 were both based on the *Transozean*, and so ultimately the costly investment in development was not in vain.

After the death of *Generalleutnant* Wever, first Chief of the *Luftwaffe* General Staff, in an air crash at Dresden-Klotzsche on 3 June 1936, the air arm had begun to be seen primarily as an extension of the ground forces. The majority of squadrons were equipped with the Ju 87 Stuka, He 111 and other medium-range bombers. The tactical short-range support role was primarily the yardstick.

Chapter 2

From the Outbreak of War to December 1940

Although great hopes had been set upon the He 177 relatively early, the new standard heavy bomber of the *Luftwaffe* was not awarded a particularly high priority in the late summer of 1939. The prototype first flew two months after the outbreak of war in Europe. He 177 V-1 (Works No. 177 0001) was powered by two DB 606 paired engines. The early flights soon proved that coupled engines gave no guarantee of early operations. Various other points of weakness, particularly as regards stability, were soon apparent. Nevertheless, *General-Ingenieur* Roluf Lucht promised on 28 June 1940 that the He 177 'is one of the most important aircraft of the German *Luftwaffe* simply because the developing political and military situation makes it essential'. From 19 July 1940 onwards the degree of priority tended to fluctuate regularly in comparison with the He 111 and Ju 88, but delays in development were now such that nothing could be promised for the experimental unit *Kampfgeschwader* (KG – Bomber Group) 40 at Lüneberg until August 1941. Not until 1 October 1942 did the He 177 receive the second highest 'SS' priority rating.

In 1940 Junkers designed for the Lufthansa *Transozean* service an aircraft designated EF 100 with six Jumo 223 engines. The motors were powerful diesels with cylinders arranged on the square, each providing some 2,500 hp at 4,400 revs/min. The machine was designed to fly 9,000 km non-stop with up to a 20-tonne payload. Wing surface of all versions was about 380 square metres, wingspan 65 metres and fuselage length 50 metres. A pressurised cabin could accommodate up to 75 passengers for an all-up weight of 80.5 tonnes. At 9,000 metres altitude the estimated speed was 750 km/hr, economic commercial speed being 500 km/hr. For short-haul trips of up to 4,000 km 102 passengers might be carried. An 80-tonne military variant with the same power plant was drawn up; 5,000 km was considered possible with a 20-tonne payload, twelve personnel and a crew of ten. The aircraft would have four gunners' positions in the forward fuselage area, each equipped with an MG 151/20Z. With a sharp eye on the Focke-Wulf *Transozean* project, it was decided to increase the fuel capacity so as to create a heavily armed transatlantic bomber with an 11,500-km range and able to carry a 5-tonne bomb-load. The EF 100 design was worked on at Dessau into late 1941.

By the end of 1939 it had been calculated that the Fw 200 had a maximum range of only 4,200 km at 22.3 tonnes take-off weight and carrying a 2-tonne bomb-load. Attacks on shipping far out to sea were supposedly the role for which the He 177 was purpose-built but the latter aircraft was so trouble-plagued that a date for operational readiness could not even be estimated. It was now becoming clear that pursuing a policy to scrap promising long-range aircraft such as the Do 19 and Ju 89 which fell just a bit short of requirements was an error when it might have been better to make a concerted effort to improve such designs.

In a letter to *Generalluftzeugmeister* (GLZM – Minister for Aircraft Production) Ernst Udet (who was a personal friend) on 12 June 1940, Professor Messerschmitt implored the delivery of the frequently promised Jumo 222 engines for the Me 261. Technical calculations had advanced so far by mid-1940 that in August full specifications for series production of the type were offered to the RLM Technical Office. These now confirmed the Me 261 as a multi-purpose aircraft for the *Luftwaffe* with possible civilian uses. It could be a bomber, a photo-reconnaissance aircraft, and also a courier aircraft capable of flying 10,000 km. Average speed was in the region of 400 km/hr. In the courier role with DB 606 paired engines, up to eight, but normally four, passengers could be squeezed into the narrow fuselage. Messerschmitt reckoned that when carrying 700 kg the range was 13,200 km, or 11,000 km with 900 kg, or at least 8,000 km with 2 tonnes. The non-delivery of the Daimler-Benz engines meant no test-flight date having been set even by mid-1940 and it was not until 23 December that year that Karl Baur took the prototype Me 261 V-1 (Works No. 2445-2610000001, BJ+CP) aloft for the first time. Besides minor problems with trim, the DB 606 engines were as troublesome as had been anticipated and their unreliability interfered seriously with flight testing. Slight damage was sustained after an undercarriage defect led to a crash landing.

On 20 December 1940 Willy Messerschmitt informed his design engineers Wolfgang Degel, Paul Konrad and Woldemar Voigt of his vision for the 'optimal aircraft', his P-1061, the Me 264. With a range of 20,000 km, the machine would be capable of fulfilling all long-distance civilian and military requirements, and in the latter case bomb-loads of 5 tonnes could be housed in a spacious bomb-bay below the central fuselage. Smaller bombs could be hung below the wings. To minimise air resistance, he wanted an 'optimal' fuselage shape as near aerodynamically perfect as could be arranged; the gunners' positions of the military version, for example, were to lie flush with the fuselage when not required – as had been planned for the Me 165.

On the maritime front, the maiden flight of BV 222 flying boat prototype V-1 (D-ANTE, CC+ER, X4+AH, Works No. 0365) took place at Hamburg-Finkenwerder on 7 September 1940. Initially conceived for Lufthansa's *Transozean* service, the machine was requisitioned after the outbreak of war as a large transport and armed reconnaissance aircraft. The three prototypes were followed by a production series of four, designated A-0, powered by BMW Bramo 323 radials. BV 222 V-7 C-0 was the forerunner of a five-machine series equipped with Jumo 207 engines.

On 5 February 1940, Blohm & Voss received instructions from the RLM to design a heavy flying boat whose performance would exceed that of the BV 222. On 17 July the RLM delivered the technical specifications as the result of which project BV P 144 came into existence. The machine planned by the RLM had a wingspan of 53 metres and was 40 metres long. Wing area was 260 square metres, hull weight 54.8 tonnes, designed take-off weight 95 tonnes. This gave a wing loading of 365 kg/square metre. As a transport the BV 238 would carry 150 troops with equipment or up to ten tonnes of vehicles. The RLM had specified in its project study four Jumo 223s but, as the machine would be under-powered with these, Blohm & Voss went for six DB 603Ns instead. The range was estimated at between 5,000 km and 7,000 km and some enlargement was required. The wingspan was increased to 60 metres, fuselage length to 43.3 metres. In the summer of 1940, the BV 238 was chosen by the *Luftwaffe* Command Staff as the spearhead for any future 'colonial war'.

At the beginning of September 1939, Hermann Göring, Commander-in-Chief of the *Luftwaffe*, had contemplated the possibility of nuisance air raids along the American eastern seaboard. Initially these ideas were purely academic and, on account of the vast distance between Europe and the United States, his staff viewed them with a gentle scepticism. On 10 August 1940, the *Seekriegsleitung* (SKL – Naval War Staff) wrote to Göring, now ranked as *Reichsmarschall*, that in connection with the proposed 'dependent German Colonial *Reich*' in Central Africa the naval bases for the fleet would require long-range aircraft with a range of at least 6,000 km. Within three days the *Luftwaffe* General Staff set out the guidelines for an extensive 'Colonial Command'. This relied primarily on flying boats being responsible for the various transport needs. In this regard great store was set on the future BV 238 since it did away with the need to build giant airfields and the service could be commenced within a short time. But the reality was rather more modest. There was no question of seizing African territories as part and parcel of a drive to expand in that continent when European enemies, principally Great Britain, remained unwilling to negotiate. Although France had capitulated, in the autumn of 1940 the opportunities for *Luftwaffe* maritime activity were restricted to naval reconnaissance flights over the eastern Atlantic from airfields along the Biscay coast. Besides a handful of Do 26 prototypes thrust into service as improvised long-range reconnaissance aircraft, only the Fw 200 Condor with a range of 3,500 km was available for attack purposes. Neither the He 177 with its 6,500-km range, nor the Heinkel-planned 'Special Development' supposedly capable of 11,000 km, both of which were much looked forward to by SKL, were yet on the horizon.

By the end of 1940, the OKL (*Oberkommando der Luftwaffe* – Air Force High Command) and the RLM – pressurised by the Atlantic war and increasing tensions with the United States – prepared detailed plans for trans-oceanic aircraft able to fly at least 12,000 km without refuelling. Flights from Brest to New York and return were considered the most desirable in the case of war with the USA. According to the German planners, the conflict with the western Allies would then soon enter a new phase. The trans-oceanic aircraft in question would be a maid of all work, for besides its offensive role it would act as a fast courier transport and perhaps import some of those raw materials the shortage of which was beginning to be felt in Germany.

Chapter 3

The Year 1941

The impending offensive against the Soviet Union scheduled for late spring 1941 shifted the focal point of the war from western Europe to Russia, and the favourable strategic position facing the Atlantic was to a large extent given up. In addition, more and more *Luftwaffe* units were relocated to Italy for operations around the Mediterranean theatre. This brought about a noticeable weakening in air cover over the Bay of Biscay and the Atlantic. Accordingly, on 22 January 1941, the *Luftwaffe* General Staff made a demand for the urgent development of efficient long-range reconnaissance aircraft to regain the initiative in the U-boat war. For this role the Fw 200, He 177, BV 222 and even the Me 261/264 were examined for their suitability. Besides flying operational missions in support of the U-boat 'wolf packs', at the beginning of 1941 Hitler had demanded bombers with the 12,000-km range which would enable them, when the time came, to attack the American eastern seaboard and return across the Atlantic. Aircraft for the task could not simply be conjured up, but the design which would have been ideal came from Arado. In 1940 the manufacturer had built the Ar E 340, a relatively well-armed bomber with two Jumo 222 engines and able to carry a 3-tonne bomb-load. The firm had no capacity for series production. From this project there developed in 1941 a rather heavy transatlantic-range bomber with twin booms, the Ar E 470, which resembled closely a Focke-Wulf design. Arado suggested five variants to the RLM, all well-armed and powered by four or six DB 613 engines with wingspan between 47.3 metres and 68.5 metres. A sixth variant, F, was a transport with a 15,000-km range. The midship's structure allowed for a large bomb-bay to be installed.

Variant E would have been powered by four or six DB 613s in pairs with exhaust turbo-chargers and could easily have carried 5 tonnes of bombs for 7,500 km and returned to France without refuelling. Top speed worked out at 530 km/hr. Operational height was 11,000 metres. The four-man crew was to have been accommodated in a pressurised cabin with remote-control gear for the defensive armament. The design would have brought the American East Coast within range, but the numerous problems with the chosen power plant could not be overcome, and the Technical Office declined to pursue the project.

Germany's long-range bomber projects were bedevilled by engine problems. By 1941 all that had been realised so far was the Fw 200, a four-engined transport designed for the commercial trade and pressed into service as an anti-shipping bomber.

The series run following Fw 200 V-10 had only a pair of MG 15s for armament. Its light construction – despite all modifications – ruled it out as a long-range bomber. Whilst Fw 200 C-1 and C-2 were powered by the relatively weak BMW 132 H-1, the C-3 received the Bramo 323 R-2 which gave it a range of 3,000 km, or so was stated on the recognition charts. The Fw 200 C-4 was better equipped for combat by mounting single MG 131s in two gun positions. (By October the following year C-5 had been successfully tested at Jarnewitz with these positions twinned-up.) Despite such improvements, the Fw 200 was an interim solution to fill the gap until such time as the standard *Luftwaffe* bomber was available. It achieved good initial results against independent Allied merchant vessels, but when the latter were armed and marshalled into convoys the effectiveness of the Fw 200 fell off. Additional fuel tanks were added from 30 May 1941 to increase the radius of action – 5,300-km endurance was aimed for, but the Fw 200 variants were never suitable for the long-distance missions which the *Luftwaffe* Command Staff was demanding.

In 1941 Focke-Wulf began design work on a successor to the Fw 200. Specification No. 256 dated 22 October 1940 for the Fw 300 described a medium- to long-range aircraft with a crew of five and powered by four DB 603s or four Jumo 222s for preference. If that were not possible, then four BMW 802s or Jumo 223s or DB 604s were to be used. The range of the four aircraft variants, all of which were designed for the *Transozean* service of Deutsche Lufthansa, lay between 6,000 km and 7,500 km with up to 40 passengers aboard. The November 1941 blueprints show an aircraft 31.2 metres long with a wingspan of 46.2 metres. Besides the civilian format, almost as an afterthought, there was an armed reconnaissance version of 277 square metres wing area. The aircraft promised to be of little use for transatlantic military operations and virtually all the development work was delegated to SNCASO in France where the design was worked on until at least the beginning of 1944 – out of sight, out of mind.

Another Focke-Wulf brain-child was a transatlantic bomber to comply with RLM guidelines issued on 5 March 1941. The Fw 238 would have a six-man crew housed in a pressurised cabin in the nose, from where the gunners would operate the four remote-controlled MG 151 turrets in the fuselage, two dorsal and two ventral. The 35.3-metre hull, tailplane and 52 metres of wing were to be of wood and plywood. The planned aircraft would have a four-part retracting main undercarriage and a tail wheel. Fitting for the motors and undercarriage chassis would be of welded steel plate.

The design provided for four BMW 803 paired-up air-cooled radials each with an output of 3,450 hp, throttled back to 2,250 hp for the most economic cruising speed, but once their availability was drawn into question Focke-Wulf opted instead for six DB 603s or four BMW 801Es. These were a poor second-best to the BMW 803s, lopping as much as 200 km/hr off the top speed. The remote-controlled weapons system threw up so many problems that it was accepted that the turrets would have to be manned. This meant an increase in crew numbers and aircraft weight, thus reducing the performance. The use of wooden materials for an aircraft of that size ran into enormous technical problems not only in the mating-up of wood and steel, but also with static electricity. For all these reasons it was decided at the end of 1941 to scrap the project leaving the manufacturer free to concentrate its efforts on the future Ta 400 design.

Another victim which had been developed primarily for the *Transozean* service was Junkers EF 100, begun in 1940. As a new design it bore a greater risk than a modification of a proven type and the Technical Office decided instead for the Ju 290. On 11 February 1941 the RLM gave Junkers the go-ahead to develop an improved Ju 90, which had an excellent record as a commercial transport. The binding contract was placed in October 1941 with a view to early delivery of thirty aircraft designated 'Ju 290 onwards from V-11'. By then the air transport situation was very tight, and all Ju 290s coming off the line were earmarked exclusively as transports for North Africa or supporting the Eastern Front. No thought was given to using them as bombers.

In the event of war with America Hitler was determined to attack targets in the USA for a reason which his Army ADC, *Oberst* Engel, noted in his diary on 24 March 1941: 'The Jews must be taught a lesson through terror attacks on the American cities.'

The precondition for this was the readiness for missions of long-range bombers such as the Me 264 when the time was ripe. During a visit to Berlin by Japanese Foreign Minister Yosuke Matsuoka in April 1941, Hitler informed him candidly that it would be his intention 'to carry through an energetic struggle by U-boats and the *Luftwaffe* against targets in the USA'. The Japanese, as Axis partners, were assured that the *Reich* would combine with the Empire of Japan to bring their main enemy, the United States, to its knees within a short time. From 1941 onwards Hitler began to think not only about terror attacks in Europe but also of reducing cities such as

New York 'to ashes and rubble'. Recognising that his U-boats were in need of support in the Atlantic, on his order in March 1941 the post of *Fliegerführer Atlantik* (Air Commander Atlantic) was set up within *Luftflotte* 3 (Third Air Fleet) to co-ordinate intensive co-operation between U-boats and aircraft, but the latter were never available in sufficient numbers to make an overall impression. Initially substantial tonnage was sunk, but the introduction by the Royal Navy of counter-measures such as anti-aircraft guns aboard merchant vessels made air attacks risky. As has been mentioned, the Fw 200, a converted passenger aircraft, was not equal to the task, but the *Luftwaffe* had nothing more efficient available at the time.

At an aircraft production conference of 19 April 1941 Udet had made an emphatic demand that the first 50 Me 264 aircraft of the series run should be included in the current production plans and the first ten machines turned out immediately (before the prototype had been test flown) for the earliest possible start to the offensive against the United States in the event of war. Hitler had demanded massive air attacks to be mounted against American heavy industry so as to weaken America's potential to wage war and to force the United States to devote more resources towards defending its coasts, cities and factory complexes. According to Albert Speer, Hitler spoke in euphoric terms as he imagined New York 'going down in a sea of flames'. He visualised the skyscrapers as gigantic 'towers of flame' and as 'blazing bundles of firewood' which finally fell in upon themselves. Manhattan, 'a bursting city', would provide a foretaste of Dante's Inferno.

The RLM technical specification of 5 March 1941 required the rapid development of a bomber able to fly a minimum distance of 12,000 km with reserve fuel for 3,000 km more. This range was just about enough for a return flight from Brest to New York without refuelling and carrying 3–5 tonnes of bombs on the outward leg. At the beginning of 1941, Messerschmitt received a binding contract for the development of a four-engined bomber. Six prototypes were wanted. Project 1061 thus became the Me 264. The first series run was to be for 24 'four-engined long-range aircraft with a 2-tonne bomb for nuisance raids against the United States'. After extensive preliminary studies, design work was undertaken throughout 1940 on the most modern German long-range bomber of the age, and by March 1941 the production files for the fuselage, wings and tail unit had been completed, the detailed work being scheduled for finalisation in November 1943. When the project files were handed to the RLM Technical Office in the summer of 1941, Professor Messerschmitt took everybody aback when he said that the first prototype (ex-weapons) would be ready for flight testing in the early summer of 1942. Udet considered this date impossible since many details remained to be clarified. As calculations of the radius of action now indicated a maximum of only 5,000 km, ways had to be found to push this up by at least 650 km more so as to reach targets inland from the US coastal strip. This was behind Messerschmitt's quest for a better aerodynamic form and other measures to better performance. These studies continued into the spring of 1942.

Besides the four-engined Me 264, Messerschmitt had embarked on a six-engined variant designated P 1075. Because of under-capacity in the Augsburg design office, some of the work, particularly on the wings and tail unit, was farmed out to Fokker at Amsterdam. As this project was intended for wide-ranging reconnaissance and offensive activities over Asia, Africa and America, five complete studies were commissioned.

On 21 April 1941 the deployment of the Me 261 as a trans-oceanic reconnaissance aircraft was discussed. It had been hoped to include the machine in the current production programme but its unsolved engine problems continued to delay progress. On 6 February 1941 Udet had ordered that the Me 261 should undergo an endurance flight to test the engine and fuel installations 'prior to the tropical operation'. Unfortunately the longitude of this tropic has remained one of the best kept secrets of the war although possibly it may have been Japan. In fact, by 9 March 1941, the Me 261 had flown a total of 25 times. Shortly afterwards it received a seaplane livery (in the RLM colours Nos 72, 73 and 65 lacquer) which suggests plans for a long flight over the sea. Why Udet thought that there were serious engine difficulties on 21 April 1941, or whether this was a subterfuge to disguise the fact that a secret mission was to be flown, remains a mystery.

What we do know is that by May 1941 Me 261 V-1 had spent 40 hours in the air without any great problems coming to light and the reconnaissance wing *Aufklärungsgruppe der Oberbefehlshaber der Luftwaffe* was already thinking of possible long-range missions for the aircraft to fly. It was believed that the aircraft could carry 1 tonne of freight to Japan. The average speed achieved in tests had been 380 km/hr at a take-off weight of 28 tonnes. For this weight a concreted runway was necessary.

During the summer of 1941 a number of engine problems interfered with the programme of tests. Both DB 606s were dismounted and returned to the manufacturer at Genshagen for overhaul and modernisation. It was therefore late summer before they were back at Augsburg in a reliable condition. On 8 November the new metal propellers were evaluated during a works flight by test pilot Karl Baur, who reported much quieter running than with the previous wooden props. However, he also had to report eight serious faults including exhaust gas in the fuselage and defective instruments and radio equipment. On a safety flight on 8 December the oil temperature rose unexpectedly during the climb and the right inner motor had to be feathered, the pilot deciding to abort the flight prematurely at 6,200 metres. The ground check revealed a defective oil gauge, excess oil in the engines and a defective undercarriage.

During the Aircraft Production Ministry conference of 21 May 1941, the representative from *Kommando Rowehl* (Test Centre for High Altitude Flight) reported that the He 177 in its present configuration was unsuited to combat operations and four independent engines were now favoured over the designed two pairs in tandem.

Modifying the previous 90 square metre wing area for the A-3, He 177B needed 108 square metres to take the four single

DB 603s or BMW 801s. Its flight weight being 38 tonnes, the machine was not described as a long-range bomber but as a heavy bomber. Its 6-tonne bomb-load was ideal for raids against distant industrial objectives but an expected maximum range of 4,500 km limited it to excursions no further than mid-Atlantic.

The Heinkel company also said it was willing to try increasing the wing area to 133 square metres to fit four DB 610s or even less powerful engines. In May 1941 it considered equipping the He 177B with four DB 613s or 615s, all these ideas being aimed at having the machine operational earlier than the end of 1943. From October 1941 the RLM became more interested in having the powerful independent engines but shrank from making the decision for lack of a firm delivery date.

At a situation conference with SKL on 22 May 1941 Hitler spoke of the need to occupy the Canary Islands and the Azores to provide a springboard for possible attacks on the USA. Within a few months Germany could have large, strategically important airfields with giant runways in mid-Atlantic. By the autumn of 1941, he foresaw, it would be possible to begin the offensive on a small scale.

After the *Luftwaffe* had transferred the bulk of its squadrons eastwards during the period up to June 1941 preceding the Russian campaign, only a modest force remained in western Europe to prosecute operations against Britain and its shipping in the Bay of Biscay and the Atlantic approaches. Bombing missions were flown generally at night against cities and ports along the English south and east coasts, and as far as Liverpool and targets in the Midlands. The raids tended to be low-intensity affairs and had little adverse effect on British industry. Armaments production continued virtually unhindered.

Even the air war at sea failed to match expectations. The number of operational missions over the Atlantic soon fell dramatically. Since the bulk of the *Luftwaffe* was to be found on the Eastern Front and in the Mediterranean theatre, and Hitler's primary aim was the rapid defeat of the Soviet Union, his interest in major air operations against Britain had diminished temporarily mainly because he feared that the Royal Air Force (RAF) would retaliate against German cities and industry.

Over the Atlantic heavy, and particularly long-range, aircraft were conspicuous by their absence. In a conversation between Professor Ernst Heinkel and Udet on 22 July 1941, the use of the He 177 for Atlantic operations and attacks on targets in Iceland was discussed. A radius of action of 2,000 km plus a reserve was deemed essential. Suddenly the He 177 was 'of the greatest importance' but the aircraft was still unready and nothing Udet could say made any difference. On 16 August the idea was first examined of fitting the aircraft with mid-air refuelling equipment to extend the range. By then targets on the American East Coast loomed large in the thinking of senior *Luftwaffe* officers. On 20 August it was calculated that an He 177 refuelled in the air would have a range of 9,500 km, enough to comb the Atlantic skies for American-made bombers being ferried across to Britain.

In October 1941 it was found that the DB 606 engines malfunctioned regularly after four or five hours running, casting into doubt the possibility of using the He 177 A-3 for long-range missions. The problem was the fit of the cowling but this was overlooked. Nevertheless the *Luftwaffe* Command Staff had decided that the flow of bombers to Britain had to be stemmed as soon as possible and on 23 December it was agreed to fit an He 177 A-1 variant with a flexible MK 101Z mid-air refuelling gear.

Neither Göring's vaunted 1941 Elch-Programme to reorganise Germany's aircraft industries, of which it was said during a General Staff conference on 12 August 1941 'there are some uncertainties', nor its successors could deliver the goods. The possibilities in Germany were limited and bore no comparison to what could be produced in the USA. Four- or six-engined bombers, for example, would only be available in small batches in the medium term. The BV 222 flying boat could only be turned out in small numbers and was considered useful only for long-distance transport work or crew training for the BV 238, not for trans-oceanic bombing. Because of the very limited production capacity at Blohm & Voss, both ObdL and *Oberkommando der Marine* (OKM – Navy High Command) realised that the output of the BV 222 would be no more than one machine per month. On 19 September the *Luftwaffe* Command Staff described the future use of the BV 222 in the following terms: 'The difficult supply and transport situation means we have to employ all long-range aircraft, including large flying boats, as transports, though we do so with reservations.'

The staff was also of the opinion that the He 177 was the better alternative and matched completely the requirements looked for in a long-range bomber. At the time, Blohm & Voss had started development work on the BV 238 but the challenge of material shortages, ground organisation and crew training, as well as numerous other problems, remained to be met. In view of the urgency, *Luftwaffe* planners decided to try out the BV 222 as an Atlantic reconnaissance aircraft while the BV 238, when it was ready, would fill the 'colonial and transport supply' role.

The first practical studies of direct co-operation between U-boats and large seaplanes were initiated in September 1941. Whereas the original idea had been for seaplanes to refuel U-boats, the principle of mutual refuelling was now established. Initially the BV 222 was to be used exclusively to refuel, re-supply and re-crew U-boats on the high seas. The aircraft was also considered suitable for shipping wounded men and prisoners back to France. The refuelling of U-boats was something of an emergency measure since a submarine had a relatively large fuel consumption. This indicated a relay of flying boat tankers but even so the idea was pursued later with the BV 238.

The BV 222 lacked the range for lengthy reconnaissance flights. On 1 November it was reported from experience with the first prototype that the radius of action was only 1,950 km, plus the reserve. It was hoped of the BV 238 that, with a 20 per cent fuel reserve, the aircraft could transport a payload of 12.2 tonnes, equivalent to eight torpedoes, to a rendezvous about 1,450 km out, or four torpedoes to 2,500 km. For refuelling U-boats two BV 238s were to be fitted experimentally with 'sea refuelling equipment' with a view to increasing the endurance of German U-boats should they be deployed near the US coast or in the Caribbean.

According to the historian Jochen Thies, it seems that, as the Russian winter approached, Hitler had his first gnawing doubts about *Endsieg* ('Final Victory'). Apparently he had decided that, if the Russian campaign failed, this would signal the beginning of the end of his expansionist aims. However, although the Soviets were gaining strength, the German Army was still advancing, and the leadership still believed that victory was at hand, at least publicly. Certainly, in the late summer of 1941, the general situation still looked fairly promising.

During the period of the early successes in the Atlantic in late 1940 and early 1941, the SKL had opted to develop both the BV 222 and BV 238 as long-range naval reconnaissance aircraft. Their radius of action would have embraced Iceland and the southern tip of Greenland, while even the sea area between the Azores and the African coast was within reason. Since it had also been planned in the late summer and early autumn of 1941 to set up 'colonial bases in Africa', the *Luftwaffe* was adopting a more offensive global policy for which German resources were clearly inadequate.

The *Luftwaffe* Command Staff had reported on 19 January 1941 its conviction that the BV 238 would not be suitable for reconnaissance or bombing missions over the Atlantic because the defensive armament was inadequate to protect a flying boat of that size against enemy aircraft. In the framework of the colonial policy, the task of the BV 238 would be to link up the various *Wehrmacht* bases along the African coast and use these to fly offensive operations against shipping. The 95-tonne flying boats were also to be used for lengthy 'special reconnaissance missions' over the sea. Besides the colonial role, according to an SKL report of 7 October 1941, the BV 238 would gradually be used more offensively as time went on. OKM thought it doubtful, however, that the machines would be produced in reasonable numbers and they also rather feared that flying boats of that size would be easy pickings for enemy aircraft.

This line of thought was the death knell for the Do 214. From the summer of 1941, the RLM had requested a change in the concept of the machine, which was now to be developed as a multi-purpose military aircraft combining the roles of U-boat tanker, minelayer, transport and Atlantic naval reconnaissance. The DB 613Cs ordered by Dornier were not available and once again a makeshift solution (DB 603s) had had to be accepted. The take-off weight of the Do 214 was 145 tonnes, 50 tonnes more than the BV 238, although the dimensions were not much different. The range of the Dornier aircraft was only 6,600 km and it was this fact more than any other which decided the RLM against proceeding with the design. After more than a dozen huge fuselage frames had been constructed the Technical Office advised Dornier with regret that it considered the BV 238 a better proposition.

Generaloberst (Colonel-General) Udet (both GLZM and Chief of the *Luftwaffe* Planning Staff) was of the opinion that, with the available aircraft, Germany could not expect to defeat the United States through aerial bombardment. On the other hand, nuisance raids against targets on the US eastern seaboard might force the Americans to build substantial defences to protect against air attack and so indirectly help to relieve pressure on German forces elsewhere. In Hitler's eyes, the machines designed for 'special cases', especially Messerschmitt's Me 264, were important in this respect. He believed it possible to strike a crippling blow from the air against an opponent as mighty as the United States. In the medium term, the long-range bomber idea would be fed on the victories won by Rommel in the Libyan desert and the success of Army Group South in the summer of 1942 in getting so close to seizing Grozny and the huge Caucasian oilfields. If these had fallen into German hands and Soviet resistance collapsed, the *Luftwaffe* would have had its springboard for trans-oceanic bombing operations.

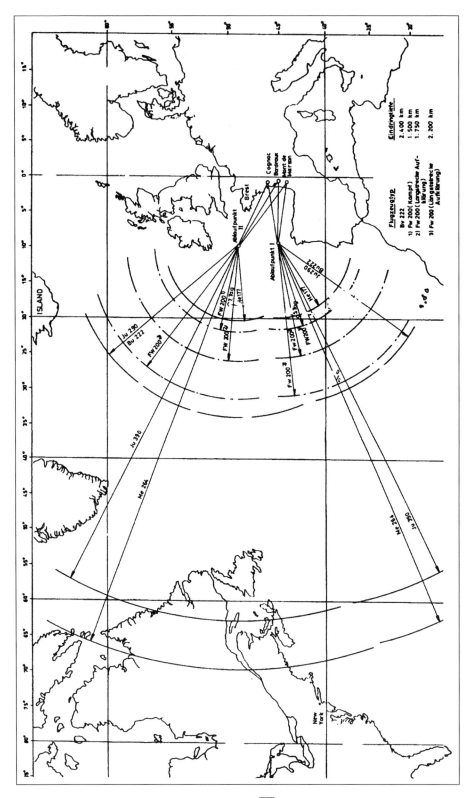

Range of all German long-distance aircraft over the Atlantic.

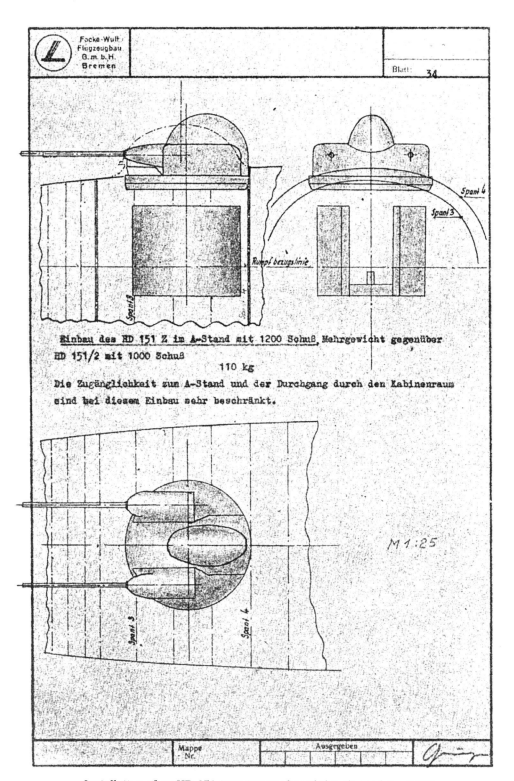

Einbau des HD 151 Z im A-Stand mit 1200 Schuß, Mehrgewicht gegenüber
HD 151/2 mit 1000 Schuß

110 kg

Die Zugänglichkeit zum A-Stand und der Durchgang durch den Kabinenraum
sind bei diesem Einbau sehr beschränkt.

M 1:25

Mappe
Nr.

Ausgegeben

Installation of an HD 151 twin-turret aboard the planned Fw 200F.

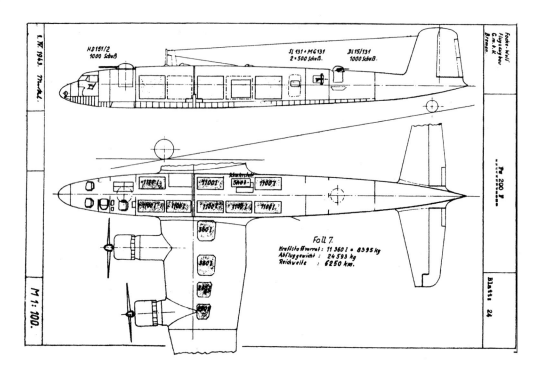

Seventh design of the Fw 200F showing a larger fuel tank system.

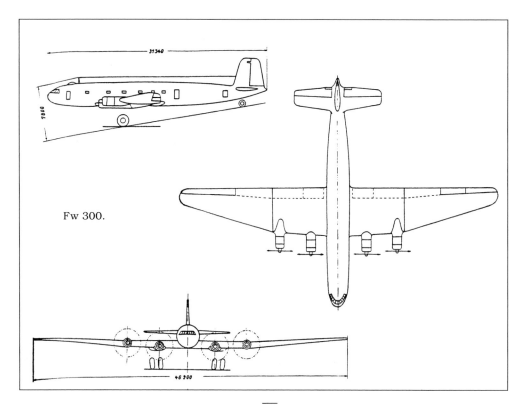

Fw 300.

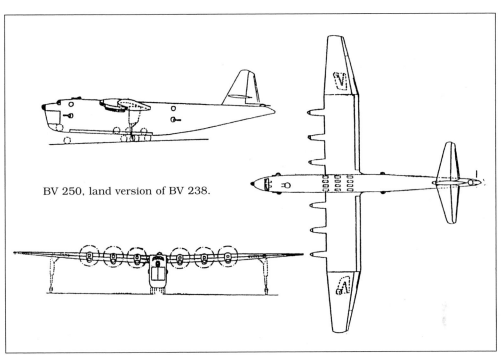

BV 250, land version of BV 238.

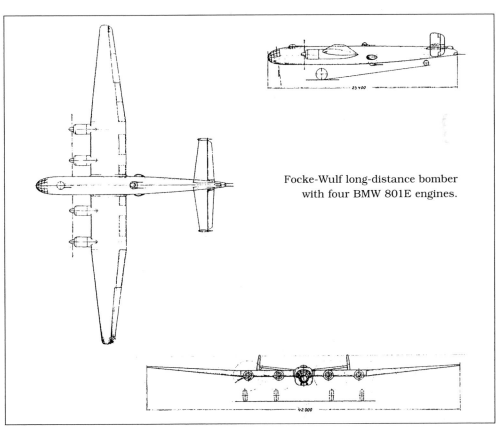

Focke-Wulf long-distance bomber
with four BMW 801E engines.

Chapter 4

The Year 1942 – First Half

POLICYMAKING

Following the suicide of Udet in November 1941, *General-feldmarschall* (Field Marshal) Milch replaced him as *Generalluftzeugmeister*. At the first aircraft production conference chaired by the new minister, on 15 February 1942, the 'America Mission' appeared on the agenda and *Flugbau-meister* Friebel, the *Fliegerstab* (air staff) engineer responsible for aircraft development, stated that neither the Me 264, nor for that matter any other machine, would prove to have the range to reach the American coast and return safely to Europe. Only air refuelling gave any promise of success. The development of the Me 264 was proceeding only slowly because of lack of workshop capacity. At the beginning of February 1942 the entire Me 264 development had been transferred temporarily to Dornier, but various bottlenecks were causing problems. For this reason the Weser Aircraft Works had become involved, but it wanted to transfer the management of the project to southern Germany and nothing came of it all. Thus the Me 264 development continued to lag behind schedule.

On 15 April Milch ordered the new head of the RLM Planning Office, *Generalmajor* Freiherr von Gablenz, to evaluate all existing long-range bomber designs and compare them against the Me 264. On 24 April a commission headed by *Oberstleutnant* (Lieutenant-Colonel) Edgar Petersen, head of the Rechlin aircraft testing centre (KdE), convened at the Messerschmitt Works, Augsburg, and on the basis of the documentation confirmed Messerschmitt's personal opinion that the Me 264 prototype was 90 per cent complete. The same day Professor Messerschmitt presented his study 'The Me 264 on Atlantic Operations' in which – aside from nuisance raids along the American coast – he suggested the aircraft was suitable: as a contact-keeper on enemy convoys; for armed maritime reconnaissance over the oceans; and for active engagement of enemy shipping targets using modern bombs.

On 7 May 1942, an even more comprehensive and optimistic Messerschmitt report was issued which promised that the 45-tonne Me 264 would have a range of 13,000 km if fitted with four Jumo 211J engines, or 14,000 km with four BMW 801 engines. Moreover, the long-awaited maiden flight of the prototype Me 264 V-1 was now as near as the autumn while V-2 and V-3 would be airborne by winter. Accordingly single aircraft nuisance raids on the American coast were possible, in Messerschmitt's estimation, from the autumn of 1943. Since these minor raids would be good propaganda, the RLM was keen to keep the option open and Milch agreed to Messerschmitt being allowed to step up the pace of development.

On 12 May 1942, von Gablenz presented to *Generaloberst* Jeschonnek, Chief of the *Luftwaffe* General Staff, a 2,500-word memorandum. It provided a unique explanation of trans-oceanic aircraft development:

> At the outset it is necessary to describe briefly the considerations and proposals which brought about the present projects. In 1940, as a result of the situation in the Atlantic and the increasing tensions with the United States, work began to increase the range of the He 177 and Fw 200. The proposal came from *General-luftzeugmeister* Udet, since at the time the General Staff did not require aircraft of that type. The minimum range required, in the case of America, was 12,000 km (the distance from Brest to New York and return), which would also be sufficient for Atlantic operations and

other trans-oceanic missions. To this minimum range was added 1,500 km as a flight reserve and another 1,500 km as a technical reserve, providing a total range of 15,000 km. A 3–5 tonne bomb-load plus normal armament and armour were also required.

Focke-Wulf and Junkers carried out in-depth analyses of these requirements and came up with aircraft having an all-up weight of between 100 and 140 tonnes. They proposed large, but as yet unavailable, engines and a development period of at least three or four years. Focke-Wulf was also asked to provide an additional design for a trans-oceanic fast aircraft. The suggestion was for a machine of wooden construction equipped with four BMW 801 engines and a light armament. The project was worked through to completion and met the specifications. No order was placed because Focke-Wulf had no capacity for the development and the use of wood seemed too risky.

At the same time, because of current development on the Me 261, Messerschmitt had received a similar invitation to tender, and the Me 264 variant was offered to the RLM in mid-1941. The design was so much better than its competitors as regards weight and performance that it was subjected to a lengthy evaluation before final acceptance. Because Messerschmitt lacks experience in building heavy aircraft, and also because, in the opinion of the RLM technical specialist, the Me 264 plan-form was too narrow, the design could not be adopted as the standard long-range bomber for the *Luftwaffe* and other firms had to be invited to tender.

In order that this new round of designs could be realised within reasonable time limits, the range requirement was reduced to between 11,000 km and 12,000 km with a total payload of 5 tonnes for bombs, armament and protection, and the specification stipulated six DB 603 engines working singly and not paired up, availability for these being promised within one or two years. The aircraft was not to be over-large;

what was not wanted was too much of a jump as regards weight, dimensions and characteristics etc., and for the aircraft to be the successor to the He 177 within a reasonable period.

A range of 11,000–12,000 km provides enormous possibilities for the Battle of the Atlantic; in the event of operations against America it is planned to increase the range by refuelling in the air. A second aircraft of similar or the same type would fly out with the first and refuel it to the maximum take-off weight at about the 3,000-km mark, providing the necessary radius of action to the target and return. Preparations are in hand to work out a satisfactory refuelling procedure and a method of effecting the mid-air rendezvous.

These new guidelines laid down in mid-1941 led to the present projects by Focke-Wulf, Heinkel and Junkers as follows:

Heinkel: 90 tonnes all-up weight, 260 square metres wing surface, 11,000 km range, 5 tonnes payload, 4.3 tonnes armament and armour.

Focke-Wulf: 80 tonnes all-up weight, 250 square metres wing surface, six DB 603 engines, range 10,000 km, payload 5 tonnes, 3.8 tonnes armament and armour.

The prototypes for these two proposals would not be available before mid-1944, thus operational readiness will lie some time before 1945.

Junkers: This is an aircraft designated Ju 390, designed for rapid development and created by lengthening the wings and fuselage of the Ju 290. All-up weight 74 tonnes, five Jumo 213 or BMW 801 engines, range 10,000 km, payload 5 tonnes, 4.3 tonnes armament and armour.

The Junkers' proposal has the advantage that it would be ready before all the others and it can be used as a transport with a 25-tonne payload. A Ju 390 prototype converted from a Ju 290 prototype could be ready by the end of 1942. The first true prototype could be available by the end of 1943, so that testing and operational readiness would occur in 1944.

To these details of the six-engined projects we must now compare the now confirmed Me 264 data and the possibilities of the BV 238.

Me 264 first variant: All-up weight 50 tonnes, four DB 603 engines, range 13,000 km, payload 3 tonnes, 2 tonnes armament and armour.

Me 264 second variant: All-up weight 47 tonnes, four BMW 801 engines, range 12,000 km, payload 2 tonnes bombs as reconnaissance aircraft, 3 tonnes armament and armour possible.

Me 264 third variant: All-up weight 43 tonnes, four Jumo 211 engines, range 11,500 km, no bombs, 1.4 tonnes armament and armour.

Investigation has shown that contrary to the assertion made by the firm, the America return flight direct is probably not possible with so little reserve. However, compared with the other proposals, the lesser all-up weights and materials requirement, plus four engines as against five or six, the design is so much better that in the opinion of the GLZM this is the aircraft to order and accordingly attempts will be made to resolve the difficulties of under-capacity at Messerschmitt.

If it is possible to resume the interrupted course of development work on the Me 264, then we can have the prototypes this year, get the programme of flight testing over with during 1943, and have the machines operational in 1944. The simplifications to the design suggested by the RLM technical centre (normal unpressurised cockpit, proven engines, no bomb-aimer's position) were made so that development could be continued despite the under-capacity at Messerschmitt (which would otherwise involve very long delays in production or cancellation of the contract) and to get the aircraft into the air. Furthermore, on account of the increasing delay in trials and introduction of the DB 603 engines, it is not expected that the engines will be ready for the 30-hour endurance run in 1943/44.

Even the Me 264 will need mid-air refuelling on the America route but this is possible with the alternative engines. Especial value is placed on this assurance as, according to the GLZM-Staff at a meeting with the Chief of General Staff, it was assumed by the GLZM that fitting alternative engine types and simplification of the Me 264 would mean giving up the idea of trans-oceanic operations.

BV 238: All-up weight 100 tonnes, 350 square metres wing surface, range 10,000 km, payload 5 tonnes bombs, 5.3 tonnes armament and armour.

As regards the BV 238, these values correspond closely to the specification and no great advantage is offered by this design against the others. Although the aircraft can be used for long distances over land as well as the sea, the GLZM suggests using the aircraft mainly in the transport role, since he understands that long-range flights over land will be better served by smaller and lighter wheeled aircraft designs and that aircraft the size of the BV 238 should then only be built if it is absolutely essential for transporting heavy loads.

It remains to add that Focke-Wulf is working on a four DB 603-engined long-range bomber designated Fw 300 which is to have a range of 7,500 km with capacity for 5 tonnes of bombs and only 2.5 tonnes given to armament and armour. The model was originally designed for civilian service but was not ordered since it offered no significant advantage over the Ju 290.

Ju 290: All-up weight 50 tonnes, range 8,750 km, payload 5 tonnes.

Modifying the transport version is not a major job according to the files. A more thorough evaluation of the possibility of this aircraft becoming a long-range bomber is being undertaken since the data look very favourable.

On the outbreak of war with the United States, the idea of operating against America directly without refuelling was naturally pursued as it had been previously. The first theoretical solution was proposed by Messerschmitt in the autumn of 1941 with the following design:

Me 264 six-engined variant: All-up weight 70–80 tonnes, six DB 603 engines, range 15,000 km, payload 5 tonnes, approximately 4 tonnes armament and armour.

The solution was theoretical because of the firm's under-capacity. Mention must be made of the special characteristics associated with these trans-oceanic aircraft and their performance. They require long runways (on average a 2-km run before take-off). On grounds of weight only about two-thirds of the fuel tanks can be protected. The aircraft are fitted with landing gear: a jettisonable undercarriage is provided for take-off. Tactically, problems of stability and lack of manoeuvrability rule out dive-bombing. For nuisance raids against American land targets, night bombing will be in the horizontal attitude. In operations over the sea, the size of the aircraft is particularly disadvantageous. Normal aerial torpedoes are envisaged but remote-controlled missiles would be best. Planning and development work is in hand to launch small parasite aircraft from these very large aircraft to carry out attacks. Test aircraft of this type are under construction and the basic trials regarding mounting them on the mother aircraft have been partly completed and should be finished during the course of the year. The parasite aircraft will be very small (6 square metres as against 14 square metres of the Bf 109) jet-propelled single-seaters designed for flights lasting from 30 minutes to an hour. They should be especially suitable for direct attacks on shipping using one or two bombs of 1,000 kg aggregate weight. Experiments to solve the problem of how the mother aircraft can recover the parasite are also in hand. Besides bombing, the parasite aircraft can be used to defend against enemy fighters. A Ju 390 for example can carry two parasite aircraft. The aircraft can be re-armed with bombs aboard the mother aircraft. To summarise therefore, in accordance with the suggestions of the GLZM in the area of trans-oceanic aircraft, the following have been approved:

(1) The four-engined Me 264 will be proceeded with as the quickest possible solution for operations against the United States.

(2) The necessary mid-air refuelling procedure will probably be worked out during 1942.

(3) For distances up to about 10,000 km, the Ju 390 is best (heavier loads, better armament, parasite aircraft).

(4) Investigations with the object of achieving a return flight to and from America without refuelling (six-engined Me 264) will be stepped up.

(5) Use of the Ju 290 for distances up to 8,000 km will be investigated with a view to using the aircraft to refuel the four-engined Me 264.

On 27 April 1942 a comprehensive written opinion commissioned by Milch was submitted by Senior Engineer Schwencke, head of the Armaments Division (Foreign) to Milch, *General-Ingenieur* Lucht and *Generalmajor* von Gablenz. The report dealt primarily with the question of distances for later trans-oceanic operations, though at this period of the war the *Luftwaffe* General Staff was not really interested in such strategic considerations, being far too tied up in the daily business of providing short-range air support to the Army. However, the report was discussed as a major item at the GLZM conference of 12 May 1942. Its purpose was not, as has been suggested by Horst Boog of the German Military-Historical Research Office, 'to unleash war on a global scale', but to evaluate the various transatlantic aircraft design projects. Schwencke indicated the enormous importance of reconnaissance flights as a prerequisite to such long-range missions, which might well include targets well inland. Here he had in mind particularly the destruction of industrial complexes behind the Urals which were of decisive significance for Soviet arms production. At the beginning of 1942 reconnaissance flights over the Asiatic part of the Soviet Union were very rare and there were few to the Urals, reliance being placed instead on the dubious statements of Russian PoWs, particularly with regard to potential targets in Siberia. Jeschonnek, Chief of the *Luftwaffe* General Staff, had referred to uncertainty surrounding the suitability of targets since, for some time, it had not been known what armaments were being produced, and where. Yet it was easily possible for He 177s to fly reconnaissance across the USSR, refuel in Japanese-controlled Manchuria and then return to German-occupied territory in Russia.

On the other hand, according to Schwencke, offensive operations against the United States scarcely entered into it. Certainly there were targets aplenty to repay the effort, the most attractive of which was the Panama Canal. If its closure could be achieved, it would cause the Allies serious difficulties with regard to the supply of raw materials and to naval movements. The same applied to numerous other targets in the eastern USA. Schwencke set out clearly the reconnaissance and bomber objectives. A survey of the American armaments industry and raw material sources provided at least twenty lucrative targets, special importance being attached by the RLM to aluminium, aircraft and propeller production and Army materials:

Potential Targets

No.	Target	Location	Product	% of total US output
201	Aluminum Corp. of America	Alcoa, TN	aluminium	30
202	Aluminum Corp. of America	Massena, NY	aluminium	15
203	Aluminum Corp. of America	Vancouver, Can	aluminium	20
204	Aluminum Corp. of America	Badina, NC	aluminium	12
205	Wright Aeronautical	Peterson, NJ	aircraft engines	15
206	Pratt & Whitney	East Hartford, CT	aircraft engines	20
207	Allison Division of GM	Indianapolis, IN	aircraft engines	10
208	Wright Aeronautical	Cincinnati, OH	aircraft engines	15
209	Hamilton Standard	East Hartford, CT	aircraft propellers	15
210	Curtiss Wright	Beaver, PA	aircraft propellers	15
211	Curtiss Wright	Cadwell, NJ	aircraft propellers	15
212	Sperry Gyroscope	Brooklyn, NY	instruments	50
213	Kryolith (mineral source)	Arsuk, Greenland	cryolite	100
214	Kryolith (refinery)	Natrona, PA	cryolite	100
215	American Car & Foundry	Berwick, PA	light armour	50
216	Colt Firearms	Hartford, CT	MG & AA guns	important factory
217	Chrysler Tank Arsenal	Detroit, MI	tank production	100
218	Allis Chalmers	La Porte, IN	heavy AA guns	70
219	Corning Glass	Corning, NY	optical lenses	important factory
220	Bausch & Lomb	Rochester, NY	optical lenses	important factory

Successful heavy bombardment of the targets – theoretically from 1943 – could have lost the Americans from between 50 per cent and 100 per cent of their military vehicle production, about 70 per cent of their aluminium production and at least 60 per cent of aircraft engines and propellers. It was important to destroy these twenty prime targets to strike a mortal blow at American war industry and thus slow output substantially. The RLM had decided not to go for the main power stations since the grid network ensured that even if five major plants were knocked out no worthwhile disruption would be caused.

The *Luftwaffe* made its plans but nothing ever came of them, and there was never once an interruption to the flow of war materials to Britain and the Soviet Union. Over 400,000 vehicles, almost 25,000 aircraft and 135,000 machine guns, to mention only a part of the material delivered, found their way to Russia by 1945. Even a partial destruction of armaments targets located along the US East Coast would have reduced massively the supplies to America's Soviet ally.

To bridge the enormous distances posed the *Luftwaffe* problems which were well-nigh insoluble. Mid-air refuelling was possible, but fundamentally too expensive. In its favour, however, *Luftwaffe* disruption of air transport between the USA and Britain, particularly strikes against unarmed American bombers being ferried across the Atlantic and attacks on merchant shipping and the raw material plant at Evigstok in southern Greenland believed to be so important to Allied aluminium production, seemed to Schwencke such ultimately rewarding possibilities that they justified the expense of mid-air refuelling.

Schwencke also argued that, instead of using transatlantic-type aircraft for offensive operations, their primary use should be the importing of those raw materials which the *Reich* lacked, particularly rubber, platinum, wolfram and zinc. Since the air and sea routes to the Far East were dominated by Allied forces, a proportion of those materials should be air-shipped from territories under Japanese control. The high prices demanded in foreign currency by Spain and Portugal for these materials militated against purchase from these sources. Using long-range transport aircraft, especially in the case of wolfram, and to a lesser extent platinum and silver, was the sensible way to avoid this extortion.

For such flights there were two routes: the 5,500-km run from Petsamo in Finland, crossing the Soviet Union to Manchuria, and the longer and more hazardous 8,900-km southern route over the Middle East and across the Indian Ocean to the Japanese-held East Indies. Schwencke advocated the mid-air refuelling of He 177s loaded with more than 10 tonnes of material.

In the RLM conference of 16 May 1942, long-range operations took up the greater part of an hours-long discussion. *Flugbaumeister* Friebel of the *Fliegerstab* repeated his opinion that operations to America involving a flight over

13,500 km were not possible without mid-air refuelling of the Me 264. This meant that all plans for an air bridge between Japan and the *Reich*, for reconnaissance missions to Siberia and to distant targets in equatorial Africa were now subject to mid-air refuelling from a tanker aircraft.

Three days later, *Generalmajor* von Gablenz presented the results of his deliberations on the future and development of transatlantic bombers. As Messerschmitt expected, Gablenz arrived at the conclusion that the Me 264 represented an extremely important stage of aircraft development. The machine simply had to be proceeded with because it was superior to, and more advanced than, the designs of all competitors. Gablenz therefore advocated a series run of thirty machines. The fourth and subsequent machines should have a redesigned nose area to accommodate a forward gun-turret, though a weapons installation of this type had been very difficult to design up to that time. Gablenz also recommended using the Me 264 as a nuisance raider with neither armour nor defensive armament. Its purpose would be to attack far distant targets, forcing the enemy to deploy men and guns in permanent anti-aircraft batteries.

That same day, Milch notified Schwencke and Gablenz that the distance from the French coast to New York was 6,700 km. The direct return flight was 13,400 km which, including a 10 per cent fuel reserve, amounted to a fuel requirement for 14,750 km. The distance was incorrect. Brest was only 5,500 km from New York, the true fuel requirement being for a flight in the region of 12,100 km.

In addition to reconnaissance flights along the American coast Milch was mainly interested in anti-shipping operations between Newfoundland and New York. This stretch of ocean was 1,500 km long, criss-crossed by much traffic and here aircraft could operate in collaboration with the U-boats. Milch observed: 'There are a whole host of possibilities there.' Once again the idea of a bombing raid on the centre of New York was raised. Using thirty transatlantic bombers the *Luftwaffe* would operate along the length of the US East Coast. The reasoning behind this outwardly unrewarding enterprise was

– as mentioned – to force the United States to erect air defences and maintain them at constant readiness. Milch explained that it was the purpose of the project:

> …to force the Americans to divert some of their armaments production to their own defences. We don't have to send a whole air fleet over there. With just a few aircraft much can be achieved. The idea is not to demolish America, but only to force the United States to erect anti-aircraft defences. Therefore, not only New York but also other areas of the United States should be on the receiving end of our bombs. Perhaps we could even fly from Petsamo in Finland over the North Pole to San Francisco. That is probably not much further. Including the 10 per cent reserve it is 7,700 km.

Regarding the bomb-load, Messerschmitt Director Theo Croneiss explained that 2 tonnes of bombs aboard a transatlantic bomber shortened its range by 1,200 km, and Milch confirmed that a single SC 1000 reduced the range by 600 km. For this reason all the armour and most of the guns aboard the Me 264 would have to be unshipped, and by the end of May the RLM was haranguing Messerschmitt for the first thirty Me 264s to be made available at the very earliest date.

By 1 June 1942 the RLM had finally succeeded in calculating the shortest distance between the French coast and New York which was now officially 5,530 km from Brest and 5,850 km from Bordeaux. The RLM wanted a reserve of not less than 15 per cent instead of the previous 10 per cent in order to ensure the safe return of the aircraft to France whatever the circumstances. Göring observed:

> One never knows what weather will be encountered on the return flight and one must always be prepared to divert for fog. At the coast, fuel for a margin of 600–800 km is required for safety and time to orient oneself over land, and finally in either direction a headwind of 40 km/hr must be allowed for.

AIRCRAFT PRODUCTION

Actual ideas for aircraft capable of flying transatlantic missions were not scarce. After it was accepted that a long-range bomber of wooden construction, such as Focke-Wulf had proposed in 1941, was for numerous reasons unsuited to the purpose, that design bureau concentrated from the beginning of 1942 on studies for a range of four- and six-engined machines able to bombard targets along the American coast or behind the Urals.

A Focke-Wulf long-distance bomber within the RLM guidelines of 22 January 1942 was of 80 tonnes all-up weight and had a wing surface of 250 square metres. The six-man crew was located three forward, three aft, all in well-armoured cabins. Standard life-saving equipment consisted of two rubber dinghies, 30 litres of water and an emergency transmitter. The planned telecommunications unit included a battery of radar and direction-finding kit: FuG 10, FuG 16, PeilG 5, FuG 25, FuBl 1 and FuG 101. Fuel for the four DB 603 paired engines was carried in fourteen armoured containers plus four disposable tanks in the bomb-bay. Optional bomb retention/release fixtures were located outboard. SC 500, SC 5000, PC 1000RS and PC 1800RS bombs, air-dropped sea mines and glider torpedoes could be carried. Bombing would be in horizontal flight. Defensive armament was sited in three hydraulically operated turrets, an HD 151Z with 1,200 rounds in a dorsal and a ventral turret, and at the tail a quadruple MG 151 with 2,400 rounds. All three turrets could bear on an enemy aircraft attacking from the rear. The best performance was reckoned to be 525 km/hr at 6,200 metres. Range with a 5-tonne bomb-load was 10,000 km, with 10 tonnes 8,500 km. In mid-1942 it was decided to use BMW 801 radials instead of DB 603s.

What interest the design provoked is not recorded but it was not long before Focke-Wulf came up with a six-engined variant as its successor. With the laconic title 'Long-Range Bomber', the design file was completed on 16 July 1942. This was a well-armed long-distance bomber with a maximum range of up to 13,000 km, powered by either six Jumo 213s, six DB 603s or six Jumo 222s. The fuselage was divided into three parts: pressurised cabin area; bomb-bay and fuel storage unit; tailplane with rear turret. The fully-glazed nose accommodated the pilot, bomb-aimer/navigator and radio operator. Remote-control gear for the side turrets was also located in the cabin which was separated from the central fuselage section by a 10-mm armoured bulkhead. The bomb area was arranged to stack three or four racks of SC 2000s in threes. The maximum bomb-load was 24 tonnes. A pressurised corridor connected the nose with the rear turret. Disposable tanks supplemented the fuel load, most of which was transported in the wings. Fuel could be increased by reducing the bomb-load. The armament was similar to the four-engined version above. As a long-range reconnaissance aircraft of 80.27 tonnes when fully equipped the machine was said to be capable of 12,000 km at 350 km/hr. The operational range of the two bomber versions with DB 603 engines was between 4,500 km and 10,600 km with an all-up weight of either 76.07 tonnes or 80.87 tonnes. With six Jumo 222s the maximum possible range was 14,000 km as a reconnaissance machine and 13,000 km as a bomber. All bomb types between SC 250 and SC 2000, or up to sixteen LMB-type mines or ten LT 1500 aerial torpedoes could be carried.

Since the required engine types were not available in sufficient numbers and the maximum range was short of the distance enabling a return mission to be flown to New York without refuelling somewhere, the projects were all discarded.

On 12 May 1942 the GLZM initiated a comprehensive review of all long-range and transatlantic aircraft projects with up to six engines. Addressing the Focke-Wulf Ta 400 project, *Fliegerstab* engineer Friebel made the observation that the aircraft's calculated performance would not exceed that of the planned Ju 390. In comparison to the Junkers' machine, the Ta 400 was a completely new, and therefore very costly, development. Accordingly, since the Ju 390 was a hybrid from the existing Ju 290, and the RLM was anxious to avoid becoming embroiled in expensive new developments if at all possible, it decided on the more easily realisable design.

The Focke-Wulf heavy bomber was an advance on the Fw 300 which had – as explained – been intended initially for the transatlantic commercial trade. The Ta 400 could have carried a 7-tonne bomb-load over part of its 9,850-km range, but again this did not allow for a return flight to New York without refuelling.

At the end of 1941, the RLM had decided to equip Germany's standard new heavy bomber, the He 177, with MK 101-Z mid-air refuelling gear in order to enhance its mediocre range. Scarcely had a start been made with this innovation than an old problem cropped up anew. Following a rapid increase in flying accidents with the aircraft, on 25 February 1942 Field Marshal Milch ordered all He 177s grounded because of engine unreliability.

The He 274 was a new high-altitude bomber design dating from the end of 1941. The first calculations showed that the radius of action would not exceed 2,900 km. Although this was of little use for strategic long-range operations, the machine could fly at great altitude and the RLM ordered a prototype for completion in the spring of 1943. After short works trials it would then be passed to *Kommando Rowehl* for operational testing.

The RLM saw this technically as an improved He 177, using parts from the He 177 wherever possible. A four-seater, the He 274 would be able to reconnoitre relatively large tracts, operating at between 13,000 metres and 15,000 metres. In gliding flight calculations suggested a speed of 650 km/hr. Nearer the ground 480 km/hr was probable. Either four DB 605 paired-up engines with additional supercharger or four DB 624s were planned. Defensive armament would be several remote-controlled gun positions (FDL 131/1 and FDL 131/2B) in the fuselage.

After the file for a twinned variant of the Ju 290 with eight radial engines – similar to the construction of the He 111Z – had been consigned relatively swiftly to the waste bin, from early March 1942 there came into being a design for a large transport powered by six BMW 801Ds or six Jumo 213s. The machine was intended to bring to Germany from the Far East those raw materials of which the *Reich* had the greatest shortage. However, the hesitant attitude of Japan, fearing problems with the Soviets should the aircraft overfly USSR airspace, was a major reason why the planned Ju 290 variants were not produced with greater despatch. The planned Ju 390 was a giant aircraft with 50 metre wingspan, 250 square metre wing surface and a take-off weight of 70 tonnes. The expected payload was 5 tonnes: 10,700 km was thought possible without defensive armament. In May 1942 the RLM began to lose interest in the transporter concept in the face of other tactical exigencies. Leading on from the basic version, the following possibilities – although to some extent not desired politically – became the focus of further development:

- Long-range reconnaissance over the Atlantic
- Mother aircraft for parasite fighters and bombers
- Long-range bomber
- Long-range transport

In May 1942 Junkers received the contract for the first three prototypes, to be equipped with BMW 801 radial engines. The later Ju 390 A-1 series was a development on the Ju 290 B-1 transport idea using the planned C-1 airframe for a six-engined Ju 290 variant. The original designation was therefore Ju 290 B-2 before the development was finally recognised as Ju 390.

During April 1942 work on the otherwise relatively advanced second Me 261 prototype, suspended because of delays involving the DB 610 coupled motors, resumed on the arrival of two DB 606s. By May, prototypes V-1 and V-2 were ready to fly 'subject to certain restrictions' according to *Generalmajor* von Gablenz, while the airframe of the third prototype was complete but lacked engines. Von Gablenz therefore recommended on 18 May that V-1 should go to the Rechlin aircraft testing centre, V-2 to the Long Distance School/Blind Flying Command at Wesendorf, while V-3 remained at the Messerschmitt works. This would defer the question of scrapping all three, as the RLM had in mind, while examining the possibility of using the aircraft as flying engine test-beds or for miscellaneous long-range work. On 14 May 1942 Göring ordered that V-1 should be transferred to Rechlin 'immediately upon completion' (as had been requested the previous summer) for a short inspection and then a 5-hour flight test.

In an air production conference on 19 May von Gablenz was categorical that the Me 261 was not suitable for any kind of front-line mission because its tanks had no protection. The fuel slopping around in the riveted wings presented too great a danger for crew and machine on operations. The usual way round this problem was to install self-sealing tanks, but this had apparently not been thought of. In the meantime the three prototypes would therefore be used exclusively for testing the DB 606 engines or, as Milch described it, 'for the hours-long flying business', endurance testing paired-up motors including the DB 610s. On account of the engine problems, however, nothing of any kind was done until 27 August, not even the runway rolling trials with maximum all-up weight.

In January 1942, while various operational uses for the Me 264 were under consideration, the possibility of using the machine as a high-altitude reconnaissance aircraft had been discussed. It was decided against the idea in February, since a few flight test results were thought advisable first. The completion of three prototypes (V-1, V-2, V-3) was now the priority in order quickly to gain some practical experience of the aircraft.

Following numerous preliminary studies begun in 1941, by 17 February 1942 a project specification had been evolved for an Me 264 with very light armament and armour and additional fuel capacity. It would have brought America within range but, despite all efforts, performance still lingered along the edges of what the RLM and OKL required with respect to range. The only answer was to enlarge the airframe and add two engines to the original four. As the new design would use mainly existing Me 264 parts, a six-engined version seemed a fairly simple proposition, and in April 1942 RLM received details of the modified Me 264 project using six engines, the types being left open. Wing surface was increased to 170 square metres since the wings would be extended by the insertion of a middle section to take the extra engine per side. The fuselage was lengthened by two frames and – as far as it was possible – would be equipped with a gun-turret front and rear. In May 1942 the Messerschmitt drawing office completed the design work, but so low a rating of priority did it receive that the most efficient Me 264 version made relatively slow progress towards fruition.

Other ideas mooted were: having a second machine tow the aircraft into the sky; mid-air refuelling by a machine of similar size; increasing wing area to accommodate two more engines; and fitting rocket boosters at take-off. Probably half a dozen such rockets would have spared enough fuel at take-off to have given the Me 264 a range of 18,000 km with a 5-tonne bomb-load, or up to 26,400 km without. The armament, if there was any, would have been remote-controlled, turntable-chassis-mounted MG 131s or MG 151s. DB 603 or Jumo 213 engines would have provided enough power for an operational ceiling of 14,000 metres and a range of 16,000 km.

Optimism played an important role in selling this aircraft to the RLM. Neither Messerschmitt, nor the Aircraft Ministry, knew when the designated power plant would be available in a reliable condition, and the RLM requirement for a remote-controlled defensive armament had not so far been complied with. In order to have the desperately needed aircraft within a reasonable time frame, the specifications were lowered to carrying a maximum 5-tonne bomb-load to the mid-point of an 11,000-km or 12,000-km return flight. As four engines would not be enough, six DB 603 single-working motors were acceptable instead. Even so, the RLM accepted that the machine would not be ready for series production until the end of 1943 or possibly well into 1944, depending on the level of priority awarded a long-range heavy bomber project. In this connection it was decided to cut the number of prototypes required from six to three and suspend ideas of building a pre-production series of 24 machines.

At about the same time the RLM received revised calculations indicating that, if the Me 264 had DB 603 engines, a range of 13,000 km was possible with a 3-tonne bomb-load and 2 tonnes of defensive weaponry including armour. With the alternative of six BMW 801s, the range with the same payload would be 12,000 km. With Jumo 211 paired engines and no bombs the range was only 11,000 km, and this would not have been sufficient in any case for a round trip to New York since there was no fuel reserve.

The long delays involved in developing the required engines meant that the Me 264 would not be produced – and even then only in a short series – until 1946/47. Horrified, the GLZM staff began to avert their gaze from the Messerschmitt project to consider instead the Ju 290.

From the beginning of 1942, Blohm & Voss had been working on the BV 250, a land version of the giant BV 238 flying boat able to carry a bomb-load consisting of six SC 2500s, this in response to an RLM requirement of 2 April 1942 which had specified a need for: a range of 2,000 km with a 40-tonne payload (in the transport role); a range of 7,000 km with 20 tonnes of bombs; a range of 10,000 km with 10 tonnes of bombs; and a range of 14,000 km as a pure reconnaissance aircraft.

The Blohm & Voss design was intended to be primarily a reconnaissance machine powered by six BMW 801Es. From fairly early on grave doubts were expressed about the suitability of the machine on account of its enormous bulk. Initially it was designed to have a wing surface of 350 square metres as against 254 square metres of the Ju 390 and 125 square metres of the four-engined Me 264. Even with six engines the machine could not get off the ground without assistance and the rate of climb was poor, all factors which did little to commend it to the RLM. Moreover *Oberstleutnant* Petersen and *Fliegerstab* engineer Friebel expressed the opinion in May that enormous aircraft of this sort which were supposed to fly more than 20,000 km could only do so with oil-cooled motors if they were intending to fly at high altitudes. Friebel explained:

> An oil-cooled engine has to be found for such aircraft. Water-cooled engines simply won't do here. Provided we aren't proposing to fly at great altitude, an air-cooled motor will be sufficient. With that I can fly at 50 per cent capacity. That is proven by the Me 264 trials with the BMW 801. In that way the machine has a shorter take-off and the great advantage of an air-cooled engine.

By then the manufacturer's first specifications were available for the giant BV 250. With six DB 603s the machine, whose wing surface had been finalised at 370 square metres, could make 14,000 km, enough for a return flight to America from France without intermediate refuelling, although this would be the reconnaissance version without bomb-load. With 5 tonnes of bombs the range shrank to 12,500 km. The calculated cruising speed of the BV 250 was only 300 km/hr. However, by mid-April it was already clear, despite all the optimism at Blohm & Voss, that the machine could only be produced with the greatest effort, using parts produced for the BV 238 and a force of 'foreign workers', and even then the first prototype was not to be expected before the summer of 1943.

Reviewing all this on 12 May 1942, Field Marshal Milch found himself in a sceptical frame of mind. He doubted that the project details as they stood would bear much scrutiny and he was dubious about the claimed range of 14,000 km. Without going too far into the calculations, he had the feeling that the realistic range lay between 10,000 km and 12,000 km. All further deliberations focussed on the fact that the BV 250, being a variant of the BV 238, was too big for transatlantic missions. Friebel noted that the aircraft would be, 'carrying along too much dead airframe weight; the wing loading is much too high.' Milch accepted this view. The immense size of the BV 250, and the likely time lag developing it, compelled him to decide that the project should be halted.

Chapter 5

The Year 1942 – Second Half

POLICYMAKING

On 1 July 1942 Admiral Dönitz, at this point head of the U-boat arm, delivered the following observation on the state of the war:

> The overall situation in the western theatre in the last half year saw great changes in that major units of the surface fleet abandoned the Atlantic and the relationship of forces seen as a whole has shifted against us. Moreover there is now a danger of enemy landings. Enemy air superiority has increased substantially. Over the Channel one can speak of enemy air supremacy, certainly by day. Also, the *Luftwaffe* with its few units is not in a position to achieve significant successes. The number of operational aircraft which *Luftflotte 3* can employ in full-scale attacks is now 50 to 60 machines...

After the end of the 'Baedeker Raids' on England (so called because the target towns featured in the famous guidebook), Hitler concentrated increasingly on the dangerous campaigns at Stalingrad and towards the Caucasian oilfields. In western Europe the *Luftwaffe* made sporadic night attacks on targets in England, but only 5.85 tonnes of explosives and 750 kg of incendiaries were dropped, a minute amount compared with the huge tonnages expended on Germany that year by Allied air fleets. Even so the British maintained fifty day-fighter and sixteen night-fighter squadrons plus 2,100 flak guns at readiness on the home front. With an average 125 operational bombers, the sum total of all that was available to the *Luftwaffe* in western Europe at the beginning of 1942, no strategic bombing missions were possible. Elsewhere there was no minelaying in the Suez Canal, nor major anti-shipping operations in the Mediterranean. Even the most important ground targets on the Eastern Front could not be pounded with any hope of long term success simply because Germany lacked a four-engined long-range bomber. Yet the *Luftwaffe* leaders expected to initiate air attacks on the American coast in the near future. Where was the logic?

Generalleutnant Walter Warlimont, then Deputy Chief of Staff at *Oberkommando der Wehrmacht* (OKW – Armed Forces High Command, Hitler's headquarters), had spent a year in the USA when a colonel and was probably the only senior German staff officer who understood the American mentality. He considered that just a few Me 264s attacking the East Coast would cause untold chaos because the nation had not been subject to attack on its mainland soil for years.

Policy makers now understood that logistics began with the import of raw materials and fuel and ended at the front, and all links in the chain were equally important. Up until late 1942 the areas occupied by the *Wehrmacht* had continued to expand – between Finland and Libya north to south, between western France and Russia west to east – and this had given rise to the concept of a 'mobile operational *Luftwaffe*' forever shifting its bases in response to demand. The desolate state of supply lines across the terrain in Russia had brought about the necessity for a real increase in air transport capacity and new bases. Jeschonnek saw in the worsening transport situation 'the core question of all future policy' but without large numbers of useful carriers such as the Ar 232/Ar 432, Ju 290/Ju 390 or the Me 323 in combination with countless Ju 52/3ms the idea had no prospect of success from the outset; it was difficult enough to replace normal wastage and losses. In the run up to war, single-engined fighters, twin-engined medium-range bombers and an assortment of other combat aircraft had had priority.

The projected Focke-Wulf transatlantic bomber would not be capable of making the 15,000-km range requirement asked by the RLM and nor could the Heinkel designs, although here 11,700 km was promised. Doubts existed about early delivery of the BV 238 seaplane and the BV 250 land version. In the words of *Flugbaumeister* Friebel, the outcome of these shortcomings was that:

> ...the America task with a direct flight (13,500 km) is not possible with available aircraft... the only possibility at present is seen as mid-air refuelling from an accompanying tanker aircraft transferring 7,000 kg of fuel about 4,000 km from the take-off aerodrome.

The aeronautical industry had made no progress in this area beyond general studies while *Generaloberst* Jeschonnek took an unfavourable view of this technique of extending aircraft range. Hamstrung by conservative thinking, he considered the idea ridiculous and Milch was more or less duty-bound to toe the line. Jeschonnek's real objection was actually to the disruption caused by refitting aircraft with fuel transfer gear. He did not oppose further investigation of the possibilities; industry could continue its research and present its conclusions. This was just as well, for hopes were being staked on having a couple of aircraft capable of being refuelled in mid-air, preferably fitted with air-cooled engines, and ready for long-range oceanic operations by the end of December 1942.

From the autumn of 1942, or at the latest by early 1943, the four-engined Me 264 would be in the process of flight testing prior to distant operations. *Flugbaumeister* Friebel had stated optimistically that such operations could commence in the spring of 1944, great faith being placed on the use of air-to-ground missiles, remote-controlled bombs (PC 1400X) and small parasite fighter-bombers. The RLM favoured the six-engined version of the Me 264 which was, however, not yet under development. Hitler and Göring had in mind not only targets in the United States but also possibilities further afield as a prelude to global air war but, even with the Me 264, most competent senior officers at the RLM knew that such a prospect could not be realised until 1945 at the earliest.

Despite all Messerschmitt's efforts only three Me 264 aircraft were under construction by mid-July 1942, the first prototype, V-1, being scheduled to fly on 10 October 1942. No date for a maiden flight was available for V-2 or V-3. Production work on the series from V-4 onwards had been halted for lack of capacity. Delayed or cancelled deliveries, especially of important parts, were preventing the completion of all Me 264s.

On 7 August 1942 *Reichsmarschall* Göring and Professor Willy Messerschmitt attended the GLZM conference for the purpose of taking part in the 'America Case' discussion. The *Reichsmarschall* surprised all of those present by not demanding – as had been expected – air raids on New York, but the deployment of the Me 264 as contact keeper on enemy shipping convoys in collaboration with the U-boat arm in the Atlantic.

> **Göring:** You won't find a pilot to fly a crate like that [Me 264] with unprotected fuel tanks for wings.
>
> **Messerschmitt:** The *Herr Reichsmarschall* is perhaps confusing it with its predecessor [Me 261]. In accordance with the RLM contract I built this aircraft with protected tanks, at least in the wings, as the British do, and this aircraft is equipped with the BMW 801 engine for about 15,000 km throttled back.
>
> **Göring:** I would hug you if you gave me just a few machines – which don't need to make it to New York – but with which I can make it to mid-Atlantic to get at the convoys.
>
> **Milch:** This is all fantasy.
>
> **Messerschmitt:** It is not fantasy. Let me show you the proof.
>
> **Göring:** If you can give me an aircraft with only 10,000 km then I will award you special priority,

because then I could fly reconnaissance over the whole North Atlantic.

Messerschmitt: This bird can fly 10,000 km. It is no big thing.

Peltz: I saw the aircraft three days ago at Lechfeld. It makes a good impression. As to its performance I cannot speak.

Göring: So I can take it that the wings won't be simple fuel tanks then.

Messerschmitt: The wings are steel plate with built-in protected tanks which are not absolutely bullet-proof.

Göring: When will the machine be ready to make a flight?

By the end of August it was clear that the date of October 1942 set by the *Luftwaffe* High Command for the maiden flight of the first Me 264 prototype was premature. Messerschmitt lacked development and skilled assembly specialists. The main undercarriage promised by the VDM firm for 1 September 1942 had run into severe difficulties and the Jumo engines had not arrived at Lechfeld at the time specified. The real problems were not confined to the prolonged development of the Me 264. The Ju 290 and the giant Ju 390 evolved from it were also victims of limited capacity at the manufacturers, even though it was Milch's opinion, or so he asserted at the GLZM conference of 20 October 1942, that the Ju 390 was amongst the most urgent priorities of the recently formulated trans-oceanic programme.

Göring had begun to take more interest in these issues and in October 1942 surprised everybody by his statement that all new bombers, including those for transatlantic duty, should follow the British example and have a rear turret equipped with four guns. Whereas the Focke-Wulf designs included a rear-gunner's position, the fuselage of the Me 264 was unsuitable for the purpose. Göring also ordered that all heavy aircraft, including the BV 222, BV 238, Fw 200, Fw 300, Ju 290, Ju 390 and the Me 264, must be developed as rapidly as possible for operational readiness. So far not one of them was likely to be available in appreciable numbers in the short term and, if they were to attack the United States, mid-air refuelling was required. The number of transatlantic bombers expected to be delivered in 1943 was so insignificant that it was inconceivable they could influence the war measurably in favour of the *Reich*. At best – and at great expense – a few nuisance raids on pinpointed targets along the US East Coast might be possible. The two alternatives were:

(1) Using an efficient mid-air-refuelled land-based bomber such as the Me 264 carrying a maximum bomb-load of 2 tonnes

or:

(2) Using a large mid-air-refuelled flying boat such as the BV 222 fitted with bomb-aiming and release gear. The *Luftwaffe* General Staff did not like this option very much because setting down on the open sea was risky if there was a big swell or much of a sea running.

At the end of October 1942 *Oberstleutnant* Petersen advised Milch that Messerschmitt had revived the subject of the six-engined Me 264 following the calculation of new figures indicating that its performance would far exceed that of the four-engined version. On account of the repeated over-optimistic assertions and promises made by Messerschmitt, Milch brushed the matter aside with a brusque, 'The Me 264 is only of propaganda value.' Accordingly, at about this time, the RLM had begun to shift its faith away from the Me 264 and towards the Ju 390. The BV 222 and Ju 290, provided they could be produced in sufficient numbers, were considered as a stopgap for Atlantic operations. After Dönitz had made ever more urgent pleas for extensive air reconnaissance in support of the U-boat offensive, the matter was given central importance on 30 October 1942.

The series-produced He 177, which was close to delivery, could range 4,600 km with a 2-tonne bomb-load, or 5,500 km without. A Ju 188 with additional tanks, both in-built and jettisonable, could probably manage 6,000 km but the conversion work was so comprehensive that the idea was never pursued seriously. Carrying 3 tonnes of bombs, the Ju 290 had a planned range of 7,250 km or 9,000 km in the reconnaissance role. The Ju 390 reconnaissance version was expected to fly 10,400 km, or 9,200 km with a 3-tonne bomb-load. With respect to the latter, though, Friebel had serious reservations:

> Well, for one thing the Ju 390 can't get up without help. Towed by an He 111 *Zwilling* it would need 1,000 metres of runway or like the Me 264 about 1,300 metres with a 4-tonne rocket for thrust. The aircraft is the first prototype so close to completion that it should fly this year. Whether these expectations will be fulfilled the tests will show. We can only console ourselves for the time being by saying that Messerschmitt can't deliver. We have transferred the Me 264 to Dornier in the hope that the firm with its great experience in long-range aircraft will be able to do the flight trials and carry through the development.

Milch decided that the Ju 290 was the most promising transport, reconnaissance aircraft and bomber. As regards the Ju 390, and more so the Me 264, the budget would not stretch to the conversion and building work required and he considered that neither aircraft would be ready for operations for years.

AIRCRAFT PRODUCTION

In the two-day discussion between the RLM departmental heads on 17 and 18 August 1942 in Berlin, the problems with the He 177 development headed the agenda. The fleet had been grounded since February and production was 144 machines behind schedule. The non-delivery of the DB 610 engines, not now expected before 1943, meant that the less powerful DB 606 had had to be accepted instead. A difficult technical problem was being met with the aileron system which had been declared unsuitable for operational use.

Professor Heinkel had deferred undertaking the necessary modifications in the absence of instructions from the RLM.

On 15 September an He 177 crashed at Rechlin, giving rise to substantial doubts regarding wing rigidity in a dive. Longitudinal stability problems had also been identified which could only be corrected by lengthening the fuselage. As a preliminary measure, He 177 production had been stepped down in favour of the obsolete He 111. As a result of these misgivings regarding the He 177, the GLZM Staff decided not only to seek constructive solutions but to conduct a critical review of the performance specification presented by the Heinkel project office. These new calculations showed that with a 2-tonne bomb-load, the He 177 had a range of no more than 4,650 km. Without bombs, primarily as a reconnaissance aircraft, this increased to 5,500 km – not even long enough to reach the American coast before the fuel ran out.

On 30 October, Milch ordered He 177 production to be stepped up. His primary concern was to get the range increased so that the bomber would be able to engage shipping targets in mid-Atlantic, although longer-range activities were still not ruled out altogether. After being informed in late autumn 1942 that the maximum range of the Me 264 without bombs would be 10,000 km, Milch decided he had to concentrate on improving the He 177. In November a programme was instituted at Brandenburg-Briest and Eger to strengthen the He 177 wings while Heinkel had been working intensively to correct problems with the twin-rudder tailplane for some time.

He 177s newly delivered for pre-operational testing continued to give cause for complaint. Flights to test performance carried out to the beginning of November by I/FKG 50 provided evidence that the first series aircraft (He 177 A-1) were distinctly slower than the pre-production series run (He 177 A-0). The range of 5,500 km categorised the aircraft as little more than a medium-distance type while the average speed of 340 km/hr was far too low for operations over western Europe. The call for more reliable and more powerful engines became ever louder, but it was not until the end of the year that the long-desired DB 610s hove slowly into sight.

By September 1942 the He 274 project was already five months behind schedule. In correspondence of 15 September, Milch ordered that the order of priority at Heinkel behind the He 177, which had the highest level of urgency, was the He 219, then the high-altitude variants of the He 111, and finally the He 274. Nevertheless the development of the He 274, contracted out to Paris, went quietly onwards. A mock-up was in existence consisting of a segment of fuselage and a set of future wings. This work was in preparation for the six He 274 prototypes which were to be built in the Schwechat Works at Vienna. On 30 September an utterly unrealistic schedule was laid down: submission of construction files and blueprints by the end of 1942; crash trials and the first prototype by mid-1944 – but by October 1942 it should have already been clear that the Paris works was an attractive target within the ambit of both the French Resistance and the Allied bomber fleets.

On 2 October, Me 261 V-1 was flown to Rechlin where the wing rivets were extracted exposing numerous fuel leaks. Further serious defects were found in the undercarriage unit and fuselage section. Me 261 V-2 (Works No. 2446, BJ+CQ) was plagued by engine troubles. In October 1942 the wingspan of Me 261 V-3 (Works No. 2447, BJ+CR) had been lengthened by 0.9 metres of wingtip extensions before the first works flight. Afterwards test pilot Karl Baur reported that at 2,200 revs/min the engines set up vibrations in the cockpit instrumentation. He thought that the reason was the wooden propellers. In his opinion the longer wingspan corrected some of the earlier yaw noticed particularly with V-1. As usual, the coolant in the DB 606 engines boiled throughout the flight.

In September 1942 static calculations for the Me 264 were terminated and the performance calculations begun in November for a long-range bomber or reconnaissance variant equipped with Jumo 211s, new RLM specifications having increased substantially the flight weight. For this reason the undercarriage had to be strengthened, but a jettisonable undercarriage was also developed to reduce take-off weight. Another new undercarriage component designed was a pair of retractable nose wheels. These were tested using a converted Bf 109 (V-3, Works No. 5603, CE+BP). It was found that taxying speed was reduced but the unit was otherwise satisfactory. Messerschmitt thought it possible that the fourth prototype would have all armament and necessary fittings and be ready for operations. The Test Centre for High Altitude Flight had also asked that Me 264 V-1 be equipped with fittings enabling BMW 801 high-altitude engines to be installed. From V-4 onwards, all Me 264s would have a stepped cockpit with nose-gunner's turret. The pre-production series run would commence the programme of nuisance raids against the United States in 1944, according to the forward-looking RLM and *Luftwaffe* Command Staff.

On 10 November 1942 the works management informed Willy Messerschmitt that V-1 was to be used solely to test flight characteristics. Only a small position would be fitted for the pilot and the machine would have no armour, armament or bomb retaining/release gear. Initially four Jumo 211Js were planned. Me 264 V-1 had the internal company designation MIII. MI and MII were unrealised engine alternatives.

Besides the Jumo power plant, the theoretical performance was calculated for an Me 264 fitted with four BMW 801Ds, DB 603Hs or Jumo 213As. The Daimler-Benz and Jumo engines had a better performance than the BMW at 8,000 metres. It was all purely academic, however, because none of them was available.

The development was limited considerably by the weak main undercarriage so that the take-off weight had to be kept below 28 tonnes. For this reason V-1 could only be fitted out partially. The second and third prototypes would have the benefit of the jettisonable additional undercarriage allowing a take-off weight of 46 tonnes. Not until the second half of the flight test programme would all three prototypes have gun-turrets and the bomb installation fitted.

After amply long taxying trials and an emergency brake

test, on 23 December 1942 chief pilot Karl Baur took the 21.175-tonne V-1 on a 22-minute circuit over Augsburg for its maiden flight. For safety reasons the undercarriage was left down the whole time. On landing the brakes failed and the flaps were damaged when the machine overshot the runway. Further trials were rescheduled to Lechfeld which had a longer concrete runway. Only one Me 264 could be stationed there, however, because there was only one hangar large enough to accommodate an aircraft that size.

By the end of 1941 the idea of mounting bombing raids against the American East Coast, particularly against important war factories and the larger ports, had many enthusiasts. The Me P 1073A project had followed a poor third to the Me 261 and Me 264 at Messerschmitt but had been given a boost with the entry of the United States into the war.

The ten-man Me P 1073A was designed to be powered by eight turbo-charged push-pull Jumo 223 diesels in four nacelles enabling the machine to fly at great altitude. Defensive armament was at least six MG 151Z positions initially manned but later redesigned for remote control from one of the two pressurised cabins located fore and aft respectively. Construction was all-metal. According to the surviving plans, length was 39.9 metres, wingspan 63 metres, height 6.1 metres. Wing surface was 330 square metres, wing loading 388 kg/square metre. The spacious fuselage had room for 6 tonnes of bombs and three midget parasite aircraft. A special mechanism existed to launch and retrieve these small machines during flight. This 128-tonne long-range bomber would have a maximum range of 18,000 km. Operational ceiling was 13,000 km, top speed 600 km/hr.

The project for such a massive machine cast all previous ideas into the shade, but as the Jumo 223 diesels were not available for the mother aircraft, nor the jet engines for the parasite aircraft, the design lost out to the Me 264. According to a Messerschmitt document of 7 July 1942, the mother aircraft (Me P 1073A) was redesignated Me 364 for a period.

By 1942 it was clear to both ObdL and the RLM that the performance of the Ju 290 workhorse would not stretch to global-sized tasks. Certainly the aircraft could range far out over the Atlantic, but to the other side was 5,600 km and a return flight of this length was impossible without mid-air refuelling. The RLM therefore looked for an improvement in the performance of the four BMW 801s which powered the machine. On 16 October, Milch established that the maximum range with 3 tonnes of bombs was 7,250 km, without bombs probably 9,000 km. Cruising speed was 340 km/hr, top speed 440 km/hr. In order to reduce fuel expenditure in taking off and climbing, Junkers suggested that the aircraft be towed up by an He 111 Z-1. Milch also had investigated the possibility of increasing the range to 11,000 km by using four rocket boosters, but before the calculations were completed, it was decided not to attempt the procedure on the grounds that if one rocket failed, the aircraft would probably crash during take-off.

Milch chaired a conference in Berlin on 20 October 1942 on the subject of long-range aircraft in which the extension of the Ju 290 programme, and the construction of the Ju 390, was discussed. The RLM specialists were of the opinion that the radius of action of the Ju 290 would be limited to 2,700 km from the coast, while the Ju 390 would manage 3,500 km. However, as the Ju 290 had already passed successfully through the full programme of flight trials, Milch decided to postpone the similarly structured Ju 390 development and the prospective series production in order to build an extra five Ju 290s per month during 1944. He also ordered an investigation into the possibility of enlarging the Ju 290's fuel capacity since he felt sure it would be possible to extend the aircraft's range to 10,000 km. Because of the increased take-off weight, a very poor rate of climb would have to be allowed for at first. Another adverse factor to be taken into account was that there were only two aerodromes in France with sufficiently long, concreted runways for such a heavy aircraft to use for take-off and landing.

On 15 December 1942, in addition to wide-ranging reconnaissance work over the Atlantic and use as tanker aircraft, a new role was devised at the RLM for the huge

Junkers workhorses. The transatlantic bomber version would have a range of 13,000 km in order to make possible attacks on the American East Coast. The discussion turned, after a long talk about the Me 264, to the Ju 390 design:

> **Milch:** What machines would we have other than the Ju 390?
>
> **Friebel:** The Me 264 under the same conditions, also with respect to armament, with armour, with four DB 603Hs.
>
> **Milch:** What does the Ju 390 need for take-off? What's its range?
>
> **Friebel:** Without the Junkers motors 1,200 metres, with them, 800 metres. Normal operational range is 11,900 km.
>
> **Milch:** What is the rate of climb after take-off and the flight weight?
>
> **Friebel:** The rate of climb after take-off is 1 metre/sec. Flight weight is 50 tonnes.
>
> **Milch:** The machine would be a practical and useful proposition if it could manage 60 per cent or even half the range you say. 15,700 km is the reconnaissance version without bombs, while 11,900 km is possible with a bomb-load of 12 tonnes. We shall have to consider it very carefully. The question is, how will it behave. To be useful for us, it will have to be able to take off or land without breaking everybody's neck. It looks possible, but we will have to go into the details much more closely...

Considering the probable performance overall, the Ju 390 did not appear an especially promising development. The claimed radius of action for the six-engined monster quickly gave rise to widespread scepticism. To quieten the doubters, new calculations were called for.

At the beginning of October 1942 Milch had understood the range laden to be 9,200 km, or 11,400 km without bombs.

The cruising speed was reported to be 330 km/hr and the top speed 470 km/hr. In a subsequent conference in Berlin on the 16th of the month, it had been explained that serious difficulties would attend the Ju 390 at take-off since its output – in view of the increased dimensions compared with the Ju 290 – was low. Another argument against the Ju 390 highlighted the fact that, whereas the planned defensive armament was responsible for a substantial increase in the weight of equipment aboard, it offered no guarantee that the Ju 390 could overcome an opponent such as the De Havilland Mosquito.

As the RLM Technical Office accepted that building the Ju 390 was bound to interfere greatly with Ju 290 production, the question of scrapping the six-engined version was soon addressed at a somewhat controversial RLM discussion on 30 October 1942. Considering the fitness of the aircraft for operations, the fact that 'the Ju 390 has to have a tow in order to get up' was a worry not only to Milch. Additionally a whole host of technical modifications had to be resolved. The Ju 390 was not just a Ju 290 with an additional wing section on either side so as to fit an extra engine. The airframe required strengthening, particularly the fuselage shell. The longer wings required new spars, and these would add to the flight weight, which in turn would reduce performance further. Many other considerations – the final armament, the fuel installation – would not be determined until later, when the more pressing problems had been resolved. Even the RLM optimists did not believe series production possible before 1946. Milch's pronouncement at the end of the discussion was as follows:

> I have said that the range difference [between the Ju 290 and Ju 390] is not great. It is 9,000 km to 10,400 km. The increase is not particularly substantial; I would settle for the Ju 290. The increase in speed of 30 km/hr is not yet certain. Despite that, the Ju 390 will have inferior characteristics by virtue of the higher wing loading. The rate of climb is less favourable by

0.3 metres/sec. And the Ju 290 has the great advantage of being able to take off unassisted, while the Ju 390 needs help, which makes our work not easier but more difficult, and it would be worthwhile only if there was a special benefit to be got from it.

An aircraft that size has to be portable. Therefore, for me, the Ju 390 is not yet 100 per cent valuable, whereas I award to the Ju 290 the predicate 'artistically valuable'. If the Ju 290 and Ju 390 were to be available at the same time, then it would be different. But the Ju 390 can't be ready until 1945, and that is an optimistic view. It is a completely new airframe. It is a question of whether such a machine justifies the great expense of manufacturing it, or I settle for the Ju 290 instead. It is not so simple as comparing it with the man-hours and other costs for a 1.5-tonne fighter or other aircraft. The ratio is not 1:3 but 1:6. It increases faster. If you could bring out the Ju 390 and Ju 290 airframe simultaneously, that would be OK. But we don't want a situation where it takes three months to bring out one machine. We could do that in one place. But for a definite task, say where we are asked for eight machines ready for operations, that is a big demand for workshop equipment and many other things involved, over a long period of time. It would be extremely costly in materials to do it. It is my belief that we should concentrate on the Ju 290.

However, at the end of October 1942, Milch ordered that for study purposes, 'a mock-up capable of flying' should be assembled, in the Deutsche Lufthansa yard at Berlin-Staaken if possible. The machine would be cobbled together out of two available Ju 290s and be ready for flight tests in the spring of 1943.

On 12 May 1942 *Oberstleutnant* Petersen had discussed with Milch the possibility of developing bombers with a range of 20,000 km. This would have enabled attacks to have been made on targets well inland from the US East Coast. The aircraft under consideration was the BV 238 which would, so it was hoped, dispense with the necessity, inevitable for BV 222 flying boats, of refuelling at some point from U-boats in mid-Atlantic. As the first BV 238 prototype edged towards completion, *Fliegerstab* engineer Wahl of the Travemünde seaplane testing centre submitted an estimate that, within a year, four BV 238s would be ready, these to be followed by a series run of fifteen. By the end of 1945, 86 BV 222s would have been produced, which would then be gradually replaced by the BV 238. These statistics led to a loss of interest in the BV 238, and no further interest was evinced in the maiden flight of the prototype. On 11 September it was decided to make no decision as to whether the seaplane should have DB 603 or BMW 801 engines since there would be long drawn-out technical problems whichever was selected, though the air-cooled BMW 801s were believed to be preferable for long-distance flights.

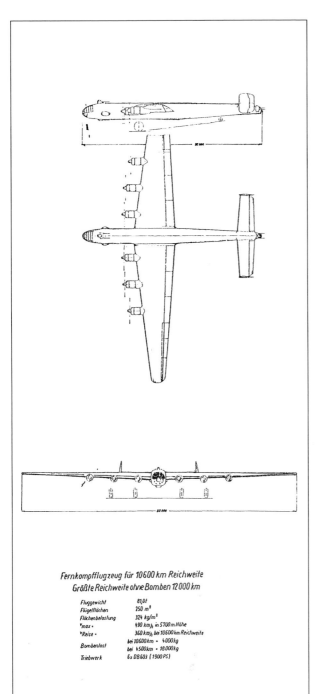

Fernkampfflugzeug für 10600 km Reichweite
Größte Reichweite ohne Bomben 12000 km

Fluggewicht	81,0t
Flügelflächen	250 m²
Flächenbelastung	324 kg/m²
v_{max} -	490 km/h in 5700 m Höhe
v_{Reise} -	360 km/h bei 10600 km Reichweite
Bombenlast	bei 10600km = 4000kg
	bei 4500km = 18000kg
Triebwerk	6x DB603 (1900 PS)

Focke-Wulf 'Long-Range Bomber' with
six DB 603 engines.

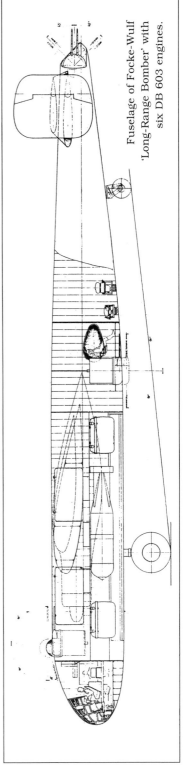

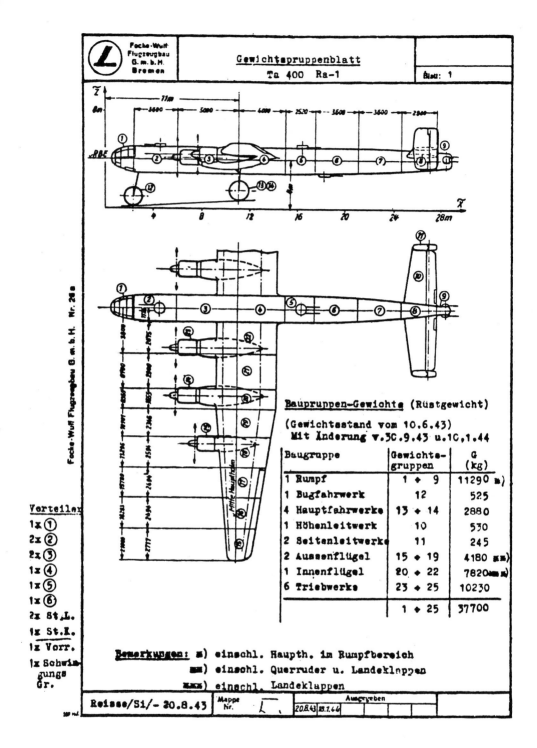

Focke-Wulf
Flugzeugbau
G.m.b.H.
Bremen

Baugruppen-Gewichte (Rüstgewicht)

(Gewichtsstand vom 10.6.43)
Mit Änderung v.30.9.43 u.10.1.44

Baugruppe	Gewichts-gruppen	G (kg)
1 Rumpf	1 ÷ 9	11290 x)
1 Bugfahrwerk	12	525
4 Hauptfahrwerke	13 ÷ 14	2880
1 Höhenleitwerk	10	530
2 Seitenleitwerke	11	245
2 Aussenflügel	15 ÷ 19	4180 xx)
1 Innenflügel	20 ÷ 22	7820 xxx)
6 Triebwerke	23 ÷ 25	10230
	1 ÷ 25	37700

Verteiler
1x ①
2x ②
2x ③
1x ④
1x ⑤
1x ⑥
2x St.L.
1x St.I.
1x Vorr.
1x Schwingungs Gr.

Bemerkungen: x) einschl. Haupth. im Rumpfbereich
xx) einschl. Querruder u. Landeklappen
xxx) einschl. Landeklappen

Reisse/Si/- 20.8.43
Mappe Nr.
Ausgegeben
20.8.43 10.1.44

Focke-Wulf Flugzeugbau G.m.b.H. Nr. 20 a

Weight groupings of the Ta 400 Ra-1, planned to be the first Focke-Wulf series-produced transatlantic bomber.

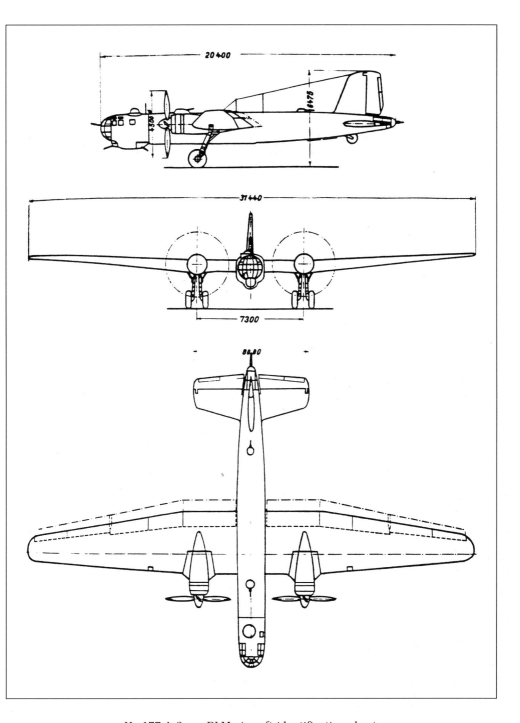

He 177 A-3 per RLM aircraft identification sheet.

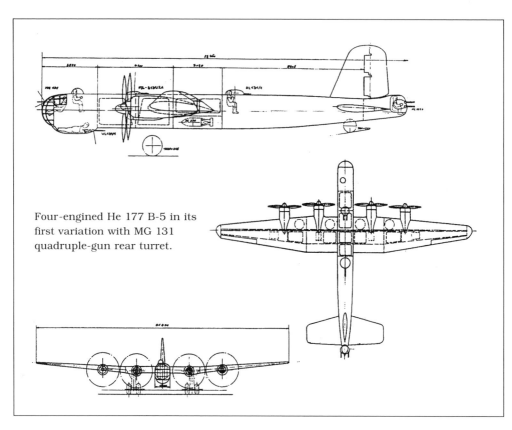

Four-engined He 177 B-5 in its first variation with MG 131 quadruple-gun rear turret.

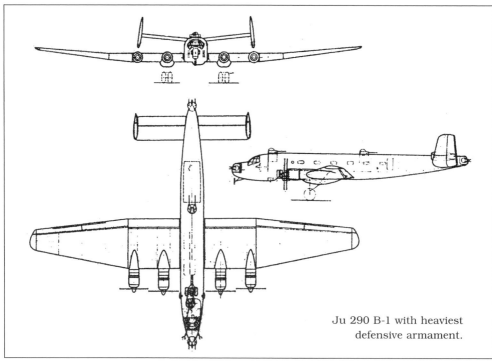

Ju 290 B-1 with heaviest defensive armament.

Chapter 6

The Year 1943 – First Half

RLM POLICYMAKING

On 15 January 1942 the *Luftwaffe* Command Staff had been of the opinion that BV 222 long-range operations were out of the question in view of the major problems experienced during trials in the Mediterranean, yet on 7 August 1942 Field Marshal Milch had been advised that the only aircraft in consideration for the planned courier run to Japan was the BV 222. The giant seaplane could cover 6,500 km with a 1-tonne payload whereas the longest range Fw 200 variant could manage no freight worthy of mention and possibly only a couple of passengers.

At the beginning of 1943, the RLM understood that production of the larger BV 238 could only be intermittent for lack of large construction hangars. The planned BV 222 production was discussed by *Luftwaffe* heads in the conference of 5 February 1943 when it was agreed that series production of large flying boats was doubtful because of the lack of construction hangars at Blohm & Voss and elsewhere. On 22 March 1943, during a development conference in Berlin, Milch confirmed that large seaplanes such as the BV 238 were desirable for use in the wide-ranging Atlantic reconnaissance role but that an independent operational command would not be possible because of the small number of machines becoming available.

The 1943 production programme stipulated that the BV 238 would gradually replace the BV 222 on the grounds of better performance. The increased range would enable larger tracts of the Atlantic to be covered, perhaps even to the coast of the United States. That same month Milch was still considering using the BV 222 for long-range reconnaissance towards American waters. He had reservations about allowing large seaplanes to touch down in the sea as planned by Dönitz (now Commander-in-Chief of the *Kriegsmarine*), for in his opinion refuelling from a U-boat was not a practicable proposition. He was not contemplating bomber raids against America at this juncture. In the spring of 1943 the production of the BV 222 flying boat had continued without any particular problems excepting the occasional lateness in delivery. This situation deteriorated at the end of May 1943 when Blohm & Voss was three machines behind schedule because fighter and medium-bomber production devoured almost all German aircraft manufacturing capacity.

On 27 May 1943 the *Fliegerführer Atlantik* at Lorient requested an influx of BV 222 flying boats for reconnaissance. Accordingly *See-Fernaufklärungsstaffel* 222 (222nd Naval Long Range Reconnaissance Squadron) was set up at Travemünde although it was given no aircraft. BV 222 V-3 was declared operational on 9 June 1943 for Atlantic sea-rescue duties at Biscarosse from mid-June but failed to arrive on time because of technical problems. At that time there were only two BV 222s on reconnaissance duty on the French coast instead of the four scheduled. On 28 June *Fliegerführer Atlantik* requested the *Staffel* be strengthened to six BV 222s and six BV 238s, and argued that the creation of a second BV 222 *Staffel* by mid-1944 was a priority for the U-boat arm. ObdL wanted to equip both these *Staffeln* with Ju 290s or Ju 390s by the end of 1944 because these would be more efficient than the flying boats. The slow production of the BV 222 guaranteed that none of these goals was ever met.

In the conference of 29 March 1943 the RLM had been sceptical that the BV 222 was suitable for operations on the open Atlantic since the aircraft could not touch down safely in a sea state greater than three. This fact, and the flammability of the aircraft, a very large target to aim at and usually a total loss once afire, were the major considerations in the eventual cancellation of BV 222 production. In August 1943, SKL also decided not to proceed with the BV 238 as no aircraft would be available in the short term.

During the GLZM conference held in Berlin on 16 January 1943, transatlantic aircraft were not mentioned at all. The longest range aircraft spoken of was the He 177 where 100 aircraft per month were promised by December 1945. Difficulties with the DB engines were continuing to cause delays, however.

One month later, on 12 February 1943, agreement was near on future policy although lack of development capacity at the manufacturers was having an increasingly negative influence. This is exemplified in a conversation between Milch, *Oberst* Pasewaldt, head of aircraft development, and General Walter Hertel, head of aircraft procurement:

> **Pasewaldt:** We discussed the long-range question regarding the Me 264 and gave the machine to Dornier. The Dornier company's staff were very mistrustful and in any case have such a work-load that they can't handle it. We then took it back, because a reluctant approach is not useful. Besides, the Me 264 is so far nothing more than a flying mock-up. They still can't make anything serious out of it. What we are supposed to do next with a project like that is causing us serious problems at the moment.

> **Milch:** Really, Blohm & Voss is most suitable for this matter when I think of the work-load the other firms have got. Dornier doesn't come into it. They must stick at the Do 335. Same with Tank [Ta 152/154]. Same with Junkers [Ju 388]. There's only Blohm & Voss left.

> **Pasewaldt:** But they are tied up with the large flying boats, BV 238, 240, 250. Not to mention the BV 222. So they've got a big work-load too.

> **Milch:** Perhaps the answer is in the machines themselves. You can use a seaplane as a long-range

reconnaissance aircraft. If you need something even a flying boat is a possibility.

Hertel: It's not much good as a bomber.

Milch: We don't want it as a bomber. That's secondary. The primary task is reconnaissance for the U-boats.

Hertel: The Ju 290 is very good for reconnaissance.

Milch: But there are not enough of them.

Pasewaldt: The others aren't available in sufficient numbers either. We must find a way to speed things up. We have to build up the numbers...

During the subsequent months, progress was slow. Too few reconnaissance flights over the sea denied the U-boats the help for which Dönitz had pleaded. At the beginning of 1943 the radius of action of the available aircraft types, as advised by the *Fliegerführer Atlantik* was:

He 177	from Bordeaux	1,500 km
Fw 200	from Cognac	2,200 km
BV 222	from Biscarosse	2,400 km
Ju 290	from Mont de Marsan	2,400 km

With these four aircraft types there could be no question of raids against the United States no matter how the matter of refuelling was approached, and this prompted a further RLM conference on 5 March 1943. The He 177 development headed the agenda. The aircraft, as currently fitted with four motors in two nacelles, had a range of 4,200 km. Heinkel calculated that this would increase by 1,000 km unladen. If the wings were enlarged and four independent air-cooled BMW 801 radials fitted, the range of the He 177B would be 6,000 km – but this was still not enough to reach America. Although a batch of He 177As was under construction, the B version would not be available in appreciable numbers until 1946, and therefore no substantial increase in range was to be expected from that quarter.

According to Friebel, the Ju 290 fitted with four BMW 801Ds would be ready as a useful offensive bomber by

August 1943 and from 1944 with the more efficient BMW 801E 14-cylinder radials. The reconnaissance version with a crew of eight had a cruising speed of 300 km/hr and a maximum speed of 450 km/hr at 6,500 metres. Equipped with a defensive armament of MG 151/20 guns the range was 6,600 km, enough to reach New York but not return.

On 25 February 1943 Göring, with an eye to the planned long-distance operations and what was presently possible, observed:

> I see the only possibility to defeat the United States and Britain in the U-boat arm. I can promise SKL their long-range aircraft for the U-boat war, but I warn them not to be too optimistic about the aircraft's readiness for operations. The development period took a very long time and the industrialists for the most part told us nothing.

Göring was hoping to have the He 177 bombers operational over Biscay initially in the reconnaissance role by autumn 1943, but he advised against setting much store by the Me 264. The machines carried their fuel in the wings and could not be risked where they would be exposed to enemy fire. In advance of the Me 264 Göring promised three BV 222s for U-boat support work. In March 1943 it was reported that the later versions of the Me 264 would have a shorter range (11,000 km) but compared with the Ju 290 a higher top speed of 540 km/hr. As there was no likelihood of Me 264 A-1s becoming available in numbers in the near future, nor even an indication of series production, Milch and Vorwald decided to rely henceforth on the Junkers' developments. Since they could penetrate well into the Atlantic, twenty available Ju 290 transports were ordered to be converted to the reconnaissance role for early delivery to *Fernaufklärungsgruppe* 5 (FAGr 5 – Long Range Reconnaissance Wing 5).

This led to the following conversation at the RLM conference of 5 March 1943:

Pasewaldt: The Me 264 must be built, we want it at all costs. But the thing is taking a long time. Meanwhile we have to make full use of the Ju 290.

Petersen: I would like to warn against exaggerated optimism over the Me 264. It needs 1,600 metres of runway with rocket assist and 2,400 metres without. That is crazy!

Rowehl: But it can fly more than 10,000 km...

Von Barsewisch [General in charge of Reconnaissance Aircraft]: Anyway, it seems from what was said in the talk with the *Grossadmiral* [Dönitz] that the U-boat war stands or falls by the reconnaissance aircraft. This has been explained to the *Führer*, he has approved it and the *Reichsmarschall* has promised to fulfil the request. Undoubtedly we must have a reconnaissance aircraft which can match the demands for mid-Atlantic cover.

So far as the *Luftwaffe* and *Kriegsmarine* High Commands were concerned, flying boats such as the BV 222 and BV 238 were from now of only limited importance mainly because refuelling at sea was not possible in anything more than a strong breeze. Only in the reconnaissance role – and then only in the remoter sea areas – were tactical operations possible. Mid-air refuelling, particularly for the Ju 290 and 390, was now back in favour. Lacking anything approaching the necessary range, the He 177 had been dropped altogether for Atlantic operations, while a number of technical experts were toying with the idea of fitting supplementary tanks to the Me 264. On 5 March 1943 both Milch and Jeschonnek were agreed that the Me 264 was unlikely to make its operational debut before 1944, perhaps a year later. The materials to build the first series run of thirty machines had been ordered at the beginning of 1943 but there was no capacity for assembly.

One of the most important conferences on the subject of Atlantic reconnaissance and trans-oceanic bombers took place on 22 March 1943 at the RLM. In view of the growing strength of Allied anti-submarine measures, Milch urged an immediate improvement in air support for Atlantic U-boats. The ever more difficult situation on the long Eastern Front and the threat of losing air superiority above it demanded an increased supply of aircraft to maintain the *status quo.*

At a conference between SKL and the *Luftwaffe* General Staff at the beginning of April 1943 the naval side opened with a request for 'permanent Atlantic reconnaissance aircraft' to support their U-boat operations tactically. Suddenly, to everybody's surprise, flying boats were back in vogue. The two largest seaplanes (BV 222 and BV 238) would now – as had often been mooted – be refuelled at sea by U-tankers so as greatly to extend their radius of search. At the beginning of 1943 intensive efforts had been put into clarifying the technical details for refuelling at sea. Previously the *Luftwaffe* Command Staff had enquired of SKL if it would be possible to station a U-tanker between the Azores and Bermuda. The *Kriegsmarine* was prepared to do this on the condition that not even one of these U-tankers should be endangered by involvement in a single 'nuisance raid against the US coast' since all U-boats were needed urgently for anti-convoy duty.

In March 1943, during a meeting with Professor Messerschmitt, Göring referred to the numerous technical difficulties with which the Me 264 was stricken and complained that it was taking too long to build.

On 27 April 1943 the BV 250 was discussed together with a lighter variant of the Ju 290E which would have an extra 900-km range as compared with the A-3 version. Unfortunately the required heavy MG 151/20 weapons installation plus ammunition increased the armament weight which in turn affected the range. As dates for fitting the Ju 290 with BMW 801E engines could not be assured, the RLM came back to the Me 264:

> **Alpers [Colonel in charge of Aircraft Department]:** Thirty machines were ordered for the plan. Finding room for an order of this size is causing difficulties in Germany because we are already beyond capacity. Junkers suggested we could take over a supplier and

use the works for assembly as well. I would like to try it. Junkers suggested the works at Toulouse.

Milch: Doesn't sound too good to me. Isn't there anything else?

Alpers: The problem is the size of the aircraft. We're getting the plans. I would like to see them. The aircraft is not included in the new delivery plans.

Milch: What else is needed to produce thirty?

Alpers: I can't say yet.

Milch: It's important to know, I gave it to the head of GL/A [Roluf Lucht] this morning. I looked over the aerodrome at Asslau. It has an 800-metre runway. Obviously that's not enough. But they have five large hangars, two of them heated. They're mainly used as a store for gas masks and a few of the Gotha gliders returned from the front. I will get them released for us.

But before these ideas could be realised, other production problems interfered with the completion of the Me 264. As noted, the Ju 390 needed at least 2,400 metres of runway for an unassisted take-off. There was no runway of such length in the *Reich* or its occupied territories. If six rocket boosters were slung below the wings, only 1,200 metres were needed and the cut in fuel consumption at take-off gave an alleged maximum range of 11,500 km. With a light bomb-load, 10,000 km was possible at a cruising speed of 350 km/hr. Nevertheless, because of the high wing-loading factor, the Me 264 was no easy prospect to handle and required the highest degree of skill during take-off.

The first prototype, the so-called 'flying mock-up', was already flying, according to Milch. Work was continuing on the next four machines. Me 264 V-2 and V-3 should be completed by the end of 1944, the other two in 1945. Before work was initiated on the series run of thirty Me 264/4ms, Messerschmitt wanted to work on the six-engined Me 264/6m if there was enough capacity. Its all-up weight was now reckoned at 75 tonnes for a wing loading of 440 kg/square metre. This aircraft could take off from western France, easily reach its objective along the American eastern seaboard at an average speed of 375 km/hr, and return with a comfortable fuel reserve. The files presented to the RLM showed that with a bomb-load the aircraft could fly 14,000 km. The Rechlin experts had calculated, on the basis of the Me 264 V-1 performance, that the range without a payload was 17,000 km. However, the machine could not be operational until 1945/46.

Only slow progress had been made on the numerous Focke-Wulf project studies for four- and six-engined long-range and transatlantic bombers. Although the later Ta 400 was equipped with the same engine type as the Me 264, the project had run more than nine months without reliable results being offered. The basic machine had a wing surface of 170 square metres. Since the all-up weight was only 60.5 tonnes, 24 tonnes of which was fuel, the wing loading of 356 kg/square metre was less than for the Me 264/6m. The manufacturers reckoned the maximum speed at 585 km/hr at 6,000 metres altitude. Range was 10,000 km at a cruising speed of 350 km/hr. The higher speed was possible because the aircraft was smaller and more aerodynamic. However, the stage of development reached by the beginning of 1943 was well adrift of the Me 264 and Ju 390. The same went for the land version of the BV 238.

During the RLM conference of 27 April 1943, a comparison of the competing designs led to the conclusion that the BV 250 was only conditionally suitable for the transatlantic operational role because it was a seaplane variant converted to land use. Its huge 350 square metre wing surface was 75 per cent larger than the 200 square metres of the Ju 290. Even the Ju 390 with 250 square metres had less. The 103 tonnes all-up weight appeared monstrous when compared to the 75-tonne Ju 290. The first BV 250 prototype was not expected until the beginning of 1945, too late to make the tactical impression required of the transatlantic bomber. On 27 April 1943 Milch decided:

I think the BV 250 can go. It gives us nothing. The bird in the hand is the Ju 290. The bird between bush and hand is the Ju 390, if we want 10,000 km.

Milch then turned to the Ta 400:

The construction side of the Focke-Wulf project seems to me, objectively, to be in order. But there are two doubts: primarily the completion date and then the question of where it is to be built. That is a big difficulty, and I am concerned that this project, if Focke-Wulf is to handle it, will greatly exceed their capacity. The Condor took an awfully long time to build, though today it would naturally come off the line much quicker than it did then. But although the firm is outstanding in the construction of small aircraft, it is not so easy to judge whether it can deal with an order of this size. It would require a major change in personnel. But we have to think about it because [Kurt] Tank is in the forefront of aircraft designers.

Milch remained dubious about the Me 264:

I think there are still many obstacles and difficulties to be overcome before the four-engined Me 264 is a practical proposition. Here again we have the same construction difficulty. What worries me is that it can only get off the ground using rockets. I am no friend of such methods. Of course, I don't blame people for using them to break world records, but they shouldn't be for everyday use. Everything depends on good luck. If just one of the eight rocket boosters fails, the take-off will come to grief and probably leave us with a write-off. That is the spanner in the works. Things are even more difficult with the six-engined version. We would be over the moon if we could use it to bomb America. With a bomb-load, America is just about within its radius of action of 14,000–15,000 km. But it is borderline, and we have to weigh up whether it isn't better to have a seaplane do it in relays.

The *Reichsluftfahrtministerium* (Aviation Ministry) where German aircraft production and *Luftwaffe* attacks against the American East Coast were planned.

Three Focke-Wulf 200Cs on the way to their appointed operational areas.

Above: The principal base for long-range reconnaissance using BV 222 flying boats under construction at Biscarosse in western France. This was the intended starting point for seaplane nuisance raids against New York. *(Bundesarchiv)*

Left: Various armour-piercing bombs being carried below the outer engine nacelles of a Focke-Wulf 200C.

Left: The radio cabin in the forward fuselage of the BV 222.

Top right: The cockpit section of a full-size wooden mock-up of the planned Ta 400.

Above: The enormous dimensions of the BV 238 flying boat are evident from this photograph.

Right: Side view of the forward fuselage section of the first BV 238 prototype.

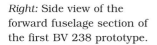

Above: In the fighter-bomber role, the He 177 was to have been used to intercept Allied bombers being ferried from the United States to Britain.

Left: Close up of the first Me 264 prototype.

Below: The striking modern lines of the Me 264 with its perspex cabin, similar to the Boeing B-29 Superfortress.

Above: Do 19 at Löwenthal near Friedrichshafen on Lake Constance.

Below: Aerial photograph of the Do 19 SV-1 during trials over southern Germany.

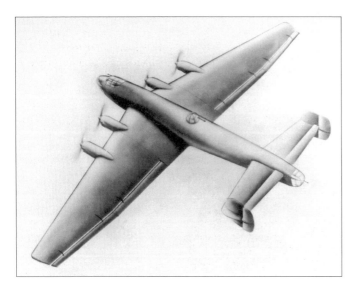

Left: Artist's impression of the planned Ju 89 A-1 long-range bomber.

Left: Ju 89 SV-1, the first prototype of the Junkers long-range bomber.

Below: The Focke-Wulf *Transozean* design inspired several civilian and eventually military variants.

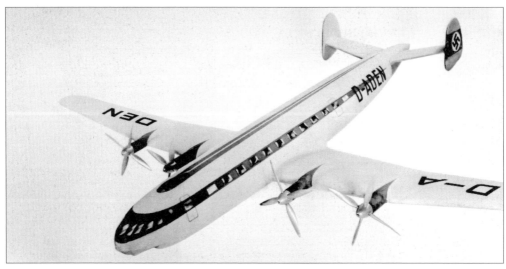

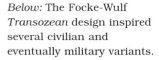

Left: Operational use of the He 177 was greatly delayed on account of engine problems and general safety questions.

Left: Wind tunnel model of the six-engined Ta 400 at the Aerodynamic Test Institute, Göttingen.

Below: On this wind tunnel model the rear-gunner's position can be easily seen.

Top: The four-engined
He 177B was produced in
France and Austria.

Above: The huge wingspan of
the He 274 is clear from this
photo.

Left: Rear-gunner's twin and
quadruple gun-turrets were
planned for the He 177,
He 274 and He 277. The
photograph shows a manned
rear chassis HL 151Z.

Above: The 4 x MG 131 rear guns of the Heinkel heavy bombers had a shorter range than positions equipped with the MG 151/20.

Right: This photo of the He 274 V-1 (AAS.01) was taken on the day of its maiden flight. The aircraft was not ready for general use until after the war was over.

Left: The four-engined He 274 was later designated AAS.01 and with the DB 605 series engines had excellent flight characteristics.

Below left: In the summer of 1944 only two He 274 aircraft were still being built in France.

Right: Giant transatlantic bombers such as the Junkers EF 100 were designed both for military use and for civilian service postwar.

Right: One of seven mock-ups of a turntable chassis for four MG 131 cannon fitted to the Ju 290 and Ju 390.

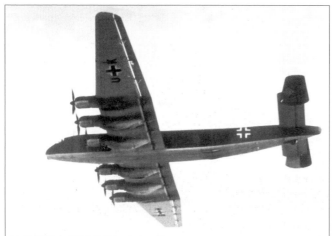

Above & left: The Ju 390 had six BMW 801 MA/2 engines but even this was barely sufficient to get the aircraft off the ground with a full load of fuel.

Above right: View from ahead of the unarmed first prototype, Ju 390 V-1.

Right: Engines unshipped, Ju 390 V-1 remained at Dessau from November 1944.

Right: French Resistance fighters destroyed the first Ju 488 prototype with explosives during its final assembly stage.

Left: Flights far out over the Atlantic involved immense risks for the crew. These two machines belonged to FAGr 5.

Above left: Crash-landing of Me 261 V-1 on 16 April 1943, following a 4,500-km flight.

Above: Wind-tunnel model of the Me 264/4m. Streamers of wool indicated the airflow over fuselage and wings.

Right: Test pilot Karl Baur (*right*) and a ground crewman in front of Me 264 V-1.

Below right: View of the Me 264 V-1 cockpit with the co-pilot's seat removed.

Below: Interior view of the Me 261.

Left & below left: The lightly damaged Me 261 V-2 survived the war and fell into American hands in 1945.

Above: The outward appearance of the Me 264 suggested the great potential of the machine.

Below: The projected six-engined Me 264/6m was to have been designated Me 364.

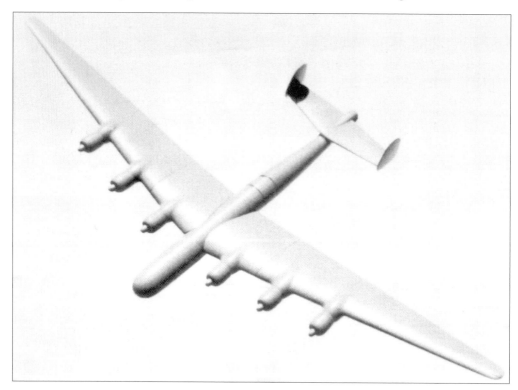

Accordingly, after having delivered final judgment against the large multi-engined flying boat, the RLM had suddenly come full circle following a few successful refuelling trials carried out with U-boats at sea. Previously Milch had dismissed the idea as 'fantasy', the use of land-based aircraft assisted at take-off if need be by rocket boosters having seemed more reasonable since then the aircraft was independent of the prevailing weather conditions.

In addition *Oberst* Pasewaldt remarked:

> We must not pass over the Ju 290. She must fly in the form in which she has been reactivated and for such time until a successor or improved version comes on the scene.

Dönitz needed at least 150 long-range aircraft for pure reconnaissance work over the Atlantic. For immediate support of the U-boats, according to *Hauptmann* (Captain) Fischer, commander of FAGr 5, two groups of six machines were required on a daily basis. This would have meant a monthly production of at least 30 Ju 290s. Milch ruled:

> Appetite grows when your meal arrives and so the BdU [U-boat Command] will have to accept that the goal is 150 machines.

Since more Ju 290s were required for reconnaissance work over the Asiatic end of the Soviet Union, the desired monthly output was put at fifty machines, far too many for the limited German capacity. The successor to the Ju 290 was here problematic, as *Oberst* Pasewaldt observed:

> In the nature of things, the Ju 290 will continue in the shape of the Ju 390. Consequently we must not pass over the Ju 390.

As far as Milch and the majority of his advisers were concerned this meant turning out both Junkers types simultaneously. As the development of the Me 264 had not proceeded to plan, there was much to be said for putting faith in proven Junkers machines even on the understanding that the Ju 290 was not a transatlantic aircraft unless a satisfactory method of mid-air refuelling could be found for it. After subsequent discussion, General Vorwald summarised the position:

> I can only second the verdicts of von Pasewaldt and Petersen. The Ju 290 and 390 are ready. How many Ju 390s can be built we can leave until later. Regarding the Ju 290 the *Reichsmarschall* has mentioned the figures. As for the Me 264, they should complete the prototypes and obtain experience with them. The Focke-Wulf bomber is so interesting that it ought to be developed despite the lack of additional capacity because it represents a considerable advance with regard to fuel consumption: 24 tonnes instead of 30.5 tonnes for a slightly more favourable range.

In conclusion Field Marshal Milch decided that all prototypes mentioned should be built and equipped with the efficient BMW 801E radial engines. He ordered thirty more Ju 290s immediately to fill the urgent need and remarked that no effort should be spared for a quick and smooth transition to the Ju 390.

On 1 May 1943 Jeschonnek issued a study of the current situation over France, the Bay of Biscay and as far as the mid-Atlantic. Beside the urgent strengthening of the fighter arm together with the setting up of an effective night-fighter arm to police coastal waters, he attributed special importance to reconnaissance over the Atlantic shipping routes and added hopefully:

> I believe that the possibilities are slowly improving. The currently available BV 222s are being prepared for operations, the Ju 290 will be operating singly from June 1943, and from August with a bit of luck we can look forward to the He 177.

Jeschonnek recorded that transatlantic bombing raids on the American coast were not being considered at present, 'because even the *Führer* is against them'. He saw this as a political decision and expected a change in future should the US step up its bomber operations against territories under *Wehrmacht* control.

AIRCRAFT PRODUCTION

The maiden flight of Me 261 V-2 took place on 25 November 1942, but what happened between that day and April 1943 is not recorded. On 16 April 1943 Karl Baur took off from Lechfeld for a ten-hour endurance flight in Me 261 V-3 with *Kapitän* Voss as co-pilot and four technical staff. The machine had 15,000 litres of fuel and take-off weight was 25 tonnes. Once in the air the right side undercarriage refused to lock while the switch was not held down manually. This problem, and the under-powered coupled DB 606 engines, led to a report which recorded that, 'the inadequacies of the machine often made themselves known'. The RLM halted the test programme and according to Baur the *Luftwaffe* handed the aircraft to *Kommando Rowehl*.

Me 264 V-1 made eleven flights totalling twelve hours in the air between 23 December 1942 and 6 March 1943. Time in flight was restricted because of problems with the twin-fin tailplane. Exhaust gas in the cabin, too-powerful aileron and rudders and faulty flight instruments were also complained of. On 22 January 1943 the machine was flown from Augsburg to Lechfeld. The undercarriage could not be fully retracted due to hydraulic failure and the lower fuselage was damaged through contact with the ground when landing. Further tests by Karl Baur brought to light defective air-brakes and nose wheel but, as luck would have it, although modifications to the ailerons and rudders were ineffective they altered the centre of gravity slightly and allowed the nose wheel to be retracted without further complications. A number of minor defects in the electrical cabling and associated systems prompted an intensive search for further problems during January and February 1943. Gerhard Caroli, head of flight testing, reported that the control surfaces remained too powerful, particularly at the higher speeds. The undercarriage and radio were reported unsatisfactory but the problems were relatively simple and soon overcome.

On two of the subsequent flight tests with Karl Baur at the controls an airspeed of 600 km/hr was attained. The defective trim and wing function indicated that a complete overhaul of the control surfaces was unavoidable. Flying on two or three engines was found satisfactory. On two test flights using the auto-pilot, the servo-motors were found to be too small for such a heavy machine. Whilst the trials dragged ever onwards, on 22 February *Oberst* Pasewaldt made a rash statement during a conference with the *Reichsmarschall* to the effect that the first series-production of the Me 264 looked like being as early as mid-1944. The first of thirty aircraft of the pre-production series, for which as yet no manufacturer had appeared, were supposed to have been operational by autumn 1943 but neither Blohm & Voss, nor Siebel nor Focke-Wulf nor Messerschmitt nor Weser Flugzeugwerke had capacity available and the problem of turning out the order remained unresolved.

Meanwhile more defects contributed to the ever-mounting development costs. On 4 March 1943, during auto-pilot testing, No. 3 engine began to stream smoke after 15 minutes and was shut down. Five days later Me 264 V-1's auto-pilot failed during a flight. Clearly there were no short cuts to solving these problems. Further tests examined the longitudinal stability after measures to correct the rudder working had been introduced. An examination of the hydraulic system passed off well but at higher take-off weights flying on two or three engines only was found unsatisfactory, contrary to earlier experience. On 23 March while landing at Lechfeld the left suspension strut collapsed, probably as a result of not having locked properly. During the repair a new control column was fitted, the wing covering reinforced, a different nose wheel and retracting gear fitted and a completely new radio unit installed.

On 27 April 1943 the planned series production of the aircraft was the major discussion point in a conference at the RLM. Only a small minority believed the aircraft capable of

11,500 km; most expected no more than 10,000 km, due mainly to all the hitches which were dogging the trials programme. The top speed was reported as 10 per cent higher than the Ju 390's, and with the exception of the rear gun-turret, of which Göring was much in favour, armament was much the same. The very high wing loading factor of 392 kg/square metre as against 254 kg/square metre for the Ju 290 was criticised. The Me 264 required 2,400 metres of runway to get up and at least 1,200 metres if assisted by six rockets.

Work on repairing the prototype lasted until 21 May and included the fitting of an improved emergency tail wheel, new wings and four new Jumo 211Js. Three workshop flights on 22 May and 2 June proved that the excessive aileron and rudder force had not been corrected. Six flights were made between 25 May and 5 June totalling 24 hours 16 minutes to measure aileron performance and examine the effect of installing two gun-turret mock-ups. On the 21st and 22nd flights the nose wheel jammed on retraction. In early June, the sun heated the greenhouse-like cabin intolerably. On flights in these conditions with a low take-off weight and not fully tanked up the relatively low top speed achieved gave rise to concern. On 11 August Me 264 V-1 was taken out of service for fitting with BMW 801 MG/2 engines and did not fly again during 1943.

In the spring of 1943 aerodynamics calculations for a six-engined Me 264 with elongated fuselage nose and a rear gun-turret were concluded in principle by the design office. At an all-up weight of 83 tonnes, range was estimated to be 17,600 km. Wing loading was 440 kg/square metre. By 27 April Messerschmitt admitted that the flying qualities of the machine did not commend it for operations. It was 'at the limit of development possibilities' and further studies for the 'optimal Me 264' were continued. It was considered unlikely that the Me 264 would enter series production before September 1944, and all Messerschmitt forward planning was being watched extremely closely for that reason.

At the beginning of 1943, General von Barsewisch envisaged

the production of between three and ten, but on average seven, He 177s monthly, for long-range reconnaissance missions. *Oberst* Vorwald informed Field Marshal Milch that the difficult situation regarding the He 177 – despite all assurances to the contrary by the Heinkel works – had not improved even after four total losses at *Einsatzstaffel* (Operational Squadron) 177. The new series from A-5 upwards with strengthened airframe, new fuselage and DB 610 engines represented a real advance in performance, and technical studies on the planned A-6 and A-7 versions, completed at Heinkel by mid-February, promised a range of 4,000 km for the former and 4,200 km for the latter, the 31-tonne aircraft being endowed with a speed of about 540 km/hr.

On 5 March Milch ordered that the A-3 and A-5 aircraft were to be fitted with two DB 610 paired engines as soon as possible for operations, and on 19th he passed down instructions that the A-7, which had the same engines but a larger wing surface, was to be taken into development without delay. It would be possible for the aircraft to get home on one set of paired engines should the other be lost, and avoiding a long drawn-out changeover to four independent engines was behind the thinking at the RLM. After numerous modifications it now appeared that the A-3 version was a useful aircraft, to be replaced shortly by the improved A-5. During the conference of departmental heads on 23 March, the A-3 received the go-ahead for mass production. This did not mean that either the A-3 or A-5 was likely to be operational very soon; A-3 was by no means close to engine-readiness and not even pilot conversion training was possible.

In mid-1943 the DB engines were still tending to oil-up, requiring the instruction that 'to avoid serious problems, initially only a very cautious use of the He 177 operationally is possible (provisionally not over the Atlantic and two to three hours per flight at most)'. This ruled out any idea of long-range reconnaissance work. On 20 May Milch laid down guidelines for the production of the planned He 177 A-7 which was now scheduled for completion in August 1943. The wings were to use steel plating so as to save on aluminium, now scarce in the *Reich*. Not until June were the DB 610s considered as reliable as the DB 605s. New seals and improved drainage for leaking oil led to hopes that long-range Atlantic reconnaissance flights would soon be a possibility.

With regard to the He 274, in October 1942 Heinkel had expressed growing concern about the workshops in France, not only because of renewed Resistance activity but because France was within easy reach of Allied bombers. For this reason a wholesale transfer to Heinkel-Süd at Vienna was wanted but obstructed by the He 219 production there. It was therefore decided on 7 February to reverse the process, and work on the He 274 cabin, engines and remote-controlled weapons systems was transferred to Paris.

On 9 February 1943, Milch decided to cancel future plans for the production of the Fw 200. This included a planned variant with a fifth engine in the nose, since the idea was not a technological advance. On 22 March Milch requested a report on how long an improved Fw 200C could be kept operational for Atlantic reconnaissance during 1943 since there was nothing better available.

In the proposed project Profile 250 in January 1943 Focke-Wulf provided the RLM with a design for a long-range bomber with four BMW 801E engines. The seven-man machine, intended primarily for operations over the sea, would have a flight weight of 53.2 tonnes and carry an average 3-tonne bomb-load, although 12 tonnes was possible as were two or three aerial torpedoes or air-dropped sea mines (LMB-type). The aircraft had shoulder-mounted wings and a twin-fin tailplane, fully retractable undercarriage and an impressive armament, primarily MG 151/20s mounted in turrets. A couple of MK 108 twin positions to protect the underside of the rear fuselage had been thought of initially although later calculations cast doubt on these because of the air resistance they created.

Another long-range bomber idea based on Focke-Wulf designs 250 and 258 was Profile 261, another machine with four BMW 801Es and of similar appearance to the foregoing. The aircraft was seen in the U-boat support role, principally for long-range reconnaissance and attacks against Allied anti-submarine aircraft. Range was 9,000 km. The file suggests: 'A purpose-built tug of the same design provides a possibility of a substantially shortened take-off.' Thus from the beginning of 1943 the idea of towing a bombed-up heavy aircraft skywards to save fuel and so lengthen its range was already current. The RLM Technical Office expressed a lack of interest in both designs on the grounds that the aircraft did not have the range to attack North America. As a result Focke-Wulf began to concentrate on designs with larger wing surface, greater fuel capacity and six independent engines.

On 9 February Milch renewed demands for the Ju 290 to be produced as a heavy bomber. The planned twelve machines for naval reconnaissance duty would not meet urgent requirements and in the spring of 1943 the first three Ju 290 transports and three more in the final assembly shop were converted to reconnaissance aircraft with a view to all six being available for Atlantic work by June. From the seventh aircraft onwards the RLM wanted the rest to be bombers. By the end of 1943, according to an instruction from Milch on 22 March, twelve should be completed. From 1944 an increase in production to an output of twelve aircraft monthly by the end of the year was foreseen, although up to 24 monthly were hoped for. Professor Hertel expressed the most heartfelt favourable sentiments about the Ju 290, but despite all admirers the maximum range of a completely fitted-out machine was only 6,600 km, in practice a radius of action of only 2,500 km. The aircraft's capability fell far short of American coastal waters without refuelling or a long tow by a sister aircraft.

Upon receipt by Junkers of the long hoped for BMW 801E radial motors sometime in mid-1944, a much more effective aircraft would be available, able to carry not only a greater volume of fuel but up to 2.4 tonnes of defensive weapons and armour. Despite the greater flight weight, the range at all-up weight ex-bombs would increase by 900 km to 7,500 km, but with 9 tonnes of bombs the radius of action fell to only 2,400 km. The P 8035 high-altitude supercharger extended the operational ceiling of the new variant to 10,000 metres, an altitude which would have made the Ju 290 a difficult aircraft to engage. Milch ordered that production should begin of sufficient aircraft of the variant to stock three reconnaissance groups, one each in Norway and on the Eastern Front, with the third on the Biscay coast also being at notice for bomber operations. Milch now began to speak in terms of thirty Ju 290s per month equipped with the new power plant.

General von Barsewisch, in charge of reconnaissance aircraft, to whom these aircraft came as a godsend, requested from Milch on 8 March 1943 at least twelve Ju 290s for the current year in the reconnaissance role. He was hoping for 174 reconnaissance aircraft for 1944 for wide-ranging cover over the Atlantic. The subject of Ju 290 production was raised on 27 April during a development conference but nothing firm could be promised. Calculations now showed that with the new BMW 801E engines the bomber version could fly 6,000 km with a 2-tonne bomb-load. Beyond the BMW engines was the possibility of the Ju 290 being fitted with the Jumo 213s – as mentioned in the departmental heads' conference of 18 May.

At the beginning of 1943 Field Marshal Milch seems to have been toying with the idea of operations involving the Ju 390 some time in 1945. After Hertel, Junkers' chief designer, had promised that the first machine would be completed by the autumn of 1943 ready for testing, Milch took him at his word. On 8 March General von Barsewisch requested a firm statement of the manner, and in what numbers, the Ju 390 would appear in the future production plan. This could not be answered satisfactorily because capacity was set within such narrow limits.

On 27 April Milch conferred with senior staff at the RLM. He had gained the impression from some quarter or other that, as well as the specially fabricated central wing additions, the outer wings, tailplane section, fuselage nose with cabin, and retractable undercarriage were all available from Ju 290 B-1 assembly material and that series production was more or less in the offing. After a relatively short development phase in 1945 the Ju 390 would be operational over the Atlantic. With the planned BMW 801Es Milch was confident, on the basis of what Junkers had told him, that the design performance, particularly the top speed, would be achieved. This was important, for on the basis of Focke-Wulf's projections of cruising speed, range and armament for their long-range bomber design, Junkers' claimed top speed for the Ju 390 of 545 km/hr was decisive, all else being virtually equal.

In that same GLZM conference the promised performance figures for the Ju 390 were revised. With extensive use of Ju 290 B-1 parts, the flight weight was 75 tonnes with 30.5 tonnes apportioned to fuel. Because of the more powerful engine plant, the rate of climb was now 3 metres/sec close to the ground and 2.6 metres/sec at altitude. On the basis of a 350 km/hr cruising speed, the range was around 9,000 km.

There are rare mentions in the literature of a flying mock-up unsuitable for distance flight built solely for study purposes cobbled together at Berlin-Staaken from two Ju 290s. This machine should not be confused with the first prototype Ju 390 V-1.

The prototype blueprints were finalised in the spring of 1943 and assembly of Ju 390 V-1 was well under way by April. Junkers estimated readiness for trials by the autumn or at the latest by the spring of 1944, provided that sufficient personnel were available at their factories in Amsterdam, Dessau, Paris and Prague. Thus it remained uncertain which of the contenders would make the running.

In comparison with the Ju 390's expected fuel consumption of 300 metres/kg, the Me 264 managed 500 metres/kg because of its better aerodynamic form. The Ju 290 figure was 420 metres/kg. The Ju 390's planned top speed of 545 km/hr at 6,000 metres altitude was 90 km/hr higher than the Ju 290's. These assertions were received with scepticism both in the industry and latterly at the RLM. In May 1943 the competing firms provided calculations showing that the economical cruising speed of the Ju 390 was only 350 km/hr for a range of 9,000 km. The machine was 50 km/hr faster than the Ju 290, the top speed being 505 km/hr as against 455 km/hr.

The Year 1943 – Second Half

POLICYMAKING

On 11 June 1943 further details were made known respecting the future defensive armament of German transatlantic bombers. The air-refuelled Ju 290 would be fitted if possible with three MG 151 turrets with a full field of fire and MG 131 turrets in a gondola below the fuselage forward. It was considered unlikely, however, that this armament would be enough to see off machines such as the Mosquito or Beaufighter, which were much better armed. Milch considered it probable that if the Ju 290 began to appear in appreciable numbers over the sea – or after bombing raids had been initiated along the American Atlantic coast – the United States would increase substantially the number of aircraft carriers of all sizes in the area.

A few days later, on 15 June 1943, *Oberst* Viktor von Lossberg, General Staff Officer to the Chief of the RLM Technical Office, delivered a document reviewing the possibility of air raids on American targets. He foresaw a BV 222, supported by two U-tankers stationed in mid-Atlantic for refuelling purposes. Although SKL agreed surprisingly quickly to support this risky proposition, the *Luftwaffe* General Staff was not interested. It had also done everything possible to prevent such flights to Japan even though these were expressly desired by Hitler himself. The same day *Fliegerstab* Engineer Berlin noted:

What we have on hand at the moment for long-range reconnaissance are the Ju 290 and He 177 which can do the job for a while. They will be replaced by the Ta 400. Accordingly this leaves the Me 264 in a poor position. I flew it recently and I believe it is the right thing to drop it.

Milch accepted this judgement immediately and took steps to have the Messerschmitt development struck from the programme permanently and as soon as possible, ordering that the Ta 400 replace it. Remarkably, the Focke-Wulf development was now the choice even though the prototype had not been started. But as Milch was shortly to discover, the process of getting decisions at the RLM implemented was not always easy because of interference from higher levels.

Although it was impossible to estimate at this stage which and how many trans-oceanic bombers could be turned out in the medium term, the current demand was for two *Staffeln* each of six BV 222s, two reconnaissance *Staffeln*, one of He 177s and the other of Ju 290s, and up to three He 177 *Staffeln* equipped with torpedoes or remote-controlled bombs for Atlantic anti-shipping operations. During the development conference on 15 June 1943, Milch advocated using the He 177 and Ju 290 for Atlantic reconnaissance within their maximum range of 6,600 km. The Me 264 would be continued as a development project only and production plans would therefore be cancelled.

On account of these manoeuvres, in June 1943 Willy Messerschmitt spoke to Hitler privately and reported on the good progress being made with the Me 264. He hoped that the *Führer* would instruct the heads of *Luftwaffe* armament to re-include the Me 264 as an aircraft important for the war effort. He struck oil and on 9 July 1943 *Oberst* Pasewaldt reported:

I would now like to mention the question of the Me 264, which will probably also interest *Oberst* Peltz. The matter has been put into a new light following the constructor's report to the *Führer*. The situation was that the *Herr Feldmarschall* [Milch] had taken the decision and reported to the *Reichsmarschall* [Göring] that the Me 264 prototype was completed and that the Weser firm had capacity. It then appeared that the capacity at Weser was not sufficient because substantial additional requirements had arisen which could not be met. At the same time there arose the urgent need for the Fw 190D, and now the Ta 152, which with regard to the general situation was very awkward for us. The remaining available capacity at Weser was given to Tank. Messerschmitt had made strenuous efforts to be allowed to look for a way to build the aircraft at his own plants. Since then, Messerschmitt has received no satisfactory reply to the question, which is to say that the question of where the aircraft is to be built is still up in the air. Since *Oberstleutnant* Diesing has now said that the Me 264 will be ordered after all, the question of where this aircraft is to be produced is naturally once again of extraordinary importance.

Because of Hitler's intervention, the Me 264 was again at the centre of interest. An interesting feature in this connection was the fact that Göring appears to have lost track of which aircraft the Me 264 was. This is clear from several statements, including that of *Oberstleutnant* Ulrich Diesing, an operations officer at *Luftwaffe* Command Staff:

After Professor Messerschmitt visited the *Führer* the *Reichsmarschall* asked me what the Me 264 was. I described the machine and added that, of the six planned prototypes, one was ready as a flying mockup without armament and equipment and that parts had been taken out or were ready for fitting. Thereupon the *Reichsmarschall* pointed out that *Feldmarschall* Milch was of the opinion that this prototype must be properly flight tested before a decision was taken about a big production run, basically because quite often with Messerschmitt's new aircraft a weakness appears requiring a big reconstruction job.

At the beginning of July 1943 the heads of aircraft production met in Berlin to discuss the increasing aerial danger to U-boats entering and leaving French bases. Since the twin-engined Ju 88C and Ju 88R heavy fighters had proved no match for British Beaufighters and Mosquitos, Milch had gone for the Ta 154 or Do 335, which were better at warding off Allied aircraft than the Ju 88. In the face of problems like these, the problem of turning out efficient transatlantic aircraft shrank into the background.

On 8 July 1943 Dönitz discussed the situation with Hitler and quickly brought the conversation round to the need for reconnaissance aircraft for his U-boats. Hitler, remembering the four- and six-engined Me 264s which might have a range of 17,000 km and a strong defensive armament, saw these as the right aircraft for the task. 'These are the machines which will later work with the U-boat arm,' Hitler said, and promised to do all he could to reverse the order cancelling their production. At the same time he made clear that he had given up his earlier idea of attacking the United States 'because the few aircraft we could send across would contribute nothing, but only incite the population there to resistance'.

Only 24 hours later, on 9 July 1943, probably after hearing Hitler's comments, Milch decided that 'for the purposes of further study' work on the Me 264 prototypes V-2 to V-4 should be resumed. Weser Flugzeugwerke would have to assist because Messerschmitt did not have the capacity for further development.

Most of the *Luftwaffe* General Staff shared Göring's ignorance about the Me 264 and other transatlantic aircraft. Even *Oberst* Petersen, commander of the Rechlin Testing Centre, still referred to it as 'a flying mock-up' and considered the machine of no significance. Jeschonnek remained disinterested in very long-range bombers; as far as he was concerned the priority was more short-range bombers over the Eastern Front, a scaling-up of air transport capacity, more fighters, night fighters and fighter-bombers. His thinking coincided with that of Milch, who, in the GLZM conference of

22 March 1943, described transatlantic bombers as a 'luxury' which at the moment Germany could not afford. Progress in producing them was slow because their development and manufacture enjoyed a low priority and they were near the end of the queue for personnel and materials. At an RLM conference on 20 August 1943, Milch and Petersen discussed progress on them with *Major* Baumbach, the general in charge of bombers, and General Hertel. Hertel was convinced that the He 177 B-5 was very important while Baumbach dismissed the He 177 for long-range work because it lacked range. For this reason he asked for a higher priority to be awarded to the Ju 290 with a view to a much larger output of machines.

Milch decided that the He 177 A-3 and A-5 should be produced as planned but only three He 177 B-5 prototypes should be produced, adding that, as the He 177 lacked range for distant operations, everything should be done as soon as possible to have a strong Ju 290 version available. He promised a final decision between the two purpose-designed transatlantic bombers, the Me 264 and Ta 400, by September 1943.

On 25 August 1943 the *Luftwaffe* Command Staff reported a cut-off in the production of the BV 238 and BV 222 so as to concentrate instead on the output of fighters. It was assumed that seaplane losses in the West was a contributory factor in this decision. The last machines would be deleted from the *Luftwaffe* active register between July 1944 and August 1945, being replaced in the West by long-range Ju 290s. The BV 222 *Staffel* at Biscarosse would be replaced by Ju 290s of FAGr 5 at the beginning of November 1943. This decision was made easier by the recent heavy bomb damage to the Blohm & Voss works. The BV 222s under assembly at the end of August 1943, together with the crew training and test aircraft stationed at Travemünde, were to be redesignated as transports in quieter theatres of war. In the West and over the Atlantic, the BV 222 was no match for well-armed Allied aircraft and under fire was quick to burst into flame. Moreover the anchorages at Biscarosse were a popular target for low-flying raiders.

Meanwhile the formation of two Ju 290 *Staffeln*, which the bomber chiefs wanted for Biscay and the eastern Atlantic, had been approved and two *Staffeln*, each of six Ju 290s, now made up 1/ and 2/FAGr 5. The deteriorating situation left no room for talk about attacking America, this idea having been put on ice indefinitely.

Professor Messerschmitt was most anxious that his Me 264 should not fall foul of this new direction in policy and argued the case on 14 October 1943 at a meeting in Berlin with Göring and Milch:

> **Göring:** *Herr* Messerschmitt, I would now like to hear your views and first of all about the Me 264. I have been told that the construction has been abandoned.

> **Messerschmitt:** I have brought with me the files respecting the entire development. The Me 264 was transferred to Dornier by *Herr Feldmarschall* Milch in a letter to *Herr* Croneiss dated 20 October 1942.

> **Milch:** Because you had no capacity.

> **Messerschmitt:** *Jawohl.* The thing then came to a halt because Dornier couldn't take it on for lack of capacity...

In the meantime, the Me 262 jet was occupying all Messerschmitt's resources. The envisaged changeover from piston engines to jet turbines for the air defence of the *Reich* had left no room for anything else. The Ta 400 case, where there was a lack of experienced engineers and assembly workers, was equally dismal. Since it was policy not to develop two machines of the same type simultaneously, a heated discussion began regarding the respective qualities of the two transatlantic bombers. Messerschmitt was of the opinion that the Focke-Wulf development would be hard put to manage 10,000 km. His six-engined prototype (Me 264/6m) would soon be ready, and this new variant would have a range of 14,000 km, or 18,000 km in the reconnaissance version. The maximum speed of the Ta 400 in Messerschmitt's view was 595 km/hr, contrary to the Focke-Wulf assertion of 615 km/hr. Göring then changed the subject to air raids on

America which had long been discarded by Hitler as undesirable.

> **Göring:** What is the shortest distance from territory we occupy to America?
>
> **Petersen:** 5,400 km from Brest to New York.
>
> **Göring:** If only we could reach it! With just a couple of bombs we could force them to blackout!

After a brief discussion of the properties of the Ju 390, talk returned to the Me 264:

> **Peltz:** What type of bomb-load can she carry?
>
> **Friebel:** Ideally two 3-tonners for 7,000 km.
>
> **Göring:** So what machine can you offer me the soonest to get at the United States?

Neither Milch nor his staff could provide a firm answer to this question, and Göring turned abruptly to another subject. Milch understood at the time that the Ju 390 favoured by Göring was not, at least as regards performance, the most suitable machine for transatlantic operations. However, neither the Ju 290, nor the Me 264 nor any of the other competitors ever received the more powerful engines they required for that purpose.

Because the Me 262 required ever more capacity for production, Milch had no option but to halt work on the Me 264, and he advocated an even lower priority for transatlantic bombers in favour of air defence of the *Reich*. In mid-October 1943 he ruled that work should also be stopped on the Ta 400, as the expense involved in transforming the initial design into a useful transatlantic bomber was too great. Production might be resumed in the unlikely event that Focke-Wulf had nothing more important to do.

This decision was followed, on 29 October 1943, by Milch's pronouncement that only the Ju 390 should be included in the current programme – without the need for prototypes – for series production so as to cover the longest operational ranges. At the beginning of November, using the harshest tones, Milch made it abundantly clear with regard to Professor Messerschmitt:

> The Me 264 will not win the war. The Me 262 can win it. Therefore everything must be risked on the Me 262. If Messerschmitt completes the Me 262 and hasn't got anything more urgent then I would ask him to sort out the Me 264 so that we know if we should proceed with it or not. I do not need a machine that is able to fly 20,000 km but breaks up on take-off, even if that only happens ten per cent of the time.

Following the retreats on the various fronts and Germany's loss of the initiative, it was necessary to concentrate resources in order to avoid being sucked into the abyss. Basically, Milch saw the only justification for long-range bombers as co-operation with the U-boat arm. It was only in sinking ever more merchant tonnage *en route* from the United States to Britain and cutting the supply route to the northern Russian ports that the greatest hurt could be inflicted on the Allies. The best to be hoped for from bombing US coastal cities was to force the Americans to erect air defences, strengthen their air and naval patrols, outraging the civilian population as a side effect.

At the same time, however, great interest had developed in opening a direct flight connection between the *Reich* and Japan:

> The overseas connection has become ever more difficult and the only practical way to maintain it is to use U-boats. Because of their low speed this takes an extraordinarily long time. The need for the connection with Japan has grown during the course of the war and must at all costs be kept up. SKL supports the Japanese requests and solicits information as to what extent and when the German–Japanese air bridge can be expected.

At first no answer could be provided because of Hitler's negative stance on the subject of very long-range aircraft.

Additionally the availability of machines within the competence of the *Fliegerführer Atlantik* from the end of 1943 was very tight. According to his operational statistics, the best he could hope for was to send out six Fw 200s and two Ju 290s daily plus one BV 222 every other day. Between 15 November and 18 December 1943, *Luftflotte* 3 mounted only 96 reconnaissance flights of which thirty were carried out by Ju 290s and eight by BV 222s. To increase the number of missions being flown, on 15 December 1943 SKL demanded an increase in the production of Ju 290s to twenty-five aircraft per month to enable at least twelve missions to be flown daily. By the end of December 1943, *Fliegerführer Atlantik* had more than sixteen Fw 200s equipped with FuG 200 ship-detection radar and ten initially without. Besides these aircraft he also had at his disposal eight Ju 290s, two BV 222s, sixteen He 177s and eighteen Ju 88s, but for the Atlantic operations specified his force was still completely inadequate.

Aircraft Production

On 8 July 1943 Me 261 V-3 sustained 70 per cent overall damage on crash-landing following an auto-pilot flight test. All aboard bar the pilot and a scientific observer were injured. The fuselage and tail section received 100 per cent damage, the main undercarriage 40 per cent, both DB 606 coupled engines serious damage. On 21 July the RLM ordered the aircraft written off, the parts to be delivered to the breaking yard at Kölleda. On 16 August the Inspectorate Division of the RLM flew Me 261 V-2, after which the machine was parked in the open since the RLM had not issued instructions as to disposal. This machine had thickly riveted wings doubling as fuel tanks, but the technicians had not been able to make the wings fully fuel-tight. During 1943 work on the type had a low priority and the fate of V-1 and V-2 is not clear. One of the two was captured by the Americans on the airfield at Lechfeld at the end of April 1945.

In the summer of 1943, while Me 264 had its engine refit, a thoroughgoing comparative study was made of the potential of combining engine types on several long-range bomber projects, particularly the six-engined Ta 400 and Me 264 variants. A BMW report dated 7 October 1943 examined the uses of the BMW 801 TM, BMW 803, the BMW 018 jet and turboprop 028 design. The report stated that, for long distances at altitude, the BMW 803 was superior to the BMW 801 by reason of lower fuel consumption. Two BMW 018 jet turbines built into the underside of the wing would provide higher operational speeds but were far more costly in fuel. In any case, the Me 264 was not suitable for turbines because the airframe was too heavy. Turboprops when available would be the best method of propulsion for long-range bombers as 700 km/hr could be achieved at 13,000 metres for over 10,000 km.

No start was ever made on constructing the six-engined Me 264 variant. The victorious powers made full use of the comprehensive studies and investigations made by Messerschmitt and BMW, much of which influenced long-range bomber design of East and West in the 1950s.

It was estimated that, by the end of October 1943, only six Fw 200 long-range bombers would be coming off the production line monthly. Such a meagre influx was not sufficient to meet the requirements of *Fliegerführer Atlantik*, who had to share the machines 50/50 with *Luftflotte* 5. Furthermore the Fw 200 C-8 range under test at the Rechlin test centre in November, and which could fire remote-controlled weapons, could not be yet be forced into service. The Fw 200 rated unfavourably against the Ju 290 but the former would still be useful in the long-distance transport role once larger fuel tanks had been installed. From the summer of 1942 there had been an Fw 200D, converted from the C-range into an unarmed transport, but its development had been aborted in connection with plans to transform the obsolete Fw 200 into the long-range bomber recommended by Rechlin. In this regard the RLM had stipulated:

(1) Fuel to be in protected containers within fuselage and effort made to avoid having supplementary tanks hung outside.

(2) Defensive weapons to correspond to C-5 and C-6 series. To improve range the fuselage gun positions C and D – ventral and tail positions respectively – can be dispensed with.

(3) The least possible conversion work. Refits should aim to use whatever is currently available.

(4) To decrease flight weight accessories not absolutely essential, such as the oxygen unit, can be unshipped.

Focke-Wulf calculated in May 1943 that the take-off weight could be kept to 25.5 tonnes and thus the airframe did not require strengthening. Engine performance of the four Bramo 323s would be improved to an output of 1,200 hp by the use of a methanol injection unit. Seven variants of Fw 200F were being worked on based on the Fw 200 C-6 airframe. The C-gun position in the fuselage would be converted to house a fuel tank, and the position would disappear from the second variant. The fuel capacity would enable the machine to fly 5,000 km. The most efficient variant was the sixth with a new, armoured fuel installation in the fuselage and a maximum range of 6,600 km. With reduced armament this could be increased to 7,200 km. Nevertheless, as the Fw 200F did not have the required range for global operations, following the Fw 200 C-8 series, a handful of reconnaissance machines, production was terminated. The final Fw 200 C-8 (Works No. 068, TO+XX) was delivered to KG 40.

In mid-1943 Focke-Wulf finalised the design for a long-range bomber with six BMW 801E rapid-change engines. The Ta 400 had dual controls and auto-pilot effective in all three axes. Armament was two twin MK 108s with 250 rounds each (nose-gunner position for lightly protected or unprotected surface targets, particularly enemy submarines); one HD 151/Z each in B-1 position, 600 rounds, and B position, 450 rounds; one FDL 151/Z in C position with 500 rounds; and one quadruple MG 131 in the rear gun-turret, 1,000 rounds. There would be room in the fuselage for a maximum of 10 tonnes of bombs, such as four SC 2500s or an equivalent load of SC 1800s or SC 1000s, or nine SD 1000s or nine

SD 500s. The fuel capacity could be increased by lightening the bomb-load.

From late summer 1943 *Luftwaffe* planners began to lose interest in the project, which was being developed in France and was well adrift of the RLM time frame, although the RLM gave the nod to a low-profile development continuing. In October Professor Ernst Heinkel warned against producing the Me 264, which he considered 'purely an aircraft for making world records'. In his opinion the only proposed aircraft which were fitted for wide-ranging bomber and reconnaissance duty over the Atlantic or North Sea were the six-engined Ta 400 and the much-modified He 177.

Despite the seeming rejection of the Ta 400, too much time had been devoted to it for the project to be given up so easily and on 13 October the RLM received revised plans for a 65-tonne long-range fighter-bomber design with wings shoulder-mounted, twin-fin tailplane, fully retractable undercarriage and six air-cooled engines. The design could be modified as a reconnaissance aircraft or heavy bomber. Wing surface would be 170 square metres, wingspan 42 metres, average bomb-load 3 tonnes. The 12,000 litres of fuel would be carried in 32 tanks, 20 of them protected containers; 24 tanks would be located in the wings, the remainder in the central fuselage.

The armament had been improved, the nose gun now being mounted on a remote-controlled FDL 103Z turntable chassis. Both B gun positions were to be fitted with a hydraulically operated MG 151Z. C position had the same chassis as the nose unit, and the rear gun-turret would be fitted with a hydraulically operated HL 131V chassis.

For long ranges the bomb-load was set at 3 tonnes, although for short-range missions up to 20 tonnes could be carried. Besides the variety of standard bomb types, two 2.2-tonne mines or a Henschel (Hs) 294 guided missile or two Hs 293 1.95-tonne glider bombs or two PC 1400X bombs were also suggested, all of which could be released from below the outer engine nacelles. A Lotfe 7D bombsight was planned for standard bomb-aiming. The machine was clearly designed for the anti-shipping role. With a range of 9,000 km the aircraft could have covered large tracts of the Atlantic and represented a serious danger to enemy flying boats.

Work on the prototype Ta 8-400 V-1 was sub-contracted to the Paris firm SNCAO at Châtillon since Focke-Wulf had neither the personnel nor the floor space to build large aircraft of those dimensions. SNCAO soon encountered problems in building the machine, and progress was also slow because the work force expected an Allied invasion of France at any moment.

The RLM had recognised from early on that the light metal construction required a great deal of manual work and was particularly anxious for the fuselage to be turned out as a single shell, rather than the designed two halves for hand-riveting, to make possible machine riveting and fitting of parts and so dispense with the need for a costly assembly shop. The RLM thought that the wings would be better in a single-beam, as opposed to Focke-Wulf's designed triple-beam, method of construction and for transport and assembly reasons it also wanted the wings to be fabricated in several sections. The RLM specialists took the view that the machine was an innovative one and would require a completely fresh approach for series production.

In the summer of 1943, the Ta 400 was far short of completion. Larger quantities of scarce materials were required for the Ta 400 than the Me 264 and because of the airframe shape far more hand work was required, and the joins between the various parts would require rigorous quality controls. The chance of the Ta 400 ever being turned out in worthwhile numbers was very slim. In contrast the Me 264 with its single-shell method of construction was a shining example to the industry. On the same day when the full specification was finalised, the RLM had cast in doubt its willingness to persist with the order for the Ta 400 prototype on the grounds that series production would need a completely new procedure, and on 15 October 1943 Field Marshal Milch notified Focke-Wulf of his provisional decision not to proceed with the Ta 400. Even before 1944 the possibility of long-range bomber aircraft construction in Germany – not only at Focke-Wulf – was fast receding. In any case, what was more pressing was the maximum production of Fw 190D-9 and Ta 152 fighters. With that pronouncement, the Ta 400 fell by the wayside.

By the summer of 1943 the Heinkel design bureau had already been informed by the RLM that contracts for the He 177 A-7 (enlarged wing surface and two DB 610 coupled engines) and other sub-variants with four independent BMW 801E engines as well as DB 603Gs (B-7) would soon be cancelled. The range of these versions lay between 4,200 km and 4,800 km, which was reasonable enough for flights over the Bay of Biscay but not to the American coast or the Far East.

On 10 August 1943, Professor Heinkel admitted that the He 177 A-7 project would not be ready in mid-1944 as previously advised, but actually a year later, principally because of the unreliable engines. What he was offering instead was the He 177 A-8, a bomber variant of the A-5 with four independent BMW 801 radial engines. Milch responded that, for as long as he could remember, he had been asking for an He 177 with non-paired engines, but to date his plea had fallen on deaf ears. Finally he had asked Professor Heinkel himself to design a variant which had either four Jumo 213s or DB 603s. He turned down BMW 801s with high-altitude superchargers because development would take too long. The RLM considered the prospects far better if Heinkel would go for the two recommended engines, and preferably the Jumo 213, because the BMW 801 had been earmarked for the Fw 190 fighter.

On 20 August Milch decided to recommend the He 177 B-5 (previously known as the A-8) using the A-5 airframe. Mention was also made in passing of an A-10 under consideration, this being an A-7 with four independent motors. At the same meeting, *Major* Hoffmann of the RLM produced performance comparisons and concluded that the He 177 B-5 with four independent DB 604Gs would be about 60 km/hr faster than the A-5 powered by two DB 610 pairs.

The top speed would then be 540 km/hr for a range of 3,850 km, a pitifully short distance which had ruled out the variant for strategic uses from the outset. Professor Heinkel interposed that precisely such a variant had been offered as early as 1938 when the RLM did not want it, and now they did.

On 20 August, Heinkel's director Franke promised that the blueprints for the He 177 B-5 would be completed within 30 days and the first prototype would be ready to fly at the end of February 1944. Heinkel reckoned to have series production under way from 1 January 1945. *Major* Hoffman pointed out that the He 177 B-5 with central tail fin only, as recommended by Heinkel, would only have a worthwhile performance if the engines had contra-rotating propellers. *Oberst* Petersen, head of the Rechlin test centre, also drew attention to the problems of paired-up engines such as had been planned for the A-5. For this reason he supported an immediate change to single-working engines for the He 177 B-5, and was against the DB 613 pairs.

During an RLM conference on 26 October, *General-Ingenieur* Mahnke raised the point about the changeover from paired to independent engines. In view of increased Allied strengths the general in charge of bombers had asked for a definitive instruction by the end of 1943 at the latest since the He 177 A-3s and A-5s serving with KG 40 and KG 100 were now flying missions with remote-controlled and glider bombs against shipping targets whilst long-range bomber missions were not presently flown.

The He 277 A-1 and B-1 developments, based on the He 177 B-5, appeared to offer a range of over 5,000 km from the early calculations. In contrast to the He 177 B-5, however, the He 277 had a larger wing surface, a fully designed fuselage and redesigned undercarriage. Even the optimists were not counting on seeing a prototype of this design until November 1944 nor anything from the production line before spring 1946. Because of the disappointing underperformance of the He 177 B series, the RLM decidedly finally for 133 square metres wing surface and four Jumo 222s or six BMW 801s should the Jumos not be available. The wing structure had been designed so that six single engines could be built in without incurring any great expense. With the appropriate locations on the wing both engine versions could be fitted at the same time. The modern airframe would receive a strong defensive armament and the best possible armour against 3-cm hits.

In July 1943 the He 277 was compared with the Ju 290 and Ju 390, and during the debate at the RLM controversy arose as to whether its extra 50 km/hr in speed was really a sufficient advance to warrant building the aircraft. The Technical Office specialists tended to the belief that it was not. Heinkel countered the argument by pointing to the unusual nose-wheel undercarriage and modern airframe. In comparison, the Ju 290 'was just a steamer, the He 277 on the other hand was an elegant and useful aircraft', and the same went for the Ju 390, which was worse-behaved in the air than the Ju 290. Heinkel director Franke conceded, however, that even in the six-engined version of the He 277 the range would be no more than 8,000 km, and it seemed questionable to him whether the machine would ever fly such a distance.

On 21 July 1943 Heinkel management had arranged for the first six high-level He 274 bombers to be produced in Paris because the RLM had not given the type a sufficiently high degree of priority. The general situation in France ensured that all work there proceeded without undue haste and the Farman company selected for the work was in any case short of suitable technical personnel. When, a month later, Heinkel realised that the RLM would not award the development a higher priority, the company decided not to step up the scale of production.

On 3 August 1943 Field Marshal Milch spoke out for more Ju 290s. Behind this lay the demands of the *Kriegsmarine*, which was keen to revive the U-boat war. On 21 August, visibly angry with Milch over Göring's decision to abandon seaplane construction in favour of more fighters, OKM pressed for the supply of long-distance reconnaissance aircraft as replacements for the BV 222 on which it had been counting. Delivery of the first of the new batch of Ju 290 long-range bombers was scheduled for December 1943. As the BV 222 would not now be available and the Ju 390 was not yet ready, the Ju 290 was the only solution. The lack of aircrew trained to fly the Ju 290 was the reason why relatively few of the aircraft were to be found over the Atlantic. *Generalleutnant* Ulrich Kessler, the new *Fliegerführer Atlantik*, indented at once for a *Staffel* of specially equipped He 177 long-range aircraft, for a second *Staffel* of Fw 200s with greater fuel capacity and a third *Staffel* of Ju 290s, the latter to be operational from 8 November 1943. On 30 October, he was promised the first ten series-produced Ju 290 reconnaissance aircraft, and as these had the same radius of action as the BV 222 but were faster, Kessler considered that the reconnaissance situation was on the up.

The reality was, of course, the reverse. On 20 November the *Luftwaffe* Command Staff advised Göring's office that the Ju 290-equipped FAGr 5 had only flown four missions. The aircraft had been in the air for between 16 and 18 hours and had remained circling a convoy for five hours unmolested because the enemy thought the Ju 290s were Allied, so long had it been since the *Luftwaffe* had operated land-based aircraft that far from the French coast. The meagre supply of Ju 290s restricted the strategic possibilities. Production of the reconnaissance version was supposed to be four or five a month from 1944 onwards increasing to ten per month in January 1945. Mass production of the bomber version was scheduled to begin in June 1944. Twenty-eight would be ready by the end of December 1944. How the planners justified these schedules remains a mystery. It had nothing to do with reality.

On 20 October 1943 Ju 390 V-1 (Works No. 390 00 0001, GH+UK) made its maiden flight at Merseburg piloted by *Flugkapitän* Pancherz. On the 28th *Oberst* Petersen flew the aircraft himself and described the flying characteristics as outstanding. Milch was full of praise next day, declaring: 'The Ju 390 has flown and was fantastic.' On account of all this,

Major Hoffmann proposed beginning the series run at once, using the first aircraft off the line for flight tests. Milch was only too aware of how time was running away from the planners and on 27 October approved the suggestion in principle that – despite the risks – the Ju 390 should be series-produced without further prototypes.

In addition to Hoffmann, *Oberst* Petersen was also in favour of turning out the Ju 390 as a very long-range bomber. Two days later Milch ordered the series run commenced. On 5 November the V-1 prototype flew at Dessau, Göring being an interested spectator, before the programme of flight tests began at Prague-Rusin. On 11 November Milch confided to Hitler's *Luftwaffe* ADC, *Oberstleutnant* von Below, that the Ju 390 would not only have an extraordinarily strong defensive armament but also 'a theoretical range of over 10,000 km. The machine has come out right at the first throw.' Gut-feelings had taken over from the slide rule.

Scarcely a month later, on 1 December 1943, the *Luftwaffe* production schedule listed the Ju 390 for series production from October 1944. There would be one machine in October, three in November and five in December 1944. In January 1945 there would be seven, in February nine and from March 1945 ten every month until March 1946. How the German aircraft industry might achieve such a miracle was not explained.

By August 1943 the *Luftwaffe* had still not managed to get the BV 222 flying boat operational over the Atlantic. Whether the naval reconnaissance squadron (*See-Fernaufklärungsstaffel* BV 222) would ever be up to strength could not be foreseen. On 21 August, the *Fliegerführer Atlantik* made a surprise request that the transfer of the next aircraft, BV 222 V-4, should be delayed because the infrastructure at Biscarosse was still incomplete. Accordingly the first of two reconnaissance BV 222 machines did not arrive there until 16 September. Shortly afterwards, both machines at Biscarosse were destroyed by Allied fighter-bombers, so that the stationing of large flying boats on the Biscay coast had to be reconsidered. At the end of August OKM had issued SKL with instructions to report on whether large flying boats were considered necessary. On 7 September 1943, in reply to an enquiry from the *Luftwaffe* general at OKM, the *Fliegerführer Atlantik* expressed the opinion that:

> Per the latest file reports today supply of further BV 222 and BV 238 no longer intended by Command Staff, *Luftflotte 3*, therefore expansion Biscarosse suspended with immediate effect. Under circumstances seems correct decision to call off BV 222s.

SKL did not agree that well-trained reconnaissance crews were better employed flying transports. At the beginning of October, SKL observed:

> To strengthen reconnaissance it seems the right thing to retain the BV 222s even after the Ju 290s are delivered. The opinion that the BV 222 is too weakly armed has not so far been proved in a fight. No value is placed on keeping a BV 238 in the Atlantic theatre. As the production of large flying boats has been stopped by ObdL – Command Staff – we can count at best on only seven flying boats of which we will not have more than three or four operational at the same time. The expansion of the ground organisation at Biscarosse therefore needs only three or four anchorages with provisional camouflage, and according to latest reports two are already completed.

With such a small operational unit, dangerous special missions with a high risk of loss, such as attacks on the American East Coast, were a doubtful proposition while the two to four flying boats envisaged by SKL for the U-boat support role was a feeble effort. Nevertheless, on the basis of operational missions already completed, seaplanes seemed suited for what the *Kriegsmarine* had in mind and lay behind its demand for more. BV 222s were wanted as soon as possible to support the U-boat war, one idea being to equip a *Staffel* of the aircraft with electronic jamming gear. A third BV 222 was promised for delivery from 20 November 1943. The C-0 version could reconnoitre a greater sea area than the earlier types, roving perhaps from France to northern Norway and back.

Chapter 8

Techniques to Increase Range

Numerous methods were tried in the effort to extend the limited range of Germany's heavy bombers. Amongst them featured rocket boosters, towed fuel containers and, in the case of seaplanes, refuelling from U-boats.

For a take-off fully laden, rocket booster tubes might be fixed below the wings. They were not favoured, being more costly than the easily jettisoned liquid-fuelled *Krafteier* (power-eggs). An He 111 Z-1 tug or similar aircraft used to tow a heavy machine into the air was another way of conserving the latter's fuel supply.

Junkers had begun testing rockets to assist take-offs in 1929. In mid-1937 successful experiments were made using two Walter SG 500 V-1 (109-500) rockets fixed below the wings of an He 111 H-1 to increase speed rapidly during the take-off phase and so save fuel. This led to the mass-production of the SG 500 A-1 with a 30-second burn and a 500-kg thrust. More than 3,000 take-offs were achieved with He 111 and Ju 88 aircraft, mostly without incident. Six SG 503s with a 45-second burn and 1,000-kg thrust were necessary for heavy gliders or four-engined aircraft such as the Ju 290.

The He 111Z tug was another means to get a heavily laden bomber airborne especially if the runway was too short. Junkers was dubious about the method on smaller airfields for fear that the tug would whip up dust and sand and so obscure the vision of the towed aircraft's crew. In further examination of the towing question in July 1942 it came to light that the Ju 390 was likely to become unstable in the vertical axis during the climb for lack of power, and for this reason Ju 290s were often adapted to the tug role. *Oberst* von Pasewaldt, head of aircraft development, gave instructions at Dessau on 18 July 1942 that all large aircraft were to have towing gear fitted at both ends of the fuselage. Additional liquid- or solid-fuel rocket boosters were available for more power if required. On 30 October that year the Rechlin test centre reported that the Ju 390 had a range of 9,000 km with a 3-tonne bomb-load, or 11,400 km without, if take-off were assisted over 1,000 metres by the He 111Z tug.

An alternative to fitting an aircraft with supplementary fuel tanks was to tow a fuel container with wings (*Deichselschlepp*). The aircraft drew on the fuel in the tank during the initial flight phase. The idea was developed originally for fighters. An He 177 A-3 (TM+IU) was employed for trials using an SG 5005 container to test the vulnerability to MG fire. It was immediately realised by *Deutsche Forschungsanstalt für Segelflug* (DFS – German Research Institute for Gliding) research engineers that much larger stabilised containers under tow could be used as a fuel source to extend the operational range of large aircraft. These towed devices were proposed for the new jet bombers from 1943 onwards, and DFS trials with an Ar 234 B-2 at Neuburg/Donau at the beginning of 1945 proved the value of the system.

In the GLZM conference of 5 March 1943 on the theme of the BV 238 it was emphasised that *Grossadmiral* Dönitz was most anxious for the seaplane to be made available very soon for reconnaissance and replenishment purposes. This idea was not accepted with much enthusiasm in higher *Luftwaffe* circles:

> **Oberst Pasewaldt:** The BV 238 is being built, though only in small numbers. But the way people imagine it just gently bobbing up and down on the ocean makes me laugh.

> **General von Barsewisch:** The Navy keeps bringing it up. They say it can refuel every so often from a U-tanker

and stay out there for weeks. [Hilarity.] No, seriously, they emphasise that particularly! For that reason it's not being shelved. But now they're coming round to the idea that only a fast land-based aircraft is going to be of use for shipping reconnaissance. Therefore we just have to find a way to get the Me 264 into service.

The U-boat arm wanted a floating fuel station in the shape of a large U-tanker from which a wolf pack and flying boats could refuel during operations against Allied convoys. The idea was discussed with great passion, but large seaplanes were not able to refuel in a heavy swell on the open sea, and eventually nothing came of it. Even in a relatively light seaway, sea state 2 or 3, refuelling was only possible exceptionally. Nevertheless, *Oberst* Viktor von Lossberg reported on 15 March 1943, regarding the possibility of bombing targets on the American mainland:

> Investigation has shown that operations against America without intermediate refuelling are not possible for three or four years. An immediate possibility is to station a U-boat 1,000–1,500 km off the American coast and when the weather is favourable it signals for the BV 222 to fly out from France with a half bomb-load and fully topped up. If something goes wrong at the rendezvous point the aircraft goes back to another U-boat in mid-Atlantic to pump fuel aboard for the flight back. The *Kriegsmarine* and Blohm & Voss both consider this method can be easily worked out. More or less fine weather and a calm sea is a precondition for the attack to enable the seaplane to load its 8 tonnes of bombs for dropping on New York or Washington. If the weather remains good the seaplane can fly back and repeat the raid the following night. The important things are: only night attacks and little or no armament. In my opinion that is the way to follow up a first-time surprise raid. Dr Seilkopf puts the operational season from March to the beginning of September. For the current year, in view of the situation in the East, it is

too late. I have spoken with *Oberstleutnant* Gaul about the possibilities of refuelling from U-boats. These would have 36 tonnes of fuel available for us. If we used two seaplanes, we would need two U-boats nearer the American coast and a safety boat in mid-Atlantic.

General Jeschonnek, Chief of the *Luftwaffe* General Staff, considered the scheme far-fetched. Even so a discussion then developed about the details of this audacious plan. Von Lossberg was completely convinced the operation would work and volunteered to lead it himself:

Milch: I would approve such a plan. It would force them over there to take unheard-of precautions. But we couldn't do it until 1944.

Vorwald: Interestingly enough, the *Kriegsmarine* is positive on it.

Milch: One would be concerned that the forward U-boat should not be too near the coastal patrols.

Von Lossberg: It would need to be at least a thousand kilometres off-shore. It could be more but then the BV 222 bomb-load would be smaller.

Milch: My only fear is that the U-boat would have to submerge if Allied aircraft were about. Then our seaplane couldn't find it.

Von Lossberg: At a thousand kilometres from the coast that wouldn't be very likely.

Milch: You also have to think that when the U-boat transmits, it will draw them out.

Von Lossberg: If the pilot receives a short-signal at 200 km, he will locate the U-boat. If the astronomical navigation is right, he will spot it at 20–30 km. He will have a half bomb-load. The biggest problem is getting the bombs aboard. They would have to be small.

Bree: We can't take high explosives, they have to be hung outside. The bombs would have to be incendiaries.

Von Lossberg: The 2.2 kg magnesium incendiary detonates after four to ten minutes. If you dropped a series of those down a New York street and they all went off like hand grenades that would be good.

Milch: What do you want to go for?

Von Lossberg: The Jewish area or the docks.

Grossadmiral Dönitz was very taken by the idea and spoke out strongly in favour. As there was insufficient time for the preparations before the weather worsened as would be expected around the beginning of September 1943, it was scheduled for the spring of 1944. By then, however, the general war situation had deteriorated. The Western Allies were firmly in control in the Atlantic, and their strong anti-submarine forces had forced the U-boats to abandon attacks on the main convoy routes. Replenishment and bombing-up operations between giant seaplanes and U-boats near the American coast were now unthinkable.

The first known successful attempt at mid-air refuelling occurred on 25 June 1923 when a US Army DH-4B was refuelled twice in mid-air in accomplishing a flight of 6 hours 38 minutes. One of the two pilots caught a hose dangled from the tanker aircraft and attached it to the fuel tank. In the 1930s, British experiments were carried out by an Imperial Airways biplane and, later, Type S-30 seaplanes in commercial service were refuelled in mid-air during transatlantic crossings.

The *Luftwaffe* seems to have shown no interest in the method until after the war began. The German Research Institute for Gliding began with coupling-up experiments in which a DFS 230 heavy glider was towed by a Ju 52, He 111 and Do 17 respectively. Next followed trials to couple-up and uncouple during flight. This was the prerequisite for mid-air refuelling. The DFS team, led by Dr Feliz Kracht, fitted a Ju 52 with an extensible hawser and drogue. 'Docking' was accomplished when a steel rod projecting from the nose of the following aircraft entered the drogue. Successful docking manoeuvres were achieved between a Ju 52/3m and

Fw 58 V-17 and these led between 18 June and 18 July 1941 to trials at Dessau in which a refuelling procedure was filmed, Ju 90 V-5 (Works No. 4917, D-ANBS) towing up and then re-tanking Fw 58 V-18 (Works No. 2207, D-OXLR).

On 16 August 1941 Heinkel design engineers and the RLM discussed ways of increasing the range of an He 177 A-3 to at least 10,000 km, the idea being that the aircraft, fitted with supplementary tanks, would fly out across the Bay of Biscay and, after refuelling from the aerial tanker 'Warsaw', operate in support of the U-boat arm by intercepting Allied reconnaissance aircraft. Additional jettisonable fuel tanks could be fitted in the rear of the bomb-bay and below the wings or fuselage. Heinkel suggested protected tanks inside the wings for which thicker riveting and fuel drainage ports would be necessary.

At the outset of refuelling the flight speed would be reduced to 220–250 km/hr and then gradually increased. The He 177 rear-gunner would be responsible for supervising the operation. The pumping equipment would be fitted aboard the tanker for weight reasons. In a memorandum of 20 August 1941 for Professor Heinkel, it was reported that an He 177 refuelled in mid-flight would easily cover 9,500 km and be able to remain aloft for 25 hours if throttled back to about 385 km/hr. The amount of extra fuel required to be shipped was at least 9 tonnes. To bomb America this aircraft would have had to be refuelled twice, the second time on the home leg, so operationally its best role was as a bomber interceptor.

Aircraft manufacturer Fieseler of Kassel carried out comprehensive tests during 1941 and displayed to the RLM various coupling-up and towing methods described by the Rechlin staff as 'very promising'. The RLM was interested in conducting further experiments at Kassel with a captured steel-nosed Potez 63 but the rear fuselage of the French machine was probably too narrow to fit the hose drum. In February 1942 it was decided that the gear could not be installed in the rear of the tanker aircraft because its weight affected its centre of gravity. On 27 November 1941 the RLM gave Transavia of Lauenburg/Pomerania the contract to design by 12 December, and supply by February 1942 a winch not exceeding 0.8 x 0.8 x 0.4 metres for a 50-metre long hose of rubber 32 mm thick. In November 1941 Fieseler was also awarded a contract to make further mid-air refuelling trials and two electrically operated hawser winches originally designed for the Fieseler air-sea rescue aircraft were fitted aboard two Fw 58s at Travemünde at the end of December. The work was given the high 'SS' level of priority but the final report of 31 May 1942 indicated that more time was needed. In the GLZM conference of 15 February 1942 *Fliegerstab* engineer Friebel, in a reference to the projected 'America Operation' of the Me 264, reported that neither that aircraft, nor the current Heinkel or Focke-Wulf 300 projects could fly an attack without mid-air refuelling. This led to a fierce discussion:

> **Milch:** Does the General Staff believe that long-range bombing missions could be carried out using mid-air refuelling, probably several thousand kilometres from base?
>
> **Jeschonnek:** There's no point.
>
> **Milch:** One can think that in peacetime, but not in war. We have got the job and have to consider best how to do it. We can't just solve it like that.
>
> **Friebel:** On the basis of the preliminary tests I don't know if we can be so strict about turning it down.
>
> **Milch:** They are wrong, therefore we won't accept it. Two aircraft flying out, how long before they do the transfer?
>
> **Friebel:** At 4,000 km one aircraft takes on board 7 tonnes of fuel from the other. The procedure is possible. Two aircraft flying 4,000 km together is also possible. If they get separated we don't lose much.
>
> **Milch:** If the General Staff changes its opinion about mid-air refuelling I would request their instructions. Until then we have to leave it aside. There is also an idea of landing in Greenland and waiting for a U-boat

to turn up with fuel. I really don't know where they get these ideas from…

Storp: Another possibility is to tow out a freight glider which is then jettisoned at sea. At least it must be operationally possible to some extent.

The conference was then shown a film of the whole process between the Ju 90 and Fw 58 mentioned earlier. Afterwards the discussion resumed:

Milch: We have carried out the operation before studying the technology. We all know they're not serious about doing it like that 4,000 km from home. The towed aircraft probably wouldn't even take off.

Friebel: We thought of doing the fuel transfer during the take-off tow.

Milch: It would be a different matter if the towed aircraft couldn't take off fully laden. If you refuelled in sight of home coming back then we could look at it in a certain way. In that film you can see the difficulty of mid-air refuelling a pregnant duck. But it avoids the real problem, the bad weather and so on. Here I see the difficulty not in the refuelling but that you have to fly a couple of thousand kilometres and then rendezvous. It's not always blue skies. As soon as you get into the soup and part company then your chances of meeting up again are pretty slim. If you could stay together it would be OK. There's two other points. First, taking the load on board and second, storing it in your tanks. If that can be solved satisfactorily then I would say we should go for it. Meeting at 4,000 km is out of the question. We have to think about that. We still have the task. How can we do it? We have to reckon on 13,500 km there and back.

Friebel: We can't do it with the aircraft we have.

Milch: If you have to fly 13,500 km it's my opinion you must have a 3,000 km reserve; 1,500 km is too little. Now we have other jobs to cover. Long-range reconnaissance over the sea, as a bomber, as a transport. Will the aircraft we have, or are expecting to have, fit the bill?

Friebel: They are the following. First, the Ju 290 which we are going to make into a six-engined job by slotting in an extra section of wing. That will be the Ju 390. The maximum range is 10,900 km with the BMW 801D. If we get the Jumo 213, the range is 12,000 km. Flight weight is 74 tonnes, payload 8 tonnes, bomb-load as according, fuel 30 tonnes. For armour 1.4 tonnes, weapons 2.9 tonnes, crew of six, empty weight 35 tonnes.

Milch: What difference would it make to the range if it had no armament or armour and just 1 tonne of bombs?

Friebel: The aircraft needs about 2.5 tonnes of fuel per 1,000 km. It would give her an extra 1,600 km. That wouldn't make much difference.

The discussion then rambled on as usual without any concrete decisions being made. Futuristic thinking on such techniques as mid-air refuelling horrified the *Luftwaffe* High Command. Jeschonnek was a mouthpiece for the scepticism of his equally conservative General Staff. The successful practical trials made no difference whatever. What the flight tests did show, however, was that the Fw 58 had had no problem docking into the Ju 52 or Ju 90. That was the real obstacle overcome.

On 9 April 1942 at Dessau, engineers from Junkers, Transavia and the Rechlin testing centre examined drawings for a hose-winch installation aboard a Ju 88 A-4 and the aperture for the DFS-designed stabiliser. It was decided that, as the Ju 88 had a relatively narrow fuselage, the Ju 86 was preferable because the larger fuselage allowed for the installation to be monitored throughout the flight. On 17 April Fieseler received a preliminary contract from the RLM for the development of an airborne fuel transfer system. The requirement was for a secure coupling technique and a procedure transferring the maximum amount of fuel possible in the shortest time.

Between 10 and 16 May 1942 Junkers worked on calculations to improve the range of the Ju 390 by mid-air refuelling from a Ju 290 and in June it was established that, by reducing the bomb-load, an extra 1,500 km could be flown, providing a total range in ideal weather conditions of 13,000 km, including a 15 per cent reserve, just enough for a return flight from Brest to New York. Further tests in flight had been made to underpin the planning, culminating in a test involving a Fw 58 and Fieseler (Fi) 167 on 15 June 1942:

> The most favourable coupling body for the higher speeds (over 170 km/hr) proved to be a ball and will be used for the new Fw 200 coupling gear. Previous tests involved a cone-shaped drogue. The hawser released astern by the Fi 167 followed the required curve from the lateral aspect but seen from behind it hangs four to six metres to the right. This is caused by aerodynamic forces acting on the twist of the hawser. Being towed by a hawser presents no real difficulties. The drawing-up of the towed aircraft by the electrical winch posed no problems. Towing an unpowered aircraft was not completely successful. The jolt at coupling is moderate. The first attempt occurred at too low a speed and the vibrations typical of this type of tow appeared. On the second attempt the need for a different coupling was realised. The tests are being continued. At our present state of knowledge it is possible for a bomber to tow a fighter-bomber with props feathered. The latter can uncouple in its operational area and fly on under its own power. The fuel transfer itself has not yet been tried.

Up to 30 June 1942 DFS had been trying to stabilise the hose by means of a slightly cone-shape drogue while attempting to insert it into the tank opening protruding from the fuselage nose. This was very difficult, particularly in turbulence. It was considered a better method to take in the ball end of a lightly weighted hose at least 25 metres long by means of a fork device with tines about 1.62 metres apart. The trapped hose end would be brought into the aircraft by hand and attached to the fuel system. Other systems considered were the 'hose-hawser procedure' (with the hose attached loosely to the hawser); the 'flexible hose procedure' (in which the second aircraft caught a dangling hose); and 'refuelling under tow by a metal tube' (where the fork caught a tube through which the fuel flowed and by means of which the tow was undertaken). A fourth possibility was 'hose refuelling by coupling up while flying below'. Here the hose was winched down, caught by the fork on the fuselage of the second machine as it flew below the tanker, and was then connected manually to the fuel tank inlet on the fuselage upper surface.

The Fieseler technical management reported on their results on 6 July 1942:

> **1.** The Fieseler catching procedure with fork and hawser was developed. In moderate turbulence it is still possible to couple up two aircraft in flight. The prerequisite is mastery of formation flying. Contact between the towing hawser and propellers during the catching phase is a danger to be aware of.
>
> **2.** The fuel transfer system using the tow method was considered but has not yet been tried in practice. What cannot be resolved is the risk of fire in the event of incorrect attachment of the hose.
>
> **3.** In order to reduce the length of hose required, experiments were made using a rigid-tow [*Deichselschlepp*] procedure. The expense in fuel of hauling up the towed aircraft justified the longer hose. Flight trials resulted in violent vibrations between both aircraft while coupled. The practical possibilities of this procedure therefore appear to be non-existent.

Once the planning stage had concluded in August 1942, airborne experiments were hindered by delays supplying machinery parts to Transavia even though they were given the relatively high 'DE' priority rating. Airborne trials at Fieseler ended in late 1942 and on 19 November the Fw 58, still equipped with the refuelling apparatus which the RLM had ordered unshipped, went to Dornier 'for ongoing studies'.

Trials by KdE Rechlin using an Fw 200 and Bf 110 for a mid-air coupling attempt were described mysteriously as 'halfway successful', the procedure being considered very difficult from an aviator's point of view, the hawser only being forked in after numerous attempts, because of the difficulty coping with a strong pendulum motion.

In a secret file note dated November 1942, *General-Ingenieur* Reichenbach (RLM LC2 head) observed:

> 1. Increasing range of normal aircraft. If a tanker aircraft refuels an operational aircraft of the same type at the extent of the tanker's radius of action, the second machine will gain from 35 to 50 per cent more range.

> 2. Fighter escort for such a flight is not possible at present. If, for every bomber or transport, a fighter is refuelled once outwards and once on the return after flying cover over the operational area, in the case of a Ju 88 with a Bf 109 this would reduce the range of the bomber by up to 25 per cent, with an He 177 by up to 15 per cent. The fighter would also need modifying to carry more lubricant and oxidant...

In a memorandum of 30 November, Reichenbach, Friebel and Scheibe (RLM LC 2/II) recommended that development centres at the RLM and KdE Rechlin should work out procedures for erecting the test equipment, determine the most favourable formation for fuel transfer and design a secure coupling system for use in flight.

The subject became current again in March 1943 when after all 'conventional' possibilities for a transatlantic bomber had been exhausted, Milch was obliged to return to the emergency solutions. Since neither the Me 264, the Ju 390 nor the Ta 400 would be available in the short term, in desperation the RLM took up the subject of mid-air refuelling once more. On 5 March 1943 the decisive talks went as follows:

Friebel: The material for thirty Me 264s has been delivered.

Von Barsewisch: It's too late.

Hertel: The machine can only be built at Messerschmitt and at the moment we have no capacity.

Friebel: That's just the point. I don't think we can expect anything worthwhile before 1945. The best we can make do with is the Ju 290 with mid-air refuelling. That is a wobbly bridge but better than nothing. I estimate it would have up to 2,700 km radius of action if we filled up two Ju 290s and a third of the way out one machine transfers half its fuel to the other. The trials were all favourable. It's only a question whether we allocate capacity to it, then it's on. Everything else is, as we see, fantasy by reason of under-capacity. Refuelling between two Ju 290s is better than a Ju 390 which doesn't yet exist and much better than an Me 264 which never will exist.

And so it came to pass. Up to four Ju 290s were converted either into tankers with refuelling equipment or long-range bombers. The aircraft involved were originally Ju 290 A-2 and A-4 reconnaissance versions and Ju 390 V-1. On 12 November 1943 at Dessau Ju 290 A-4 (Works No. 0169, PI+PW) and Ju 290 A-4 (Works No. 0170, KR+LA, possibly the sixth prototype attached to KdE Rechlin between 2 December 1943 and 14 April 1944) flew a refuelling exercise. According to the Ju 390 V-1 log, refuelling trials were carried out at Dessau with Ju 290 A-4 (Works No. 0151, CE+YZ) between 10 and 15 January 1944, and at Prague between 17 and 23 January 1944. The tests were filmed from a Ju 88 V-7 for the benefit of Junkers technicians. Between 24 and 29 January 1944 Junkers received mid-air refuelling equipment for installation aboard Ju 290 A-2 (Works No. 0157, SB+QG) and Ju 290 A-2 (Works No. 0157, SB+QH) and further trials were flown from the Biscay aerodrome Mont de Marsan over the Atlantic. How far these two aircraft ranged in these trials is not recorded.

The development of *Mistel* aircraft began with a patent registered by Hugo Junkers in 1929 for a design he prepared two years earlier. DFS took up the idea at the beginning of the 1940s and its first practical trial involved heavy glider DFS 230 B-2 (CB+ZB) and a Klemm (Kl) 35 (D-EXCM) on top as the motored unit. Later an Fw 35 (CA+GN) replaced the Klemm. From June 1943 a Bf 109 was mounted atop a DFS 240 (D-IEXX) and test flown, the results being sufficiently satisfactory for an operational unit, a Ju 88 A-4 airframe carrying a large hollow charge being transported by a Bf 109 F-4, to be placed with KG 101 over the Normandy area in 1944. Subsequently plans were drawn up for an He 177 airframe carrying a 4-tonne hollow charge for pinpoint raids but the idea was abandoned at the end of 1944 for lack of capacity. Ultimately only the Ju 88 *Mistel* ever saw service, being used, with mixed results, in attempts to demolish Rhine bridges and attack targets on the Eastern Front.

The *Mistel* design prompted the idea of carrying the unpowered airframe on top of, or below, the fuselage of the carrier aircraft, or having midget bombers slung below the wings. It was even seriously argued that transatlantic bombers should carry their own fighter cover, or small jet bombers. After the attack the daughter machines would then return to the carrier aircraft.

This thinking culminated in plans to stow aircraft such as the Me 328 or Me P 1073, with retractable or folding wings, in the interior of machines the size of the Ju 390 or the projected Me 264. Early in the war, before the development of supplementary disposable fuel tanks, Messerschmitt worked on the scheme of having short-range bombers tow their own fighter defence to the target on a short hawser. The first practical trials on the ground involved a Bf 110 C-1 (Works No. 959, CE+BU, D-AEGJ) towing a Bf 109 E-3 (Works No. 1953, CE+BM). After this went off well, the first airborne trial took place on 18 April 1940 from Augsburg to Munich-Riem and return, the propeller of the fighter being feathered.

Once jettisonable 300-litre fuel tanks became available for the Bf 109 in 1940, the towing idea was abandoned but the experience gained led to the notion of small 'parasite' fighters and bombers being carried within the fuselage of giant 'mother' aircraft. The Ju 390 design appeared particularly suited to this role and on 4 April 1942 the RLM Technical Office asked for fighters and bombers with pulse-jet propulsion to be developed for it as parasite aircraft. The Ju 390 would be a kind of flying arsenal to which the midget machines returned after a raid to re-bomb in preparation for a fresh sortie. Retrieval was by means of a slip-coupling or by landing on the back of the carrier aircraft for lowering into the interior by lift. Consideration was also given to carrying the bombed-up small aircraft piggy-back on the Ju 390. On release of the securing coupling, the smaller aircraft would soar off 'like a kite'. Unsurprisingly, this involved some risk of collision with the wings or tailplane of the mother aircraft.

Junkers' design for a single-seater parasite did not find favour at the RLM and the ministry preferred the Messerschmitt file. As Junkers lacked design office capacity, it abandoned its own project and accepted the Messerschmitt design for use with the Ju 390. On 2 April 1942, when Junkers showed the RLM this plan, the ministry accepted the combination of Junkers mother aircraft and Messerschmitt parasites. In 1943, with the worsening war situation, the concept gradually lost importance and from the early summer of 1944 the midget fighters underwent a metamorphosis and emerged as machines such as the He 162.

The first parasite aircraft was the Me P 73 (later Me P 1073B) purpose-built to operate from the eight-engined Me P 1073A. This single-seater turbojet fighter was designed to carry two fixed MG 151/20 cannon. The air intakes were located left and right of the fuselage. The aircraft had an oval cross-section and a low-wing configuration. The sturdy, laminar-profile wings had a 35-degree sweep-back. Wingspan was 4.4 metres, the fuselage was 5.9 metres long and 1.8 metres high. When the wings were folded upwards, the body fitted easily into an area of 3 square metres.

How the carrier aircraft would have recaptured the parasite is not stated. The plan can only have been that it would have landed on the back of the mother aircraft, but if so the airframe would have required substantial strengthening which would have increased flight weight and reduced the range. The idea of this particular parasite fighter was abandoned and led to the He 162 *Volksjäger* fitted with BMW 003 engines.

Amongst the most interesting Messerschmitt designs was the Me P 79 series (later Me P 1079 and later still Me 328). The project set out in June 1941 to evaluate the propensities of pulse-jet propulsion as an alternative to turbines. The various Augsburg designs resulted in single-seater fighters, bombers and parasite aircraft.

On 31 March 1942 the RLM Technical Office approved Messerschmitt's portfolio of plans for six variants:

Me 328 A-1: midget fighter with two MG 151s.

Me 328 A-2: midget fighter with two MG 151s and two MK 103s.

Me 328 A-3: parasite fighter with armament as for the A-2.

Me 328 B-1: midget bomber with 1-tonne bomb-load.

Me 328 B-2: as B-1 but with A-2 airframe.

Me 328 B-3: midget bomber with 1.4-tonne bomb-load.

After Messerschmitt had completed the basic project study, the papers were passed to Jacobs and Schreyer Flugzeugbau (JSF) at Ober Ramstadt near Darmstadt and the mock-up was turned out in close collaboration between the two companies. The wind-tunnel models were built in Darmstadt and tested by the Aviation Research Institute (LFA) 'Hermann Göring' at Brunswick. JSF also carried out the static trials. Two prototypes (Me 328 V0-1 and V0-2) were planned initially, the Messerschmitt design blueprints to be passed to JSF for construction. The RLM Technical Office ordered ten prototypes for trials (Me 328 V-1 to V-10) to be built by DFS at Ainring near Bad Reichenhall with an option for ten Me 328 A-1s to be exercised provided trials were completed successfully. The Me 328A was only ever a single prototype. In March 1943 the JSF static tests were only 60 per cent completed when the work was stopped. This was the last attempt to build a parasite fighter for the Ju 390 or similar carrier.

In mid-December 1942 JSF received orders to build 20 Me 328B prototypes, V-11 to V-30, with a view eventually to series-produce about 280 aircraft at Darmstadt. The airframe was the A-1 re-conceived as a 'Special Development for the Fast Bomber Role' and would be used for low-level attacks on pinpointed targets. The aircraft were viewed as 'flying coastal artillery' for use primarily against the expected invasion. The development was well advanced by 25 November 1942. The project was for a single-seater fast bomber propelled by two Argus pulse-jets and able to carry an SD 500 or SC 1000 bomb. Top speed was calculated at 810 km/hr unladen, 630 km/hr with the maximum bomb-load. On test the Argus engines were found to be less powerful than expected and the maximum speed with 1-tonne bomb-load was put at 560 km/hr.

The Me 328B design was approved by KdE Rechlin on the basis of the project files submitted between 15 December 1942 and 4 January 1943. Flight testing of the prototype was scheduled for the Messerschmitt aerodrome at Lechfeld in Bavaria and at Rechlin. Pre-operational squadron trials were also listed to be held at Lechfeld. The aircraft would take-off in the *Mistel* mode, DFS at Ainring having decided on the Do 217 M-1 as the best carrier. Wind-tunnel tests were virtually completed by August 1943 and naturally brought forth a number of design improvements. As a result JSF began work on the prototypes, BV-1 and BV-2, of which the first was completed but not actually fitted out until April 1944. After vibration trials the machine arrived at Hörsching on 18 May 1944 for testing from the summer. It was planned to build eight more of the type, BV-3 to BV-10, as un-engined training aircraft although BV-3 received two pulse-jets as an experimental measure. The other aircraft of the series were in fact never constructed. In June 1944 the Kittelberger firm at Höchst-Bregenz took over the construction of BV-2 as JSF had been contracted to develop the wooden version of the Me 262A rear fuselage.

The Me 328B had meanwhile become a manned flying bomb with a 2.5-tonne payload. The aircraft would glide into the attack after being towed into the sky. In March 1944 trials were made using BT 1800 or PC 1400 bombs. Engineers of DFS, where from ten to twenty of the machines were to be built, were responsible for the preliminary tests. Ju 88 S-3s or Ju 388 K-1s were to be the mother aircraft. Work on these continued until September 1944. After two prototypes had been completed and a third, BV-3 partially so, the work was halted even though the pulse-jets had finally arrived. All further activities were concentrated on the Me 328 V-1, the first prototype of the bomber version.

As an advance on the Me 328 A-3 which was designed to be refuelled in flight, Messerschmitt designed a variant capable of carrying a bomb-load of between 500 kg and 1.4 tonnes. Three of the aircraft were to fit aboard a Ju 390. Partially retractable wings were part of a scheme to enable comfortable stowage aboard the mother aircraft. By summer 1942 work was relatively well advanced. A Messerschmitt memorandum of 7 July that year reported that the planned parasite bomber would have an SC 500 RS rocket-assist. The designed speed of the V-1 variant was between 950 km/hr and 830 km/hr. The procedure was to be one of the following:

1. The parasite aircraft would be towed into the air by the mother aircraft, taking station behind and below it by virtue of the parasite's higher wing loading.

2. Once airborne as in (1), the parasite aircraft would be hauled in and hitched below the mother aircraft rather like a exterior-hung bomb. If the mother aircraft had enough clearance on the ground, the parasite machine would be underslung before take-off.

3. The parasite aircraft to be carried in the fuselage of the carrier aircraft.

The hauling-in procedure was DFS-proven. An advantage of method (3) was that maintenance, refuelling, re-ammunitioning and re-bombing could all be performed by airborne ground staff during the flight. Retractable wings were seen as preferable to a folding-back mechanism. Such small, fast aircraft would have been a difficult target for enemy anti-aircraft batteries and fighters. The manned V-1 version was earmarked for suicide operations but nothing came of this through shortage of machines and Hitler's dislike of *kamikaze* tactics.

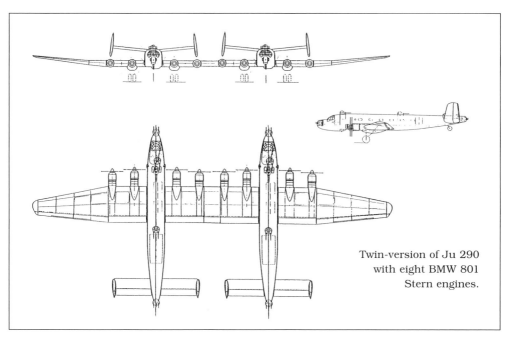

Twin-version of Ju 290
with eight BMW 801
Stern engines.

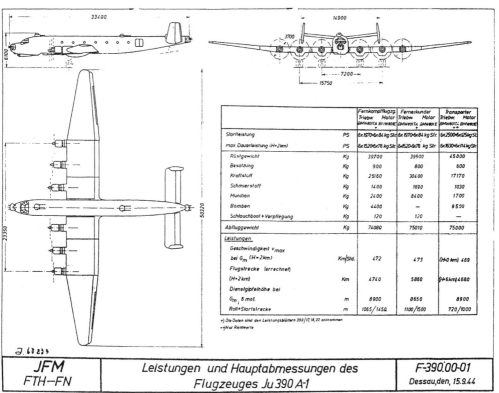

		Fernkampfflugzg. Triebw. BMW801TA / Motor Bl.(W801E)	Fernerkunder Triebw. BMW801TA / Motor BMW801E	Transporter Triebw. BMW801TA / Motor BMW801E
Startleistung	PS	6x1970+6x84 kg Str.	6x1970+6x84 kg Str.	6x2500+6x125kg St.
max.Dauerleistung (H+2km)	PS	6x1520+6x76 kg Str	6x1520+6x76 kg Str.	6x1630+6x114 kg Str.
Rüstgewicht	Kg	39700	39500	45000
Besatzung	Kg	900	800	800
Kraftstoff	Kg	25160	30400	17170
Schmierstoff	Kg	1400	1690	1030
Munition	Kg	2400	8400	1700
Bomben	Kg	4400	—	9500
Schlauchboot + Verpflegung	Kg	120	120	—
Abfluggewicht	Kg	74080	75010	75000
Leistungen				
Geschwindigkeit v_{max} bei G_m (H=2km)	Km/Std.	472	473	(H=0 km) 469
Flugstrecke (errechnet) (H=2km)	Km	4740	5860	(0+6km) 4680
Dienstgipfelhöhe bei G_m, 6 mot.	m	8900	8650	8900
Roll+Startstrecke	m	1065/1450	1100/1500	720/1000

+) Die Daten sind den Leistungsblättern 390/17, 18, 22 entnommen
++)Nur Richtwerte

JFM FTH–FN	Leistungen und Hauptabmessungen des Flugzeuges Ju 390 A-1	F-390.00-01 Dessau,den, 15.9.44

Planned series production version of Ju 390 A-1 propelled by six
BMW 801E engines.

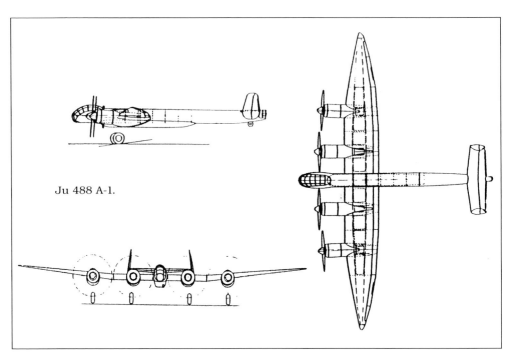

Ju 488 A-1.

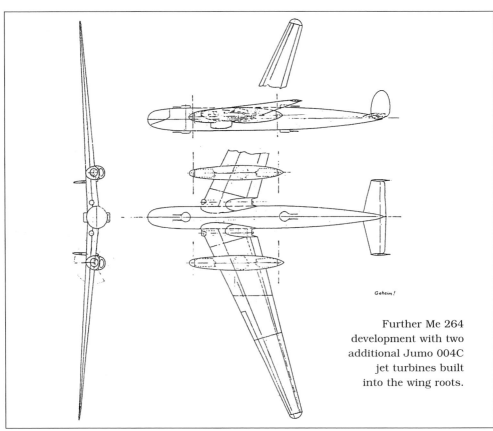

Geheim!

Further Me 264
development with two
additional Jumo 004C
jet turbines built
into the wing roots.

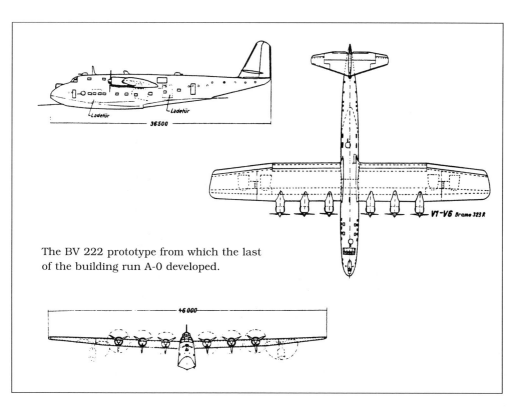

The BV 222 prototype from which the last of the building run A-0 developed.

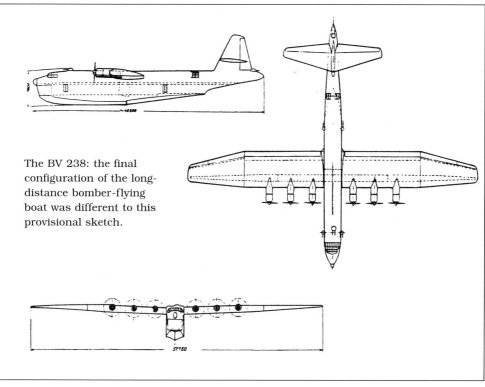

The BV 238: the final configuration of the long-distance bomber-flying boat was different to this provisional sketch.

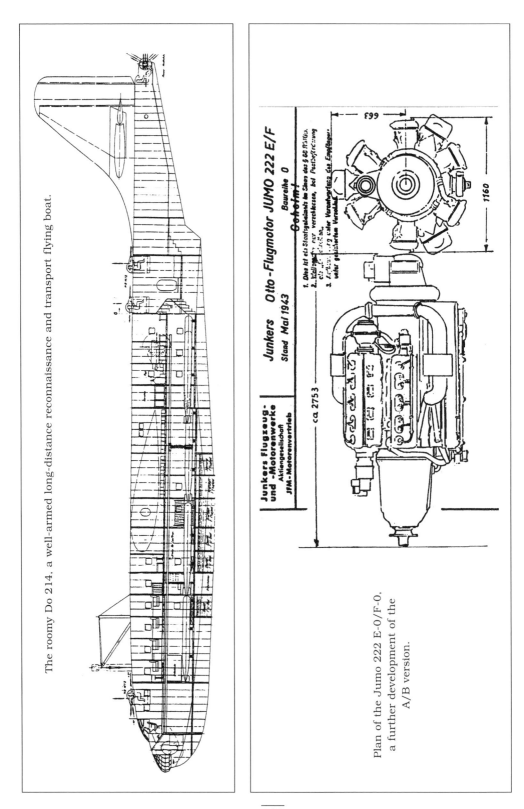

The roomy Do 214, a well-armed long-distance reconnaissance and transport flying boat.

**Junkers Flugzeug-
und -Motorenwerke**
Aktiengesellschaft
JFM-Motorenvertrieb

Junkers   Otto-Flugmotor JUMO 222 E/F
Stand Mai 1943

Baureihe 0

Plan of the Jumo 222 E-0/F-0,
a further development of the
A/B version.

Chapter 9

The Year 1944 – First Half

At an Aircraft Production Conference in Berlin on 28 January 1944, *Hauptmann* Fischer, commander of FAGr 5, supplied Milch with a comprehensive evaluation of the Ju 290 which had flown operationally in recent months in the poorest weather conditions over the Atlantic, the four-engined aircraft proving itself 'excellent to fly'. However, in order to penetrate to regions less well defended by the enemy, a longer range was necessary. Moreover, aircrews were asking for better defensive armament in the form of hydraulically-operated remote-controlled 20-mm gun-turrets. Upon hearing this, Milch at once ordered work on the six-engined Ju 390 to be accelerated although, in deference to Fischer, he also mentioned the need to improve defensive armament by installing remote-controlled weapons and missile firing equipment.

In the conference of departmental heads of 29 February 1944, Milch, Vorwald, Hertel, General Adolf Galland (commander of the Luftwaffe fighter arm) and over thirty technical specialists discussed the future armament of the Ju 290. *Hauptmann* Fischer stated in this regard that even the MG 151Z rear gun-turret due for the Ju 290 reconnaissance version at the beginning of 1945 was inadequate. This shortcoming was to be addressed during series production, but in the opinion of FAGr 5 this was too late. Even an MG 131 quadruple turret, which had a range of almost 1,000 metres, was no match for a Mosquito attacking from astern, for the 20-mm weapons of the enemy aircraft were effective at 2,000 metres. *Oberst* von Lossberg was of the opinion that the quadruple turret was more effective than the twin turret over the intermediate ranges because of the heavier concentration of fire. A better MG 131 with a higher rate of fire would soon be available while an MG 151Z twin unit had been given preferential status and was now under test at Tarnewitz. In March 1944 another twin unit was examined which was substantially superior to the MG 131V and MG 151Z. These units would soon be installed in the Ju 290 and it would be decided by the end of the month if they should be fitted to current operational aircraft.

Following the Ju 290 A-3 and A-5 reconnaissance versions, the much more heavily armed C-1 had been developed from the A-5. This was to have an MG 151Z revolving turret front and rear plus three more gun positions on the upper and lower fuselage. It would also have a greater fuel capacity and range. The D-1 was the bomber version of the C-1 and would be able to launch remote-controlled bombs but the second fuselage tank had been unshipped to increase the bomb-load, thus reducing the radius of action fairly substantially.

On 28 January Milch issued an order transferring resources from the Ju 290 to the Ju 390, which came as a surprise. The heavily armed bomber was to carry underslung remote-controlled bombs over the Atlantic to attack ground targets in the United States. It was not a new idea, yet despite these plans at the RLM the construction of the Ju 390 series had not advanced all that far. The prototype, Ju 390 V-1, was under test at Prague to the end of March 1944: V-2 was to be completed by September and undergo practical trials from November. Despite the tight capacity at Junkers, according to a report circulated in March 1944, 26 Ju 390s were to be produced at Dessau and by May 1945 111 more. But by June 1944 the aircraft would be history.

On 3 July 1943, the RLM had discussed an aircraft wanted by Hitler which was an unarmoured two-seater with a large radius of action and able to fly at 15,000 metres. As a result Junkers submitted plans for an extended Ju 188 airframe with enlarged wings and propelled by four BMW 801Js. A speed of 700 km/hr at 14,000 metres was offered. As, in the opinion of *Fliegerstab* engineer Friebel, the conversion costs would be too high, the design was not proceeded with. Junkers was not to be outdone and now came up with the Ju 488, a machine made from cannibalised parts of the Ju 388, Ju 88 A-15 and Ju 288 C-0. All unmodified pertinent material was gathered up at Bernburg and sent by rail to France for assembly by Latécoère, Breguet and SNCA Sudest.

The *Jägerstab* (Fighter Staff) came into being by virtue of an edict from Armaments Minister Albert Speer of 1 March 1944. Under the joint direction of the Armaments Minister and Aircraft Production Minister Milch, measures were to be taken greatly to enhance the production of fighter aircraft. Bombers were now of minor significance. Directly subordinate to the joint heads was civil service engineer Karl-Otto Saur who ran the day-to-day business.

During the Atlantic winter storms of early 1944 the number of reconnaissance flights dwindled. RAF and United States Army Air Force (USAAF) bombers also regularly bombed *Luftwaffe* bases along the French coast, preventing missions being flown. Between 29 February and 23 March 1944, FAGr 5 was stood down from operations for recuperation and repairs. Allied air superiority over western France and Biscay had become so strong as to rule out operations by large flying boats, and within four months the BV 222 would be seen over those waters no longer. Another victim in France was the He 274. On 20 April 1944 the RLM decreed that only the first three of the six prototypes and the crash-test airframe under production exclusively in France were to be completed. Such work on them as there was slowed even more after the Allied landings. The second and third prototypes were captured by the Allies and completed by them at leisure for flight trials.

On 15 March 1944 *Oberstleutnant* Sorge presented a review of the strategic air situation over Europe under the provocative title 'Accordingly, How Should The War Be Continued?' Contrary to the usual rose-tinted opinions, Sorge delivered judgment on the war aims of the earlier policy-makers as 'not achieved'. Not only the falling-off in U-boat successes but the growing superiority of Allied forces on all fronts and over the *Reich* had lost Germany the initiative. This was true for all theatres including the Atlantic and the shipping tonnage war. Whilst the Allies had surplus fuel, iron, steel and aluminium, and were only short of rubber, in Germany only coal, iron and zinc stocks were definitely in excess of current requirements. Doubts existed regarding aluminium, all non-ferrous metals, rubber, copper, fuel, manganese and zinc. Oil production in particular was vulnerable to the Allied air forces. To disrupt imports coming into Britain – and simultaneously weaken the American foothold there – Sorge suggested building at least 50 Ju 290s and 300 He 177s to regain the initiative over the Atlantic and introduce nuisance raids along the American East Coast. Haunted by the spectre of defeat, an old, unforgotten dream revived in the German *Reich.*

The fountain of ideas never welled dry. The Ar E 555 project consisted of no fewer than eleven different drawing board variations. None was ever built and it is doubtful if they qualified for the label 'long-range aircraft'. The calculations completed in May 1944 gave the aircraft a maximum range of 5,000 km but a top speed of 950 km/hr. None of the required power-plant options, including the preferred HeS 11 turbines, nor the turboprops (not in general service anywhere until after the war), were ever available.

From the end of 1943, the Heinkel-Süd design offices at Vienna-Schwechat had worked intensively on variants of the He 177 B-5. A new variant was the He 177 B-6, armed with three twin turrets with MG 151/20s and a further five MG 131s. At the beginning of 1944 a novel idea was mooted, of creating a design not only from two different aircraft types, but from two different manufacturers' types, the He 177 B-5 and B-7 fitted with Me 264 A-1 wings. The development, together with a version having a wooden twin tail fin, was passed to the Farman company in Paris. On 18 February 1944 the Heinkel project bureau presented a study for the modification of the He 177B. The work, including the augmented defensive armament, strengthening the airframe and increasing fuel capacity, also fell to the Paris firm. The aircraft now required a wheel skid for take-off to compensate for the increased flight weight of 44 tonnes. A big step in development was the prospect of adding the Me 264 wings to a modified He 177B fuselage made of steel to save on aluminium. Range was to be 8,000 km. Conditions being what they were, the Paris firm was unable to supply a definite calendar. The first He 177B blueprints with standard tailplane and twin-fin assembly were shown to the RLM Development Chief, *Oberstleutnant* Knemeyer, at Schwechat in February 1944. The version with Me 264 wings was never designed.

In mid-March 1944, Göring set down the specifications for the future He 177 B-7 which was now to be primarily a long-range reconnaissance aircraft for Atlantic duty. On 20 March the RLM gave Heinkel the contract to build the variant and turn out the first prototypes, one of which was to be ready for flight tests by the end of the year. As required by the RLM, this prototype would have had four independent DB 603Es, the glazed nose and cockpit of the B-6 variant, and a greatly enlarged fuel capacity. By April 1944 work on B-5 and B-7 was in full swing. The RLM was increasingly interested in the latter version which would have an MG 131V quadruple turret front and rear. The B-1, B-2 and C gun positions would each have an MG 151Z. This made for an extremely strong defensive armament but the increased weight curtailed the range.

In August 1943, the Me 264 prototype had been refitted with BMW 801 MG/2 engines and serious problems with these had led to delays. After an Allied air raid on Lechfeld on 18 March 1944, the programme was transferred to Memmingen on 16 April. In the first taxying trial at Lechfeld on 14 April 1944 the brake shoes tore off. Two days later a propeller defect was noticed but it was not serious enough to prevent the aircraft's 38th flight, to Memmingen, where more damage was sustained by too rough a landing on the new tail-wheel. During the repair some of the vibrations were eliminated by work on the tail fins. In a file note the same day, *Oberstleutnant* Knemeyer and *Flugzeugbaumeister* Scheibe of KdE Rechlin both remarked on the good flying characteristics of the first prototype but Scheibe criticised the poor visibility from the cabin caused by reflections and serious vibrations in the airframe. For long-range work an auto-pilot and emergency compass gear were indispensable; they were both fitted but did not work.

In a subsequent flight General von Barsewisch condemned the aircraft as too slow for operations even though it was now 10 per cent faster than originally designed after the engine refit replacing the Jumo 211 plant. A third opinion submitted by Knemeyer was unequivocally positive; he was certain that the reported defects would be overcome providing there was capacity at the series-production stage. Scheibe also recommended refitting the aircraft with yet more powerful engines such as the Jumo 222 A/B radials. Knemeyer agreed but in general considered the Me 264 the only suitable long-range bomber he had seen to date and urged that the remaining prototypes be completed as soon as possible.

Flight trials were continued over southern Germany in April 1944 during which a definite tail-heavy tendency was detected. A new tail-wheel was fitted and additional tests made for wing stability. Between 28 April and 2 May unrewarding efforts were made using weights in an attempt to eliminate the vibrations in the airframe and avoid having to design new wings. The long-planned examination of flight characteristics and performance was now postponed while consideration was given to having new wings.

On 5 June a flight was made to take stability readings. Next day *Flugkapitän* Baur noticed a pronounced trembling of the control surfaces at speeds between 380 km/hr and 450 km/hr. He was also critical of the poor accuracy of the auto-pilot and recommended that a replacement system be installed. Work by engineer Wegener confirmed Baur's earlier impression that the wings were too small for such a large machine leading to stability problems. Wind-tunnel tests to examine roll and pitch in the period up to July 1944 provided clear evidence of what the optimum wing size and profile should be.

On 9 June 1944, three days after the Allied landings in

Normandy, the head of the *Jägerstab*, Otto Saur, still clung to the belief that an air raid against Manhattan by thirty He 177 aircraft would have a marvellous effect. Despite the new, grave setback on the Western Front, the transatlantic bomber still managed to find a spot on the agenda of the *Jägerstab* meeting of 10 June 1944:

Diesing: The General of Reconnaissance Aircraft is of the opinion that the Ju 290 and 390 will not be operational in the Atlantic next year. Knemeyer has suggested not mass-producing the longest-ranged reconnaissance aircraft but instead special aircraft built as prototypes which each series follows, thus keeping them always modern. There are various possibilities, the Hütter project, the Ju 488 and so on.

Saur: I spoke with a Knight's Cross holder yesterday, one of the best U-boat men. He told me that, at the decisive moment, there would be no greater success if we've got the machines ready – even if there were only twenty of them – than to fly to New York and bomb them. He said he had been there three times and knew very well how things stood.

Diesing: There is a political question here. Maybe we would be supporting Roosevelt by doing that. Up till now we could use the propaganda line that we haven't done anything so far against America.

Saur: I believe it would have an unbelievable effect. The U-boat man I mentioned told me it would be most effective if it succeeded in getting their people to reject the invasion when three days after it happened we bombarded England with the Fi 103 [V-1 flying bomb] and twenty aircraft bombed New York.

Interruption by unrecorded person: In my opinion we could sacrifice twenty He 177s and let the crews parachute down afterwards.

Saur: It wouldn't be against the rules of war to drop bombs there.

The idea that an He 177 could bomb a target city, and the crew would then bale out and surrender, found few enthusiasts. In Speer's general report of 23 June, the *Jägerstab* decided 'rigorously to decelerate' production of the He 177 with coupled engines in favour of versions with four independent motors – considered a better proposition for long-range bomber operations. The general war situation was, however, unfavourable for strategic bomber building. When the *Jägerstab* reconvened on 28 June 1944 under the chairmanship of Saur, the He 177 was again on the agenda. The decision to step down production was confirmed. In June 1944 SKL would only agree to this step, which had been proposed by Milch, if sufficient Me 264s were turned out instead. No advice was offered on how this was to be achieved.

Consideration of the quickest way to reverse Germany's evil fortunes preoccupied Milch in the summer of 1944. He wanted to institute nuisance raids against the US sooner rather than later although he was uncomfortable with mid-air refuelling to the extent that he was reported as having suggested ironically:

> I think it might be best to just fly over there, drop the bombs, crash the aircraft and simply ask them, What PoW camp am I going to then?

The final development of the Ju 290 was the proposed Ju 290 E-1 night bomber. This was a C-1 with bomb-bay and armed with three MG 151Zs. It never came to fruition. After the definitive cancellation of the Ju 290B series and the planned Ju 390 A-1 by the *Luftwaffe* Command Staff in June 1944, only the He 177 B-5(F) remained on the programme for long-range reconnaissance work. The commanding general of *Luftwaffe* reconnaissance, General von Barsewisch, and *Oberstleutnant* Knemeyer considered it possible to have a weakly armed version of this aircraft ready for operations in the medium term. Four prototypes were being produced at Zwölfaxing near Vienna, and then the series would follow. Nevertheless, the RLM had not abandoned hope that the Me 264 with its 10,000-km range would appear instead of the

Heinkel aircraft; by the time it was ready there would probably be six He 177 B-5 *Staffeln* in existence, but that was scarcely more than a token presence.

Von Barsewisch, representatives of the *Luftwaffe* General Staff, and the RLM discussed the use of the Ar 234 jet and the Ju 388 for coastal and Atlantic reconnaissance in a conference of 10 June 1944. It emerged that in view of the daily worsening shortage of materials and capacity within the German aviation industry there was no longer a possibility of having well-armed formations of heavy aircraft. In this connection the *Luftwaffe* High Command was unanimous that long-range aircraft were needed which could operate singly. These would need a cruising speed of 700 km/hr, the cabins being fully pressurised. The operational altitude would be between 12,000 metres and 13,000 metres. Effective radar would assist their search capability over the oceans. *Oberstleutnant* Knemeyer was of the opinion that only the Me 264 qualified for this role.

In the meantime the general situation meant a halt to Ju 390 production because of insufficient resources. Apart from the Me 264 prototypes and a few aircraft for which not even the prototype run was in sight, the Ju 488 seemed the likeliest candidate for long-range work in 1945.

On 19 June 1944 the RLM determined that the Ju 290B would be operational from late summer onwards with a limited range of 5,500 km. This version had been supposedly struck out of the production programme some time previously. The RLM had also investigated an improved Ju 390 with more powerful engines providing a range of 10,000 km at a cruising speed of 350 km/hr. On 29 June, KdE Rechlin made a surprise pronouncement that the Ju 390 was unsuitable for long-range operations since the wing loading was too great. Furthermore, according to the technical specialists, the designed undercarriage was inadequate for the planned take-off weight. The defensive armament, long considered satisfactory, was now deemed too weak, and revolving turrets with 30-mm guns were now thought indispensable. The estimated top speed was 500 km/hr, and as this was also below requirements, deletion from the programme was close. Shortly before the termination of all work on the Ju 390 programme, Junkers received orders in June 1944 to build Ju 390 V-2 to V-7, but this may have been simply an invoicing measure to balance the books for work already carried out. *Oberstleutnant* Knemeyer suggested for the interim:

(1) The Ju 290 will continue; the modified version, Ju 390, will be struck out.

(2) The He 177 with a range of 5,400 km will be introduced temporarily.

(3) The capacity freed by these measures will be given over to the Ju 388 and Ju 488 which can make 680 km/hr by reducing the armament.

(4) A further increase in speed makes possible the Hütter project (700 km/hr) using Ju 388 parts.

(5) These measures will enable 18–20 Me 264s to be completed from available materials until the Ju 488 and an aircraft for Atlantic reconnaissance become operational.

Although this solution was purely an emergency measure, more radical ideas were afoot. Strangers to all reality dwelt at *Führer Hauptquartier* (FHQ – Hitler's headquarters) and Saur, who had taken part in several conferences in Hitler's presence, declared on 21 June 1944:

I understand from conversations with the *Führer* that he is convinced we should be decisive about having centres of concentrated effort [*Schwerpünkte*]. If we know that this line is right, that we have here revolutionary improvements and not just amateurish things, then I suggest that we should forge ahead with the Me 264. The Me 263 shows us possibilities of absolutely revolutionary significance in combining piston engines and jets. By their carrying capacity and range they seem suitable to discharge all tasks and in small numbers.

The BV 222 A-0 was only suitable to a limited extent for long-range reconnaissance work.

View of the flight deck of the BV 222.

Above: Despite regular increases in defensive armament, because of their flight characteristics large flying boats had little chance against fighter-bombers.

Below: The camouflaged BV 238 V-1 in front of the Hamburg-Finkenwerder assembly hangar.

Above: The Gö 8 served as a one-fifth scale model for examining flight characteristics of the projected Do 214.

Left: Several captured flying boats, for example the Potez CAMS 161, were immobilised by the *Luftwaffe* after testing for lack of replacement parts.

Below: This Latécoère 631 large flying boat remained out of commission for a long period following an accident soon after falling into German hands.

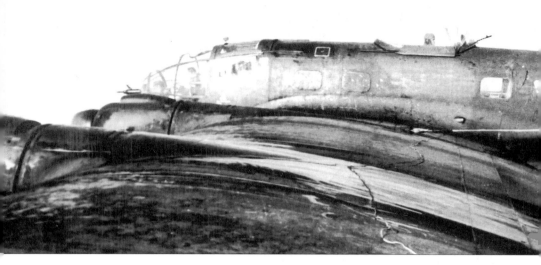

Top: The He 111 Z-1, besides serving as a tug for large gliders, was earmarked to tow heavily laden transatlantic aircraft at take-off.

Above: Another way of taking along supplementary fuel tanks was by towed containers.

Left: An SG 5041 V-1/V-2 towed fuel tank hung astern of an Ar 234 B-2. The method extended the aircraft's range from 1,420 km to 2,540 km.

Left: The first mid-air refuelling experiments were carried out by a Fokker-Grulich FII. The rolled fuel hose can be seen in the open door.

Below: Two aircraft coupling up for fuel transfer purposes used a method similar to the naval taut towline.

Above: The first BV 238 V-1 prototype flew un-engined to test its gliding qualities.

Right: Wind-tunnel model of one of two pulse-jet driven Me 328s.

Right: The Me 328 AV-3 was tested on a Do 217 K-0.

Top left: One of the first *Mistel* operational combinations, involving a Ju 88 A-4 and Bf 109 F-4.

Left: During a test flight the Bf 109 parts from the mother aircraft.

Above: Me 328 AV-2 was the second prototype and was propelled by two pulse-jets hung below the wings.

Below: Me 328 model, conceived for later use as parasite aircraft aboard a mother aircraft, was designed with partially retractable wings. Here new wing roots are under test.

Above: The Ju 287 A-1 was the first jet-propelled heavy bomber of the *Luftwaffe.* This is a model of an early version.

Below: Mock-up of the crew compartment of the Ju 287 V-3.

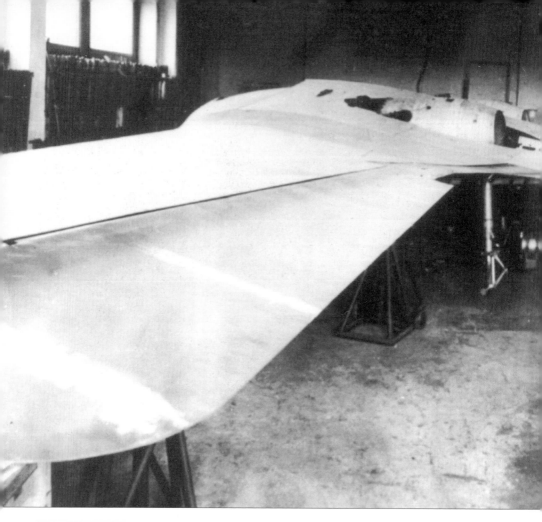

Above: Wernher von Braun (in civilian suit) with other members of the Peenemünde staff.

Top left: A mock-up of the Horten IX used to examine the feasibility of fitting two jet turbines.

Left: The engine section in the Horten IX V-2.

Below left: Model of the planned three-engined version of the Ju 287 V-3 to V-6.

Below: The Heinkel-Hirth HeS 11 jet turbine.

Left & below: The A4, also known as the V-2, was towed into launch position by a Meiler truck. In place of its conventional warhead, 'special loads' were also considered. These could have included battlefield gases.

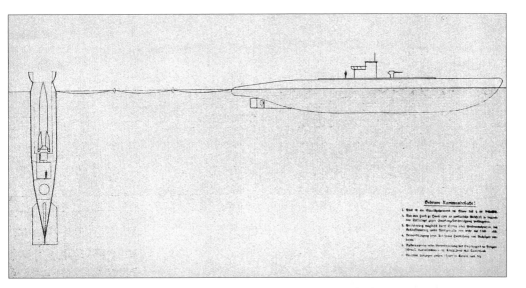

Above: The sea-launched version of the V-2. After the submersible barge had been tilted upright, the V-2 would be fired from below the water surface.

Right: Sketch of the barge in position ready to fire its V-2. The exhaust-gas pipe is clearly visible.

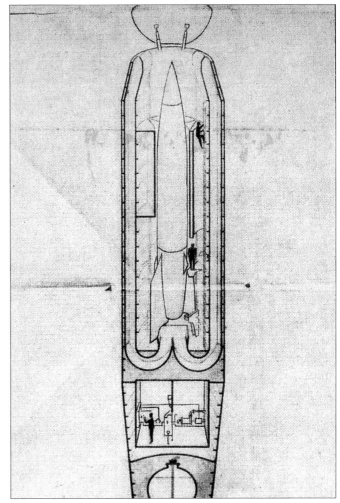

Left: Sänger's experimental apparatus for testing the proposed launch installation for his rocket bomber. Note the rifle in position to fire the projectile up the ramp.

Below: Model of Sänger's rocket bomber.

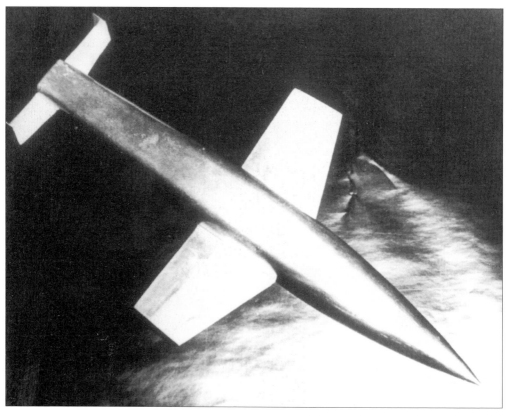

Above: A rocket engine under test. These had to be tested on a very reduced scale.

Below: The bomb bay of the He 177 V-38 may have looked large enough to carry an atom bomb but was designed to test the bomb installation of the Ju 287 A-1 series run.

Left: SS-*Obergruppenführer* and *Waffen*-SS General Dr (Ing) Kammler in 1944.

Below At the beginning of 1945, yoked oxen were used to bring 'high tech' weapons to the runway because fuel was so scarce.

Even so, America would still not have been within range of an improved Me 264 without mid-air refuelling, not even without the 'weapons of annihilation' of which *Generalmajor* von Rhoden, former head of General Staff Section 8, spoke shortly after the war. Despite the loss of the French Atlantic bases, such ideas were still rife at FHQ, but they looked none too good against the harsh reality of the production situation regarding these transatlantic aircraft. When the talk at FHQ came round to the future performance of the He 177, the B-5(F) order was cancelled because, on the basis of the calculations, the Me 264 was the one aircraft which could cross the Atlantic alone and at night.

On 26 June during a steep ascent the pilot of the Me 264 prototype had been forced to level out after losing all fuel pressure for both inner engines. This was due to defects in the respective fuel pumps. The auto-pilot and electrical system were also checked over during the repairs and a full overhaul was found advisable.

The halting progress in the flight test programme, the shortages of raw materials, production work on the Ar 234 and the difficulties attending the production of the Me 262 fighter were all contributory factors in the decision of the *Jägerstab* on 28 June that the Me 264 should only be turned out in modest numbers, and this despite the fact that the aircraft was the only design suitable for the longest-range work after the decision not to proceed with the Ju 390 and He 177B. The Me 262 enjoyed absolute priority and dominated all Messerschmitt's resources. The staging for the final Me 264 assembly at Augsburg was dismantled to make space for the jet fighter and stored because of Me 410 production, for a short period, at Gersthofen in Bavaria. After Professor Messerschmitt had reported that a proper production area with the right personnel would not be available for the long-range bomber, the *Reichsmarschall* accepted that nothing more could be expected in that direction, at least in any numbers.

On 29 June 1944, SKL pondered the future equipping of the long-range groups which would operate alongside the improved U-boats then being developed. Because of the general war situation, heavy aircraft could only be counted on within a very modest framework. The inventory of long-range bombers at 1 June 1944 consisted of only the fifteen Ju 290s at FAGr 5. Even with a step-up in production it was expected that six months would be needed to bring the unit up to strength.

Twelve He 177 B-5(F)s were scheduled for delivery before 1 May 1945 as the basis for a new long-range reconnaissance *Staffel*, and another six were expected by 1 September 1945 as a stop-gap for long-range operations. Because of the collapsing fronts and infrastructure even these modest plans were purely academic, though the aircraft was the only Heinkel-Süd design advanced enough to merit thoughts of how to increase its range. The series model with supplementary fuel tanks in the bomb-bay could fly 5,000 km on 10.7 tonnes of fuel. With two additional external tanks increasing the fuel volume to 13 tonnes, a flight of 5,800 km was possible. If the number of guns in the front and rear turrets was reduced and two 1,200-litre containers slung below the wings instead, the range was now 6,500 km. If the defensive armament was cut to MG 131 twins in the B-1 position and the rear turret, and an MG 131 in C gun position, fuel could be increased to 14.3 tonnes for a range of 7,100 km. With no defensive armament and three disposable 1,200-litre tanks plus a supplementary tank in the bomb area, 7,500 km was within the realms of possibility.

Chapter 10

The Year 1944 – Second Half

On 8 July 1944 Armaments Minister Speer ordered the rapid running down of all heavy bomber projects, as only in this manner could the production of fighters be guaranteed. In his opinion, 200 He 177s took up the production capacity of at least 1,000 fighters. Since the Allied invasion of France, and the imminent loss of the Atlantic bases, there was basically no other way to proceed. As with the He 177 variants with coupled engines, the He 177B fell victim in June 1944 to an impotent production programme which had no room for long-range bombers.

On 18 July 1944 KdE Rechlin expressed its opinion on the vices of the Me 264:

> The aircraft in its whole conception is not useful on the grounds of its too-high wing loading, the complicated nature of its undercarriage, the exceptional length of runway required for take-off and the need for rocket boosters to assist in the endeavour, and the poor defensive armament. The basic idea of developing and then building the machine in a purpose-built fighter factory lacking any heavy aircraft experience is flawed and in our opinion it cannot be produced today without prejudice to the urgent Me 262 fighter production at Messerschmitt. The promised dates seem impossible to keep as still no kind of test data is available.

The same day an Allied air attack destroyed the factory at Memmingen. Me 264 V-1 and most of the material for the next two prototypes, and the subsequent numbers, were written off. Metallbau Offingen, a Messerschmitt subsidiary at Neu-Ulm, was also severely damaged. Some 80 per cent of the production installation was destroyed, putting back the date of the second prototype to no earlier than February 1945. On 26 July 1944 *Hauptmann* Nebel of KdE set up a special unit in order to find some way to turn out the replacement prototypes. How KdE with its limited resources was supposed to achieve this goal was reasoning known only to OKL which decided, on 15 August, that *Sonderkommando Nebel* should devote itself to 'technical tasks with regard to coming prototypes' rather than the Me 264 exclusively. What was actually meant here was the Do 335 fighter and the four-engined Do 635.

On 11 January 1944 during a long conference between the RLM, Messerschmitt and Heinkel in Vienna, the ministry had made the surprising announcement that it was impressed by the concept of an He 277 fuselage with Me 264 wings. This would enable a 56-tonne take-off-weight bomber to be produced relatively quickly. Its range with a 3-tonne bomb-load would be 12,500 km, which could, in the eyes of the RLM planners, enable it to attack New York. The machine required a wheeled skid as undercarriage and rocket boosters for take-off or the range would be only 10,000 km.

The use of Me 264 parts would have meant a costly conversion job on the He 277 fuselage. The twin-fin tailplane and rear-gunner's position which the RLM required categorically, since this was the preference of the *Reichsmarschall*, needed no modification. It was discovered, however, that only free-fall bombs could be carried in the bomb-bay. On 23 August 1944 the RLM ordered all work stopped on the He 177 and further variations, excepting He 177 V-103 B-5. The final test version of the He 277 was blown up at Heinkel's Eger works.

The first unarmed prototype Ju 488 V-401, metal-built with wooden twin tail fins, was at the final assembly stage at Latécoère, Toul, when, on the night of 17 July 1944, the French Resistance destroyed the airframe. The second prototype, V-402, was discovered beside a French railway track in August. Ju 488 V-403 to V-406 formed the first short series-run equipped with defensive armament and bomb equipment, Jumo 222 A3/B3 engines being preferred over the original BMW 801TJ-0s. OKL had had great hopes for the design, which was to replace the Ju 290 reconnaissance aircraft. After the loss of the Junkers works at Toul, the firm had no means of proceeding with the project and the RLM ordered it abandoned in November.

On 10 July Speer reported to the *Führer* on his deliberations respecting concentration of *Luftwaffe* production resources for 1944/45 in which the following measures appeared most important:

> In the process of re-evaluating the *Luftwaffe* programme, the whole ground apparatus must be subjected to detailed and penetrating scrutiny with a view to disposing of all mechanisation unnecessary under the present circumstances. In order to bring about the concentration in fighter production as rapidly as possible, on the suggestion of the *Reichsmarschall* the *Führer* has ordered that the aircraft types which are to be halted must be stopped with immediate effect, even to the extent of scrapping or converting parts to other uses, and that the relevant managements, workers, machines, other capacity and transports be transferred for the maximum output of fighters, especially those types recently ordered...

Although the RLM spared no effort to keep Me 264 production alive on a small-scale, the aircraft had to make way for fighter production in the short term. After the disastrous air raid on Memmingen, Messerschmitt picked up the pieces and was soon at work on three new versions of the Me 264. Variant A was a reconnaissance aircraft, variant B a long-range bomber, variant C a special long-range reconnaissance aircraft. With effect from the planned Me 264 V-4 at the latest, all future prototypes and the first series run would be fitted with four turbo-charged BMW 801Es with a GM-1 fuel system, the tanks for which were located in the central fuselage. Design work on the project had been started in the spring of 1944 and by August 1944 a dossier entitled 'Special Long-Range Reconnaissance Aircraft Me 264C' had been completed. A long-range transport version with FLH 151 twin guns and able to carry up to 17 paratroops or agents was also planned.

The reconnaissance Me 264A had a range of 13,600 km thanks to two external supplementary tanks. At 6,300 metres altitude the machine had a top speed of 580 km/hr. Maximum flight duration was in the region of 40 hours. Three camera units were to be installed at the rear. It had not been decided by the summer of 1944 whether the cabin should be pressurised.

The so-called 'special' version, the Me 264C, had two additional Jumo 004-TL or BMW 801 E/F engines and had a remarkable claimed performance for its time. With the GM-1 supplement the machine could operate at 8,000 metres at over 600 km/hr for 25 minutes and stay aloft for 45 hours. Armed with a 2-tonne bomb or several FuG 302C radio beacons, the range would have been 11,000 km and the cruising speed around 350 km/hr. Three Rb 50/30 cameras were planned. Defensive armament consisted of an MG 131 in A and B turrets (the latter mounted on a turntable chassis), an HD 151/Z in B-2 and an MG 151 in C turret. Two MG 131s were considered for the side windows. In an attempt to comply with the RLM guidelines, Messerschmitt also offered the Me 264 with four Jumo 222s and the GM-1 installation.

Me 264B, the long-range bomber design, would have had four BMW 801Es and two additional Jumo 004C turbines although four Jumo 222s were thought better later. Armament was as for the reconnaissance Me 264A except for an MG 131 instead of the MG 151 in C turret. The range of the bomber with a 3-tonne bomb-load was 11,600 km. Maximum bomb-load was six SC or SD 1000s. TL-drive would have been fitted. This increased the speed by 80 km/hr but was expensive in terms of weight. With its pressurised cabin the bomber could operate at an altitude of 14,500 metres.

At this stage of proceedings the need was surely to be clear on one single purpose. Instead the destruction of the defect-ridden Me 264 V-1 resulted in a replacement project of three variants, allowing even more major tinkering. The defensive armament of the bomber version was even revised on several occasions during July and August 1944. It was decided that 360-degree revolving turrets for two MG 213s needed to be designed, manufactured and installed. The reason was that, as the cabin but not the fuselage was to be pressurised, the aircraft might have to proceed unarmed or be equipped with remote-controlled weapons for operations at altitude.

On 5 August 1944, Hitler intervened to demand the urgent production of the Me 264, and eventually on 30 August Speer ordered vaguely: 'With all haste and urgency (Priority SS 4940) the Me 264 is to be built combining active industrial concerns.'

On 5 September 1944 General Staff engineer Roluf Lucht was appointed chairman of the Aircraft Commission. Amongst his immediate tasks was to ensure the continuation of work on the Me 264 now prioritised as urgent by order of the *Führer*. On 7 September at a conference involving *Grossadmiral* Dönitz, *Major* Fischer, commander of FAGr 5, and *Hauptmann* Müller of General von Barsewisch's staff, the future operational role of the Me 264 was discussed with the *Kriegsmarine* for the last time. Delivery of five aircraft was expected by the end of 1944 but they no longer had special appeal to the *Kriegsmarine*. The machine was so inferior in armament that single Me 264s would be easy pickings for numerically greater formations of enemy night- and long-distance fighters even over the sea. Moreover the high wing loading of 440 kg/square metre and the costly assembly work were also unfavourable factors. Nevertheless no order was issued cancelling the production run. How and whether it was still considered possible, at night or in fog, to reach suitable targets on the American East Coast even with small bomb-loads was a question which remains unanswered.

On 10 September 1944 a conference involving *Oberst* Gaul, liaison officer to the *Kriegsmarine*, representatives of the U-boat Command and of the general of reconnaissance aircraft decided that small numbers of Me 264s could be used for long-range operations, but only out of Norway, since the machines could not safely overfly Britain, France or the western Mediterranean. If Norway were lost then the Me 264 would no longer be of operational use. Hitler's view was that: 'With its range we can use the machine to punish America a thousand times over for the destruction of our cities!' Whether by this he was referring to a 'miracle weapon' is unknown. On 18 September Speer reported that Me 264 variant production would begin shortly. In the overall report of all important current Armaments Ministry projects is listed laconically: 'By decision of the *Führer*, V-1, A4 [V-2] and Me 264 urgently.'

Despite all wordy exhortations to speed up production, progress remained very slow under war conditions. Messerschmitt persevered in attempts to turn out the second and third Me 264 types but nearly all factories above ground had been bombed to ruins. In September in order to maximise the range, Messerschmitt had had disposable tanks designed. These were over 5 tonnes in weight and had to be slung below the wings near the fuselage.

Metallbau Offingen had been 80 per cent destroyed in the air raid two months previously yet it was still possible for Messerschmitt to continue work there well into December on a courier aircraft with a range of 12,000 km, Japan being within its compass with 4 tonnes of freight. Whether this aircraft could have done reconnaissance work as well as the Me 264A and C is an interesting question. Thoughts of long-range bombing raids diminished sharply in September 1944 once the idea of evacuating National Socialist leaders and top secret projects from *Reich* territory became current. To avoid having to make do with whatever aircraft were still available for the purpose, the Me 264 was now farmed out to sub-contractors. Henschel of Schönefeld, for example, received a contract to turn out wing parts for delivery by November. The RLM changed the quantity ordered on seven occasions before the whole production contract was cancelled in October.

At the beginning of 1944 Messerschmitt had drawn up an improved version of the six-engined Me 264 of swept-wing design propelled by four piston engines plus two jet turbines or turboprops. Further project studies followed which concentrated exclusively on the use of jet turbines. Defensive armament was four MG 151Zs in turrets. Project Me P 1085 was incapable of realisation for lack of capacity not least with regard to the piston engines. The two variants, and a later all-jet engined addition, eventually served as a basis for more studies.

Professor Messerschmitt's recommendation that it would be a good idea to add two or four more jet turbines to the Me 264 design came to the ears of General von Barsewisch. The extra engines would have so vastly increased fuel consumption that the range of the Me 264 fell to barely 5,000 km, much the same as a Ju 290 or He 177. It was the final straw. In view of the possibility of a renewed U-boat offensive planned for April 1945, von Barsewisch's patience was finally exhausted and, cancelling the Me 264, he settled for the Do 335 *Zwilling*. Dönitz had also advised Hitler that the Me 264 should be cancelled, and on 23 September work on the project was stopped for good. Confirmation followed a month later, on 18 October, in the '*Reichsmarschall* Technical Order No. 2' in the unmistakably terse: 'Work on the Me 264 is terminated absolutely.'

The testing of winch installations for tanker aircraft was terminated in August 1944. By then an effective system had been developed in which the second aircraft approached the rear of the tanker from which a coupling drogue projected. At the right moment a locking device hooked the two machines together and it was then an easy matter to transfer fuel. DFS reports from 1 August 1944 onwards make no further mention of the activity, although at that stage it was claimed that only two more months would have been needed to perfect the fuel transfer procedure. By refuelling at a point 3,000 km westwards from a Biscay base the Me 264 A-1 would have had the range to bomb New York or another suitable target and fly back. The loss of western France in August 1944 brought all such plans to an abrupt end.

In the aircraft production programme drawn up by Saur

on 12 December 1944, neither the Me 264, nor any other long-range bomber was mentioned. The small He 162 fighter, the Me 262, the Ta 152, Me 163/263, Ar 234, Do 335 and Ju 388 were the last Third *Reich* warplanes in production under the control of the Armaments Ministry. Thus, at the end of 1944, the possibilities of *Luftwaffe* operations towards the American coast transferred to bomber projects of a new era, the planned multi-stage rocket and the Sänger jet bomber which was planned to cruise at an altitude of 120 km.

It remains to report the demise of the last giant seaplanes in *Luftwaffe* service. The first BV 238 prototype V-1 made its maiden flight at Hamburg on 11 March 1944 after sea trials on the Elbe the previous day. Despite continual rain and a strong current 'strikingly good manoeuvrability' was reported. Top speed was about 260 km/hr. After an air raid on the production yard the seaplane was 'evacuated' to Schaalsee near Lübeck, camouflaged and moored near the river bank where it was discovered by Allied aircraft in 1945 and destroyed.

At least three French heavy flying boats were captured by the *Wehrmacht* and flown to Germany. Because the aircraft were one-offs, maintenance and repair was problematical. In 1936 the French Air Ministry had contracted for six-engined transatlantic commercial flying boats able to transport up to 40 passengers. In 1938 the first prototype of the Latécoère 631 powered by six Gnome & Rhône P.18s was ordered. At the 1940 armistice it fell into German hands in an uncompleted condition and did not make its first flight, as F-BAHG, until 4 November 1942. On completion of this flight the aircraft was found to have 20 per cent damage and the later history of the machine is unknown.

A Potez 161 (F-BAGV) was developed in 1936 and after being captured near-complete by the *Wehrmacht* was turned out in Vichy France as VE+WW. It was initially moored near Friedrichshafen on Lake Constance but later Rügen island in the Baltic was considered a safer anchorage. There were plans to use the machine as an un-piloted flying bomb in *Mistel* mode for an attack against the American mainland. Nothing further is known about this intention. The Potez 161 was rarely flown after 1941 for lack of spare parts and was eventually located at Rügen by Allied aircraft on 17 September 1944 and destroyed.

The third French flying boat in *Luftwaffe* hands was the unfinished Lioré-et-Olivier H-49 later redesignated SE 200, a 70-seater passenger seaplane powered by six Gnome & Rhônes. With fuselage markings 20+01 it was flown in January 1944 to moorings at Friedrichshafen and shot to pieces by Allied fighters in April that year. Parts of the wreck were trawled up by fishermen in 1950.

Three Ju 290s were built 'for special purposes' by Junkers from September 1944. Whether these machines were intended to fly to the Far East, South America, or to parachute spies or were for use as last-ditch bombers against America is unknown, as are their works numbers or other reliable information. It is believed that a Ju 290 took off from Beneschau airfield on 8 May 1945 for an unknown destination. Nothing is known about the cargo nor the *Waffen-SS* officers aboard as passengers.

That a second Ju 390 prototype was completed seems a possibility but there is no proof available from the manufacturer's documentation. Ju 390 V-2 is mentioned twice in the log of *Oberleutnant* Joachim Eisermann. Subsequently this aircraft allegedly made a 50-minute flight from/to Rechlin on 9 February 1945 and then made a second flight the same day to Lärz, where Eisermann left the aircraft. After completion of air trials Ju 390 V-1 remained for a long period propellerless on the edge of the airfield at Dessau and was put to the torch there in April 1945 to prevent the machine falling into American hands.

Chapter 11

The Year 1945

Along with Alexander Lippisch, the brothers Reimar and Walter Horten were the foremost proponents of the flying-wing principle in Germany. The various glider designs of this kind and the later twin-jet Horten (Ho) IX led them into heavy bomber manufacture. On 15 June 1944 the SS ordered twelve Ho III glider aircraft as the forerunners for a much larger flying-wing bomber. Six of the machines were intended for the diplomatic courier service. Here the designs were to be modified to transform the original glider into a jet aircraft. Two Jumo 004 B-2 turbines were under consideration. The Horten team was headed by Professor Naul.

During a three-day conference involving Horten, Junkers and Messerschmitt in the autumn of 1944, the RLM requested a new and more efficient bomber which could reach targets on the American eastern seaboard and return to Europe safely without the need to refuel in mid-air. It emerged that the longer range Ju 287 was unable to fulfil the demands made of it in this respect. A comparison of the performance estimates of the three existing projects showed that the Horten design had a 60 per cent greater range than all competitors including Junkers. Although no contracts had been placed by November 1944, Horten decided to prepare the groundwork for the Ho VIII, a modified Ho III. The machine had a wingspan of 40 metres and 150 square metres of wing. Its glide factor was about 30 but exact figures could not be supplied to the RLM without first making the necessary wind-tunnel tests. Six Argus (As) 10 pulse-jets integral in the wing were planned provisionally for the Ho VIII. The strong wings were to be of double-spar construction similar to those of the earlier Ho VI; the body was to be a wooden monocoque structure such as was already used on the Ho IX. Since much technical detail could be extracted from earlier design work, the brothers thought it possible to have the Ho VIII ready within six months. The steps employed would facilitate building a much larger long-range flying-wing bomber for *Kommando IX (Horten)*.

Because of the relatively low wing loading of only 53 kg/square metre, the Ho VIII would have been useful as a training aircraft for the bigger but little-heavier bomber. Work began in December 1944 and progressed surprisingly quickly during the next three months. On 12 March 1945 *Reichsmarschall* Göring told the Horten brothers and the *Kommando IX* head that he intended to place a firm order for the flying-wing bomber but he did not set concrete terms for completion. At the same time he did order the Ho VIII, and this was worked on at Göttingen.

Despite the war situation, work on the transatlantic version of the Ho VIII continued. The three-seater aircraft was designed for a maximum range (including a 1,000-km fuel reserve) of 13,000 km. With four SC or SD 1000 bombs, the Hortens calculated a radius of action of about 4,000 km, more with a reduced bomb-load. Six Jumo 004B turbines were designed integral to the wings after four BMW 003s had been found to lack sufficient power. Some 16 tonnes of fuel could be carried. Thought was given to the idea of having two turboprops but the development was unready. When American forces arrived at Göttingen in April 1945 the assembly was virtually ready, the first airframe being about 50 per cent complete.

It would appear that *Amt X, SS-Führungshauptamt* placed an order for another Horten design, the Ho XVIII, on 12 March 1945, and by 23 March Horten had prepared a design specification and presented it in Berlin. It was planned that the Ho XVIII with a 4-tonne bomb-load would have a maximum all-up weight of 32 tonnes although, for an America operation, the load would have been reduced to a single tonne or less in order to reduce fuel consumption and increase the fuel carried. For short-range missions there were three bomb bays, one in the fuselage and two between the outer wing section and the engine block, but for a long-range mission bombs could be replaced by disposable fuel tanks. The aircraft could have been refuelled in mid-air by a Ju 290 or similar. Horten expected a top speed of 820 km/hr in horizontal flight with an absolute limit for safety of 900 km/hr bearing in mind the steel/wood construction.

Although the preliminary work had not been completed by March 1945, the TLR (Technical Aircraft Production) head suggested that, in view of the rapid Allied advance, the development should be continued at Kahla in the Harz region. To build such a relatively large aircraft in the warren of tunnels inside Kahla mountain was not considered possible, and in any case Kahla was the principal Me 262 fighter production centre. A furniture factory at Stuttgart owned by the firm A. May where frames for the Ba 349 and minor He 162 parts were produced under licence had been planned for emergency use in 1944 by the SS, but the Allies were too close to Stuttgart at the beginning of April 1945 when the Ho XVIII was ready for assembly.

In contrast to all other Horten flying-wing designs, the Ho XVIII featured a large vertical tail surface which swept back from the crew cabin faired into the forward section. Remote-controlled gun positions with twin MG or MK cannon were to have been fitted at the nose and rear of the 19-metre long fuselage. The planned variants had a hand-operated 20-mm twin-gun position fore and aft of the cabin. In the last days of the war, most of the personnel engaged on the Ho XVIII project were more concerned with surviving past the end of hostilities than finishing the job and the great Ho XVIII was never completed.

In the autumn of 1944, *Reichsmarschall* Göring's staff invited aircraft manufacturers to attend a conference at Dessau to discuss the criteria for a new long-range bomber – a 12,000-km range was required for this aircraft, 13,000 km including the reserve, and a 4-tonne bomb-load. This indicated that a thoroughbred strategic bomber was now planned for as soon as possible, and in great haste.

Five days after the Ardennes Offensive was abandoned on 20 January 1945, Hitler ordered the immediate development of a giant high-speed bomber with great range and corresponding bomb-load. The available jet aircraft were meanwhile to fly to the limits of their range using large jettisonable or towed fuel tanks for bombing operations 'to bridge the period until a series-produced large bomber appears'. To date there is no document extant suggesting that these transatlantic jet bombers were to be designed for some purpose other than the disruption of the Atlantic sea lanes and to support German U-boat operations there.

The development of jet bombers in Germany and elsewhere began with the construction of fast fighters. After the slow progress of the He 280, of which only a few aircraft were produced, and the Me 262 A-1a, which came off the line in relatively large batches from 1944 onwards, the Ar 234 B-2 was the first useful jet bomber. The four-engined variants such as the Ar 234 C-3 and the C-5 prototype led the way to the heavy jet bomber, of which the Ju 287 V-1, which first flew on 8 August 1944, seems to have been the only example which took to the air before the capitulation. To meet the need, designs covered the broadest field to include swept-wing configurations and the 'flying wing'.

The forerunner of all these was possibly the Espenlaub E-2. Between 1927 and 1934 there came the Storch series of which Storch I flew successfully in 1927. A year later Storch III was flight tested. The later machines of the series flew until 1929. Of a more swept-wing appearance was the flying-wing Storch VII tested in 1931 while Storch VIII flew as a glider only, followed in 1934 by Storch IX with an engine in the nose. The development of flying-wing designs was concentrated primarily at the German Research Institute for Gliding. Between 1927 and 1937 seven different delta-winged aircraft were developed and flight tested. Included amongst these was the Delta V also designated DFS 40. Under the directorship of Dr Alexander Lippisch, there followed in 1943 the Delta V-1 (P-11) and in 1944 the Delta VII, which was seized at Chiemsee by American forces in 1945. All these test aircraft represented a valuable next step to the strategic bomber.

The RLM had declined Messerschmitt's P 08 project for a heavy bomber of flying-wing design as proposed on 1 September 1940. Insofar as they were worthy of the title, the available long-range aircraft of that period had a relatively low ratio between bomb-load and aircraft weight. Shortly after the outbreak of war it was apparent that a 500-kg or 1-tonne bomb was insufficient to inflict serious lasting damage on a capital ship, and that only the heaviest bombs could put a battleship out of action. Germany's operational long-range bomber was the Fw 200 which lacked a bomb-bay spacious enough to accommodate a heavy load.

Project 08 had a surprisingly large bomb-bay and payload capacity which even allowed for remote-controlled bombs and, for the first time in German aircraft design, gun-turrets for all-round defence operated from a central fire control point in the flight cabin. The manner of construction permitted modification for other purposes within a relatively short time. But it was not wanted at the time, and the seven profiles which developed from it only emerged in the last year of the war.

The design study for Messerschmitt project Me P 1107 was completed on 15 January 1945. The aircraft came in several variations as regards purpose and fuselage shape and was to be a long-range bomber equipped with four Heinkel HeS 011 turbines for a range of 9,500 km. The machine was a further development of the Me 264 incorporating the most recent advances in aerodynamics. By this time Messerschmitt's Augsburg offices had been transferred to Oberammergau, where work on this and the succeeding project, Me P 1108, was begun.

Because of the extremely difficult situation as regards raw materials, the aircraft was of a mixed structure, the fuselage being of steel and duraluminium, the wings of wood. The wings were designed to be of box construction with a central reinforcing spar for stability and strength. This was a temporary measure to cover the prototypes and proposed short series production run only. Aircraft weight for all versions was 9 tonnes, but the bomber had tanks for a maximum of 15 tonnes of fuel whereas the reconnaissance variant carried 19.4 tonnes in fuselage side tanks. The use of such tanks gave a maximum range of 10,000 km. The estimated endurance was between 8.45 hours and 11 hours.

According to the manufacturer's files, the wingspan of the P 1107/I was 17.3 metres and the wing surface 60 square metres. Length was 18.4 metres and the height 4.96 metres. The initially unarmed and unarmoured machine was designed to carry in the fuselage bomb-bay a 4-tonne payload of four SC or SD 1000s or one SC 1500 and two SC 500s. One or two remote-controlled PC 1400X 'Fritz X' bombs or aerial torpedoes were other possibilities. Electronic equipment was to have included one each of FuG 10, FuG 15, FuG 15a, FuG 101, FuG 120 and FuG 240 'Berlin' radars. This array would have enabled operations against distant seaborne targets and land and sea reconnaissance missions far afield even by night and in poor weather conditions. The radars were to have been fitted to all P 1107 variants.

The two basic tail designs were the *T-Leitwerk* 'T-Tail' integral with the fuselage on the P 1107/I version and the *V-Leitwerk* 'V-Tail' of P 1107/II. The two designs differed substantially. The retractable undercarriage, the bomb bay and some of the protected fuel tanks were located within the metal fuselage of the conventional version. The principal flying-wing version was mainly of wood with far fewer metal parts. This would have allowed at least a short series production despite the acute shortage of materials. The first prototype from Oberammergau was scheduled for mid-1946. For transatlantic work the P 1107 would have required mid-air refuelling.

Another Messerschmitt development at about the same time was a bomber offered in traditional and flying-wing versions, Me P 1108/I and II respectively. Both designs were outside the guidelines for the jet long-range bomber demanded by Hitler on 20 January 1945. The preliminary studies completed eight days earlier revealed a two-seater flying wing powered by four HeS 011 turbines and capable of 980 km/hr. The maximum range was 7,000 km, far too short for transatlantic operations. The conventional version had a round fuselage cross-section and four heavy jet engines paired up at the rear of the wings. The machine was 18.2 metres long with a 20-metre wingspan. Messerschmitt preferred the conventional version from the outset. It resembled the later De Havilland Comet and was expected to reach New York from Europe in six hours. One infers from this that the manufacturer was already thinking beyond the war's end; his immediate task was in any case the production of sorely needed Me 262 jet fighters.

The Heinkel design bureau in Vienna also began drawing board work on a jet bomber at the beginning of 1945. Led by Professor Günter, a modern flying wing was aimed for, propulsion being provided by four HeS 011 turbines. A relatively early series run was hoped for. Although no direct requirement existed for a range to enable raids to be mounted against the American coast, the prototype begun in February 1945 did have a trans-oceanic range. Complying with Göring's specifications of 22 February 1945, the aircraft had a range of 28,000 km. Allowing for a 20 per cent fuel reserve the radius of action was 12,000 km. The wing was of a new form, incorporating a two-stage sweep resulting in a bi-convex profile with a 10 per cent relative thickness, and bore a close resemblance to the legendary British Victor V-bomber conceived during the same year. The planned machine had a wingspan of 31.5 metres and an overall length of 19.85 metres. The spacious fuselage had ample room for several armour-protected fuel tanks and a bomb-bay for 3 tonnes.

Heinkel's major preoccupation was turning out the He 162 *Volksjäger* fighter and so development work on the 'jet-engined bomber' was pedestrian and came to an abrupt halt at the beginning of April 1945 when Soviet units arrived at Schwechat near Vienna. The Heinkel-Süd design office was evacuated to the Tyrol with its most important files and a few days later these became Allied war booty.

Junkers' four-engined *Entwicklungsflugzeug* (EF – Development Aircraft) 130 was an elegant flying-wing design with four mounted HeS 11 jet turbines. The plans for the 38-tonne machine show a bomber with a 24-metre wingspan and a wing area of 120 square metres. Because Junkers lacked capacity, the development was transferred in part to DFS at Ainring near Bad Reichenhall. In contrast to the Horten designs, EF 130 had a metal fuselage and an extensive wing surface of wood. A bomb bay for 4 tonnes and several armour-protected fuel tanks were located in the fuselage. The roomy cabin was pressurised, its three occupants included the gunner who remote-controlled the gun-turrets in the fuselage. The initial plans were for four HeS 11 turbines but as delivery of these was uncertain consideration was given to four BMW 003 C-1s instead, although even these were in short supply. The retractable main landing gear was located below the wings, the retractable nose wheel below the forward fuselage. Top speed was 950 km/hr. Carrying a full bomb-load the range was 5,500 km, with only 1 tonne 7,500 km. In view of the advanced developments at Horten and the work being done to bring the Ju 287 to readiness, the EF 130 had no priority and was cancelled at the beginning of 1945 by the TLR head, personnel being transferred to the EF 126 and EF 131 developments.

Despite the dramatic downturn in the war situation, at the beginning of 1945 the Junkers design office began planning an all-metal 90-tonne transatlantic bomber able to cruise at 1,000 km/hr. Radius of action was to be 7,500 km with 10 per cent fuel reserve and 8 tonnes of bombs, the range of 17,000 km being easily enough to bomb American coastal objectives without mid-air refuelling. The giant machine had a wingspan of 51.3 metres, was 31 metres long and 11 metres high. The spacious fuselage was integral to the wing structure and accommodated the bomb-bay and voluminous retractable 8-wheel undercarriage. The nose gear retracted rearwards. The six second-generation Heinkel or

Jumo turbines were buried within the wings, three each side. Air intake was located in the nose and flowed through the undercarriage casing to the six linked turbines. The wings had a 35-degree sweep-back and resembled in strength and size those of the smaller Gotha P60. The design could carry three to five turrets with twin guns for defence but which weapons were intended is not known. Theoretically the aircraft was well suited for strategic operations but it was all too late and construction work was never started.

Junkers' EF 132 was one of the heaviest jet bomber designs. Three Jumo turbines were planned for each of its 35-degree swept-back wings. Jumo 012 turbines were intended originally but were never available and six BMW 803Cs or Jumo 004Cs were decided upon instead. Wing surface was 160 square metres, wing loading 400 kg/square metre. Optimal airflow was achieved by burying the turbines in the wing roots. The four- or five-man crew would have been grouped into a spacious pressurised cabin. Three revolving gun-turrets equipped with twin 20-mm cannon were remote-controlled by gunners in the cabin where a modern periscope and remote aiming unit was planned. Although similar installations had been designed for other projects, by the end of 1944 the development team at Siemens, Mauser and Rheinmetall was still not satisfied that a successful result had been achieved. There was room in the bomb-bay for ten 500-kg or five 1-tonne projectiles. Aircraft weight was about 65 tonnes and with a full bomb-load range was about 9,800 km. The expected top speed was 925 km/hr. Work on the Ju EF 132 began shortly before the war ended. After the Americans occupied Dessau at the end of the war some of the files were kept hidden but were discovered by Red Army specialists in the summer of 1945 after US forces withdrew from the area.

Desperate times called for desperate measures and, considering the lack of capacity, non-availability of engines and shortage of fuel, at the beginning of 1945 Focke-Wulf came up with an ambitious idea for a fast jet bomber able to carry a 30-tonne bomb-load. The two- or four-man aircraft had a 22-metre wingspan. The all-up weight was 70 tonnes, fuel accounting for 17.8 tonnes, bombs in the six bomb-bays 30 tonnes, empty aircraft 22 tonnes. Propulsion was to be by jet turbines producing 13,000–15,000 kg thrust. Its speed would approach the sound barrier, so easily out-pacing enemy fighters that no armament was considered necessary, and making it a difficult target for anti-aircraft batteries. Range with a full bomb-load was 500 km, but the unladen reconnaissance version could have covered 10,000 km. Every possible economy was taken into account in the design.

For such a small aircraft to reach the designed top speed with a relatively large bomb-load of 30 tonnes required innovative thinking. The take-off speed alone would have been 500 km/hr and the very high wing loading of 500 kg/square metre would have made the aircraft a tricky proposition to get up. There was no room in the fuselage of the bomber version for the disproportionately large undercarriage and an independent take-off would have needed a rocket-assisted sled. Some critics consider this would have been very risky, although the runway required was not particularly long. Landing was to be on an integral skid. The wing loading at landing would have been in the region of 200 kg/square metre which Focke-Wulf considered adequately low.

The alternative take-off was in *Mistel* fashion with a mother aircraft to take the bomber aloft without it consuming fuel, the larger aircraft obtaining extra lift from the bomber's wings. The two-seater carrier aircraft had a 54-metre wingspan. All-up weight with the bomber underslung was 122 tonnes. Propulsion would have been six DB 603N piston engines or several DB 201 turboprops. Three tonnes of fuel was enough for the ascent.

On 13 January 1945 Focke-Wulf turned its attention to the idea of fitting five small bomber aircraft into the carrier for pinpoint bombing raids using 2.3 tonne hollow-charge bombs. These single-seaters had a very high wing loading of 500 kg/square metre and were intended principally for attacks against merchant vessels and tankers. Kurt Tank explained his philosophy as follows:

A 15,000-ton tanker sunk denies the enemy fuel for three major bombing raids on Germany. The thought that, by the sacrifice of one man and one machine, or, if remote-controlled, then of one machine alone, one can prevent three great air raids is in my opinion a considerable one.

Because neither the giant mother aircraft nor the required HeS 011 engines were available at the beginning of 1945, the idea remained confined to the drawing board and in any case Hitler was basically opposed to *kamikaze* tactics. The rammers of *Sonderkommando Elbe* were the exception rather than the rule.

One of the most interesting futuristic projects to emerge in Germany during the Second World War was the two-seater *Raumgleiter*, a rocket-propelled space bomber designed by Dr Eugen Sänger (b. Pressnitz, Bohemia, 1905). A graduate of the Technical University of Vienna, Sänger's ideas on space vehicles and flight beyond the Earth's atmosphere were first brought to public attention in 1933 in his book *Weltraumflug*. Sänger was engaged on rocket research at DFS from September 1942, where his main aim was to develop an efficient liquid fuel engine. His resulting plans for a rocket bomber were received with mixed views by the DFS directors. On 18 February 1943 he presented the head of DFS, Professor Walter Georgii, with a manuscript detailing his ideas for 'a long-distance bomber rocket engine'. It was not until 26 August 1944 that Georgii returned the manuscript in abridged form as publication UM 3538 of the German Aviation Research Institute, endorsed *Geheime Kommandosache* ('secret') and distributed to a wider research circle.

The design was for a 28-metre-long 'space glider' with a 15-metre wing span and a fuselage 3.6 metres wide and 1.8 metres high. each wing surface was only 44 square metres, the overall total lift surface being 125.5 square metres including contributory sections of the fuselage. The fuselage itself contained the pressurised cabin, all four fuel tanks, the retractable undercarriage and a spacious bomb-bay. Flights beyond the Earth's atmosphere were made possible by combustion chambers with a special cooling system. The evaporation system for the rocket motor was ordered in 1944. The 90 tonnes of fuel provided 100,000 kg of thrust for a maximum of eight minutes. Experiments with a smaller 1,000-kg thrust version were carried out at Fassberg on Lüneberg Heath and provided a burn of five minutes' duration.

Because of the limited fuel capacity, take-off would have been by use of a powered sled. Practical tests to establish friction data were made using a round fired up the ramp from a Karabiner 98 rifle at 800 metres/sec. No damage to the projectile was reported after numerous firings. The aircraft and sled propulsion motor were designed to be placed on the sled chassis for firing up an inclined concrete ramp 3,000 metres in length and aimed to the west. The bomber would have accelerated up to 12,500 metres altitude where the pilot, who would have been subjected during the one minute of acceleration to a G-force of 12, would ignite the rocket motor and continue to climb.

The rocket start-up speed was about 3,000 metres/sec, and the maximum speed was calculated at 10,000 metres/sec (36,000 km/hr) at 120 km altitude. Now in a glide, the machine would have used the deflection of the Earth's atmosphere to optimise the flight path. The ricochet effect of thicker layers of air would have continually repelled the aircraft into a continuous wave movement until the desired exit point was reached on the other side of the globe.

The rocket bomber was a step into a new dimension. No defences existed in the mid-1940s to meet an attack from space. It brought the whole of the United States within range, and even in small numbers such an aircraft would have made a global war strategy possible, provided that the various scarce raw materials necessary for construction could somehow have been conjured up. At a speed of 4,000 metres/sec (14,400 km/hr) at 50 km altitude there would have been no problem in carrying a bomb-load of 11 tonnes a distance of 7,000 km. At 100 km altitude, a smaller payload made a range of 20,000 km possible. Bomb-loads between 500 kg and 65 tonnes were considered.

Sänger's idea for a single-seater version would have had a take-off speed of 800 metres/sec and a constant airspeed between 3,000 and 5,000 metres/sec. This would have enabled ranges of between 300 km and 29,500 km to have been achieved. Periods of gliding lay between eight minutes and 29 hours. The absolute ceiling on the approach path to the United States would have been around 800 km altitude. An especially rewarding target was the densely populated area of Manhattan in the centre of New York. A 10-tonne conventional bomb impacting at between 500 and 800 metres/sec would have caused widespread destruction in which few structures were left standing. To destroy Manhattan completely, taking into account the bomb release height, it was reckoned that between 420 tonnes and 5,000 tonnes of bombs were required, although by virtue of the tremendous impact speed, even 1-tonne cylindrical bombs would have caused great devastation. The possibly insurmountable obstacle to all this wishful thinking, however, was how the bombs were to be aimed accurately.

The pilot of the space glider had to aim his bombs by eye 'at a relatively low speed' or simply drop off numerous projectiles in the form of a carpet bombing raid over half the country. From a height of between 50 km and 150 km above the Earth's surface, well beyond the enemy's reach, at a speed of 28,800 km/hr, the bombs would have been dropped with a zero possibility of hitting any particular target. If one had been specified, it would probably not have been visible to the pilot at that altitude and he would have had to aim by astronomical navigation. At impact the bomb-load would have been subject to substantial dispersal so that the aircraft would probably have carried a number of individual payloads. Sänger's complex calculations revealed that a stick of bombs dropped from between 50 km and 150 km at relatively fast speed would fall for between two and five minutes and would impact between 175 km and 1,500 km apart.

It was planned that the machine should complete its flight

either in the Japanese-occupied Marianas Islands, where it would be checked over and refuelled, or return to Europe without a stop if one of the two rocket motors had enough thrust left. The practical problems regarding the rocket motor and flight trajectory appear to have been resolved satisfactorily, but beside the bomb-aiming, the problems of friction from heat and where the heat-resistant metals were to come from remained unresolved. Protection of the retractable undercarriage, the four fuel tanks, the bomb-load, the pressurised cabin and controls – all these were required to withstand forces about which little was known.

The threat to the United States and other targets was therefore purely academic. This rocket bomber was required to be built in 1944/45 by an aviation industry which, despite several years of effort, had been able to produce only one flying prototype of the modern but conventional four-engined Me 264.

In 1946 the rocket bomber design was considered by the Soviets to be one of their most important armaments projects, but Sänger could not be lured away from France and eventually the Soviet interest in the idea was abandoned.

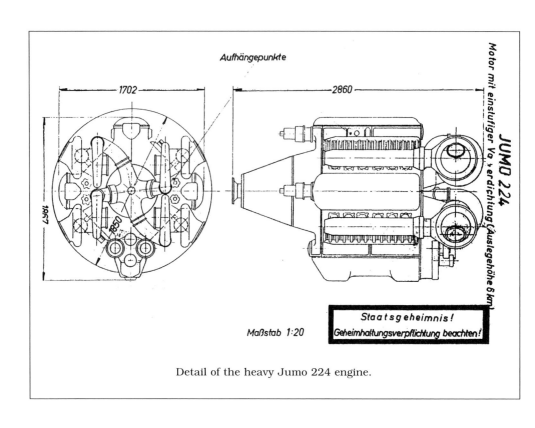

Detail of the heavy Jumo 224 engine.

Description of the fork-locking procedure for mid-air refuelling.

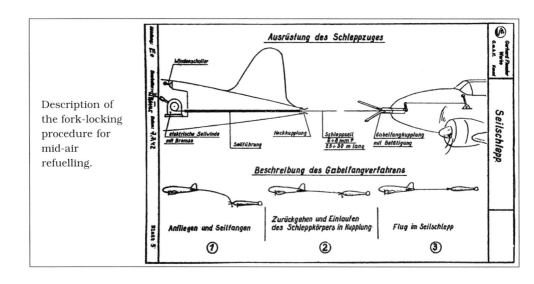

How refuelling was achieved by the tube-tow procedure.

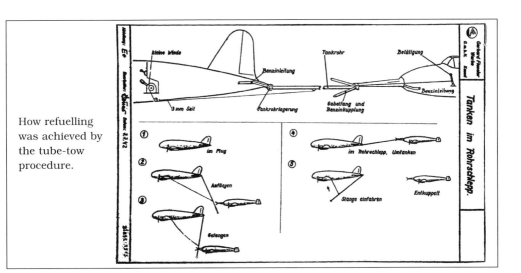

Simpler than the tube-tow was refuelling by a fuel hose.

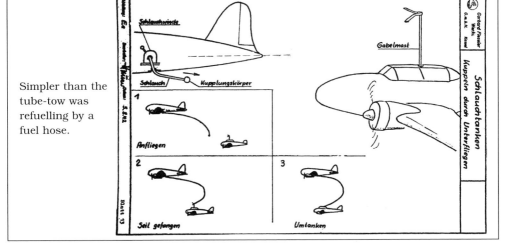

In the combined hose-hawser procedure the tank hose was passed over by means of a wire.

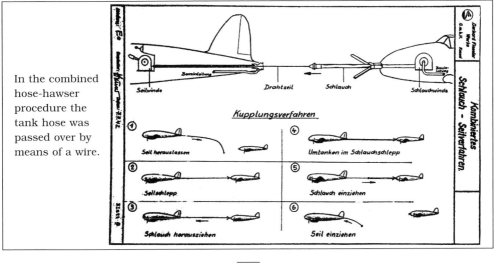

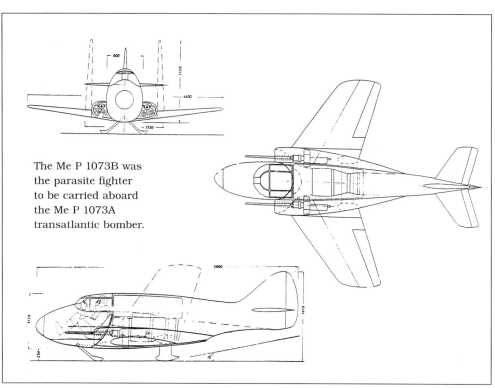

The Me P 1073B was
the parasite fighter
to be carried aboard
the Me P 1073A
transatlantic bomber.

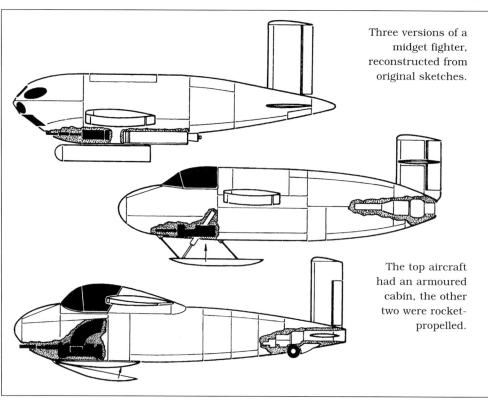

Three versions of a
midget fighter,
reconstructed from
original sketches.

The top aircraft
had an armoured
cabin, the other
two were rocket-
propelled.

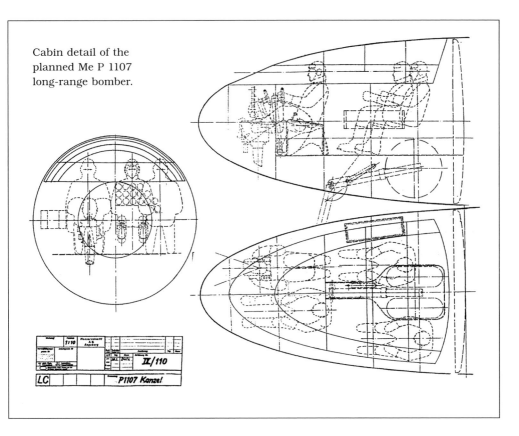

Cabin detail of the
planned Me P 1107
long-range bomber.

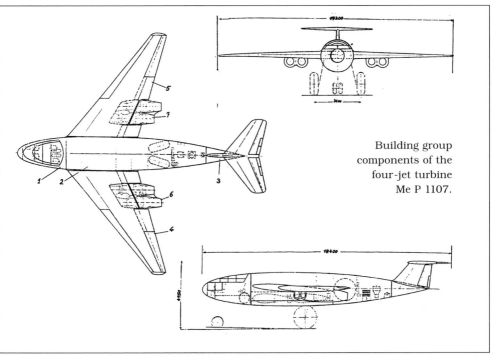

Building group
components of the
four-jet turbine
Me P 1107.

Chapter 12

Rocket Attack

The use of artillery rockets has a long tradition and, in Europe, stretches back to modest beginnings in the Napoleonic Wars. After playing little part in the Great War, their importance grew with advances in technology. In 1931 the *Heereswaffenamt* (Army Weapons Office) ordered a small liquid-fuel rocket motor of about 20 kg thrust. An assembly in working order was supplied three years later, and on 3 August 1934 *Aggregat* 1 (A1) ran for 50 seconds producing a constant thrust of 130 kg. A2 was tested on the East Frisian island of Borkum and in 1936 work building the long-range A3 began at the Kummersdorf testing ground outside Berlin. For security reasons it was tested at Greifswalder Oie, a small island in the Baltic off Peenemünde on the Usedom Peninsula. The first successful test launch of an A3 took place on 8 December 1937, and from then until 1942 a whole series of proving tests followed using the simple reduced-scale A5 while the future operational attack rocket, designated A4, was under development at Kummersdorf and Peenemünde. The immediate problem had been to design an efficient rocket motor that was neither overweight nor unwieldy. The first such propulsion unit, of 25,000-kg thrust, ran on the test stand on 21 March 1940.

On 20 August 1941 the project was presented to Hitler and OKW head Field Marshal Keitel at Hitler's *Wolfschanze* (Wolf's Lair) headquarters by *Generaloberst* Fromm, head of Army Weapons Supply, and *Oberst* Walter Dornberger, Dr Wernher von Braun and Dr Ernst Steinhoff of the Peenemünde test facility. After seeing a film about rocket development at the partially built site, Hitler was very enthusiastic. Dornberger noted in his file:

> The *Führer* emphasised that this development is of revolutionary significance for our global war policy. An offensive with a mere few thousand rockets annually is not enough. If it came to an offensive, then we had to make and fire off hundreds of thousands of rockets each year.

Dornberger observed that the construction of giant rockets required not only a skilled work force and the manufacture of costly or scarce materials but also a long development period. The first phase of tests would not be likely to be finished before the end of August 1942. A precondition was that the rocket programme receive the highest category of priority and that Peenemünde be expanded as soon as possible. The temporary de-prioritisation of the work in 1940 had been very adverse. In conclusion Keitel promised all possible support for the project.

The complexity of the development held back progress at Peenemünde. The first completed A4 rocket on Test Stand VII on 25 February 1942 was used to test the propulsion unit. The fate of the unit is unknown. A series of failures followed; many A4s exploded on the launch pad or shortly after taking off, or deviated from the set trajectory. Frequently the most minor defect was responsible. Not until 13 June 1943 did the specialists achieve a completely successful launch and flight. A training battery was then formed and eventually the first A4, also known as the *Vergeltungswaffe* 2 (V-2 – Revenge Weapon 2), impacted in London on 8 September 1944. About 5,500 A4 rockets fell on London and on cities in Belgium, Holland and France. The A4 had a limited range of 320 km, but this would eventually change, if only in the planning.

Relatively early, in the course of 1936, the *Heereswaffenamt* was already working on plans for a successor to the projected A4. Initially the intention was that the rocket designated A10 should have a motor fuelled by a mix of liquid oxygen and alcohol for 100,000 kg of thrust. The missile would carry a 4-tonne warhead over a range of 500 km. The installations erected at Peenemünde between 1936 and 1939 were made to measure for this device, but the work lost urgency from 1939 after the short-range A4 found favour. Only in 1940, when the A10 was seen as one stage of an intercontinental rocket still to be designed, was interest gradually revived. For a range of 5,000 km, the calculations showed that a much more powerful plant capable of developing at least 180,000 kg of thrust would be necessary. This new missile was known as 'the America Rocket'. Scientists at Peenemünde were anxious to discover a method of increasing the range of individual rockets, and on 29 July 1940 Graupe, an engineer working on the A4, submitted calculations for a two-stage ground-to-ground rocket provisionally designated A9/10. On the basis of his figures it was quickly decided to design an intercontinental rocket which could hit the United States. The complex technology and other problems hindered progress and as in any case the *Heereswaffenamt* considered that more theoretical work needed to be done, a few months later an improved version with longer range emerged.

By the end of 1940, long before the successful first launch of an A4, rocket specialists had also concluded that the 8,000 km/hr impact speed and its enormous kinetic energy could be usefully converted to lengthen the range. Wings were added for better aerodynamic lift and an undulating trajectory. On 31 January 1941 Graupe submitted a dissenting opinion regarding the 'glide-body' although in the course of the year he worked on another two-stage project which 'glided' and on which he reported to the *Heereswaffenamt* on 20 October 1941. Nevertheless, all these ideas were beset by the immense problems being thrown up by the A4.

It was known on 18 December 1941 that the motor for the start stage of the intercontinental rocket would not be available before the end of 1944, possibly into 1945. Peenemünde rocket scientist Dr Thiel expressed the opinion that the choice lay between having a motor producing

180,000 kg of thrust made up out of six 30,000 Salbei Visol (50:50 benzol/petrol mixture with nitric acid oxidant) combustion chambers or designing a new unit altogether. The advantage of the former was that it had already been decided upon for the purpose of attempting to improve the A4 performance. There was no possibility of the intercontinental rocket being realised, although work did continue from 1942 on a small scale. Other ideas to fall under the hammer were the A11, a further development of the A9/10, and the A12, a purely hypothetical concept for a three-stage carrier rocket probably destined for a flight out into space.

The winged A4 was designated A9 and also known as 'Glider A4' or 'the winged projectile'. On Dornberger's express order no work was carried out on the A9 between October 1942 and June 1944 in order to concentrate all energies on the A4. Once the latter was considered ready for operations, the A9, now re-designated A4b, received increased attention. In a letter to the *Heereswaffenamt* on 11 August 1944, von Braun attributed a range of at least 450 km to the A4b. (The standard A4 with wings was also designated A4b but was not a variant of the production unit.) Practical work on developing a winged rocket with great range was begun from December 1944 and it was planned as an interim measure to use the A4b as the second stage of an intercontinental rocket. The first flight took place on 27 December 1944, the rocket losing directional stability at 50 metres. The first satisfactory flight was at Peenemünde on 24 January 1945 when the A4b reached an altitude of almost 80 km and a maximum speed of 1,200 metres/sec. This seems to have been the last attempt to come up with a more efficient second stage using the A4b than would have been possible with the standard A4. The test vehicle was a scaled-up A4 of 26 metres length with a maximum body diameter of 4.1 metres and 9.1 metres across the stabilisers. Take-off weight was 85 tonnes and the warhead was designed for 925 kg. The rocket motor developed 30,000 kg of thrust for its 600-km range. These practical tests were abandoned in February 1945 following the decision to evacuate Peenemünde.

Chapter 12

In theory, the initial thrust at launch of an A9/10 was 180,000 kg, the burn lasting 50 seconds at which point the second stage, an A4 or winged A9, separated from the A10. Calculations indicated a ceiling of 350 km for this second stage. The final speed at the end of the burn would have been at least 3,000 metres/sec, and the winged second stage could fly at least 5,000 km. From Biscay launch sites the A9/10 would have had the range to hit New York or Washington and targets all along the American eastern seaboard from Canada southwards. It was a weapon against which no counter-measure existed. Modern-style rocket silos of extremely thick concrete were built in northern France during 1943. The most advanced was 80 per cent complete when the area was overrun by the Allies in the summer of 1944. The Wizernes silo had the height to accommodate fully the A9.

By that time the gyroscopic navigation system for the projected 'America Rocket' was under manufacture in the 'Polte 2' underground factory at Rudisleben in the Harz mountains, and the giant A9/10 and its power plant could only have been built in protective bunkers or underground from the summer of 1944 onwards. After Peenemünde had suffered its first heavy air attack in August 1943, a large section of the Army weapons testing centre, including the development work on the 'America Rocket' was transferred to Ebensee. The camp of that name was a satellite of Mauthausen concentration camp in Upper Austria and supplied the labour for an extensive underground weapons factory code-named 'Zement' where about 18,000 luckless inmates worked on *Sonderbauvorhaben* (Special Project) B-1. About 40 per cent of this work force died of accidents, lack of food and brutal treatment. Galleries bored into the rock were supported and water-proofed by prefabricated concrete sections to get the construction work over with quickly. Zement had a floor area of about 300,000 square metres, of which Zement A took up 220,000 square metres in which the *Heereswaffenamt* had decided to turn out twenty *Wasserfall* flak rockets monthly and possibly the same number of long-range rockets.

Underground factory Zement B, with a floor space of 70,000 square metres, was the testing facility for rockets developed in Zement A. The intention was to have ready by December 1944 a rocket testing area of 20,000 square metres under reinforced concrete, to replace another range at nearby Schlier. After non-rocket fuel production at Ebensee had been awarded a higher priority than rockets, the planned series production of a German two-stage rocket would certainly have been shelved in favour of using the available protected floor space for fuel production.

The Third *Reich* had in the region of 200 underground weapons facilities, and the location of a few of them, particularly in Poland, remains a task for archaeologists. Nevertheless, German and English-language authorities on the subject are virtually unanimous that there was no 'America rocket' production in the spring of 1945. Although theoretical draughtsmanship may have been concluded by then, it seems very doubtful that the technology had made such giant strides in three months that an 'America Rocket' could be successfully flight tested. These is no mention in any declassified document of the existence of a two-stage intercontinental rocket. Moreover the recently established *Jägerstab* had been vehement from the summer of 1944 onwards in its demands for the supply of high-performance fighter aircraft to the *Luftwaffe*, bunker-type assembly hangars being required for this purpose, and the same applied to the production of aircraft fuels. Following these in priority came important war material such as ball bearings, motor parts or assembly shops for remote-controlled weaponry. The basic priorities left no room for the giant A9/10 or any of its five successors.

There is, however, one archive source from the former East Germany containing sworn testimony to a DDR tribunal in 1962 which strongly suggests the test of an unusually large rocket near Ohrdruf in March 1945. In 1962 the Arnstadt/Thuringia municipal authorities took sworn depositions from many residents for a quasi-judicial DDR tribunal whose task was to compile a Second World War history of the region or, more probably, find out what the Americans might have learnt about strange Nazi technologies at Ohrdruf. The statements may be viewed at Arnstadt town hall under the heading 'Befragung von Bürgern zu Ereignissen zur örtlichen Geschichte'. Four depositions, two by former technical workers at Polte 3 (a fuel-tank maker and a rocket-scaffolding worker), one by a former concentration camp inmate and the last by the custodian of the Wachsenburg watch-tower, were unanimous that a very large rocket was fired at Rudisleben on the night of 16 March 1945.

Werner Kasper worked with the civilian team while the concentration camp prisoners were supervised by officials of the *Reichspost*. Kasper gave evidence that he was involved in the making of tanks for liquid oxygen and a nitrogenous substance for a two-stage rocket of approximately 30 metres' length. He also stated under oath that the rocket was fired at about 11 o'clock on the night of 16 March 1945 by engineers from Peenemünde. Its bearing was to the north. The other two statements by persons working at Rudisleben corroborate this testimony. Frau Cläre Werner was custodian of the Wachsenburg watch-tower north-east of Ohrdruf. In her deposition she stated:

> Towards nine on the evening of 16 March 1945, the same group [plain-clothes officials from the *Reichspost* and other services] was on the tower with binoculars. We looked towards Ichtershausen [a village to the east-northeast directly in line with Rudisleben]. About eleven o'clock there was a very bright glare and then something soared up into the sky with a great tail-fire. It went higher and higher and then headed away to the north.

There were several projects commencing around the middle of the war which envisaged firing rockets from U-boats or from submersible barges towed by a U-boat, at targets along the United States' coastline. In the first test of one of these, in May 1942 off Greifswalder Oie near Peenemünde, the Type IX U-boat *U-511* commanded by *Kapitänleutnant* Fritz Steinhoff, brother of Peenemünde scientist Ernst Steinhoff, fired while submerged twenty 21-cm solid propellant artillery rockets from a launching apparatus fixed to the after-casing. The rockets flew a 3,000-metre trajectory satisfactorily, convincing SKL that the method was feasible to attack targets on a distant coast such as that of the United States. With the advent of superior Allied radar technology, consideration was given to the possibility of firing rockets from the torpedo tubes at enemy anti-submarine vessels. A rocket-propelled anti-ship missile with a 3,000-metre range capable of holing a destroyer was soon in the design stage.

The basic experimental work code-named 'Ursel' was handled from the summer of 1944 by the *Chemisch-Physikalische Forschungsanstalt der Kriegsmarine* (CPVA – Navy Research Institute for Physics and Chemistry) on Lake Toplitz near Bad Aussee, Salzburg province. CPVA head was Dr Ernst Steinhoff, who since 1943 had been departmental head for shipboard remote-control and radar-ranging at Peenemünde.

The missiles were aimed at a cliff from a launcher up to 100 metres below the surface of Lake Toplitz. The systems were produced by the Westphalian firm WASAG. Tests continued to the end of 1944 by when the projectiles had acquired various experimental wings. In February 1945, Dr Lindberg, a CPVA scientist, inspected a Type XXI U-boat equipped with a launch tube for the Ursel underwater rocket. This was to be a purely defensive armament for use against oncoming enemy warships.

The statement made during an interrogation at Dachau in 1947 by former SS-*Obersturmbannführer* Otto Skorzeny, head of sabotage, SS-RSHA/Amt VI, that it was planned to deploy underwater rockets with a 15-kg warhead against American coastal targets seems ludicrous if the explosive substance was not to have had a terrific destructive effect.

The idea of launching a V-1 flying bomb from the deck of a U-boat was discussed but never attempted. The chances of hitting New York at a range of 200 km from the rolling deck of a U-boat were not considered favourable unless somebody ashore turned on a homing device. Agents' reports received around 5 November 1944 by Allied Supreme Headquarters in Europe spoke of four U-boats having departed for the American coast with remote-controlled V-1s. A number of US carrier-supported anti-submarine groups were positioned in coastal waters. The main concern was that the V-1s might have a fission warhead of some description for use against the centre of New York. An insinuation made by Armaments Minister Speer lent credence to this fear, and German radio promised that the first rockets would hit the United States on 1 February 1945. This led to some unrest at the potential receiving end and thus, at least in a psychological sense, the offensive was successful.

Besides the use of small projectiles and the V-1, thought was given at Peenemünde to firing the V-2 against land targets from a submersible barge towed into position by a U-boat. The suggestion was made originally by Otto Lafferenz, a leading member of the *Deutsche Arbeitsfront* (DAF) to *Oberst* Dornberger, military director of Peenemünde in the autumn of 1943. Using the Volkswagen works at Wolfsburg as a cover-address, the entire correspondence was given the designation Prüfstand XII. By flooding various tanks, the metal submersible barges could be stood upright in the water in a position suitable for the launch of the V-2 within. The idea was to bombard American coastal cities from a position about 300 km off-shore. Development of the rocket lagged, however, and by late 1944 the idea of towing the barges to the coast of the United States may have been abandoned when it was discovered that the rocket fuel, which was partially organic, being produced in some measure from potatoes, lost its potency after three to four days. Since a transatlantic tow would take thirty days, the project to attack the United States would not then be feasible. Although there is no proof, the subsequent development from December 1944 was probably intended for use against the British coast only.

During a conference at Peenemünde on 9 December 1944 involving *Generalmajor* Rossmann (Departmental head, weapons testing-10), Dr Dickmann from the Vulkanwerft company of Stettin and director Riedel Ill of EW Karlshagen, the theme of 'firing A4s from the sea' was discussed. These seem to have been the first talks between staff of the A4 development division and the shipyard responsible for building the submersible barges. Apart from the basic questions, the launching procedure had to be explored thoroughly. Vulkanwerft presented its first designs and plans showing how the tow was to be effected and how the slow tilting of the barge in the water to reach the optimum firing position was to be achieved.

Meanwhile Peenemünde engineers – following consultation with the *Kriegsmarine* – had come to the conclusion that a Type XXI U-boat could tow up to three submersible barges each containing an A4. The rockets would be loaded into the barges ashore, the 500-tonne barges then being floated off the loading dock. Shipyard manufacture actually began at the end of 1944. The barge had a form resembling an A4 with a roundish cross-section narrowing towards the stern and stabilised by four fins. The nose of the barge, through which the rocket would be fired when upright, was capped by a massive watertight cover. The exhaust gases from the rocket at launch would be discharged upwards through a piping system. In the stern was a pump room with ballast tanks. To fire the rocket from as calm conditions as possible the same depths would have been chosen as those pertaining at Lake Toplitz for the tests. It appears that the intention was to fire the rocket from a depth of 100 metres.

According to Markus Köberl, *Kapitänleutnant* Stephan, commander of the Type VIIC U-boat *U-1063*, carried out a towing trial with a submersible barge. According to unconfirmed reports one such barge was completed at Schichau Werft, Elbing, in the spring of 1945. The planned trials with a barge, both empty and loaded with an A4, and towed by a Type XXI U-boat, were abandoned in February 1945 when Peenemünde was evacuated.

Attacks against Britain and the US East Coast using barge-launched V-2s with battlefield gas, radioactive material or other unconventional warheads would have been technically possible from the end of 1945. One can imagine that using that kind of material – in view of the dramatic war situation – began to dominate German strategic thinking but the devastating Allied air raids made it impossible to realise the objective at the last minute.

At the war's end numerous partly immobilised A4 rockets were discovered at Leese, a village on the eastern bank of the Weser, at an installation manufacturing battlefield gases. At an underground munitions factory at Espelkamp in northern Germany, numerous A4 projectiles were found. The warheads were missing. Until the beginning of 1945 Espelkamp had been a centre where artillery shells were filled with chemicals and stored. Information filtering through to US agencies may have led to the taking of precautions there.

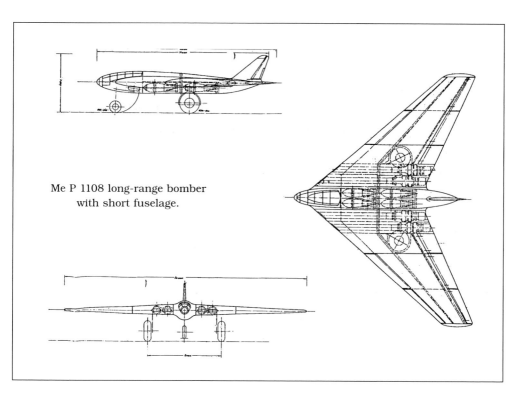

Me P 1108 long-range bomber
with short fuselage.

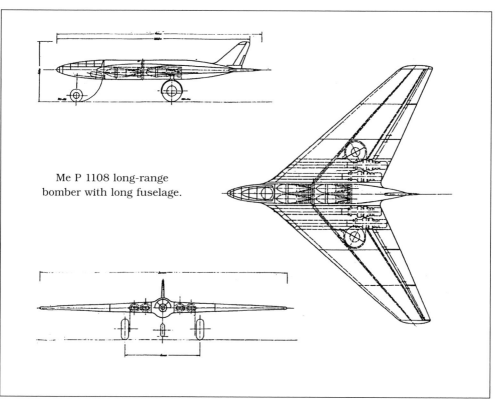

Me P 1108 long-range
bomber with long fuselage.

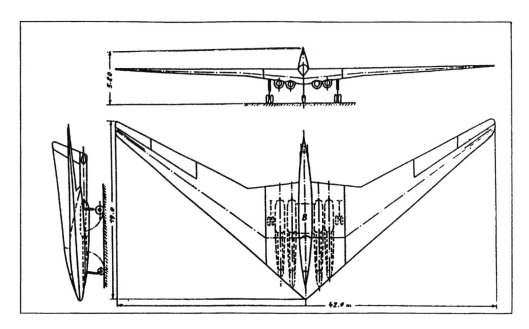

Horten XVIII bomber with four jet turbines and glazed cabin integrated into wing.

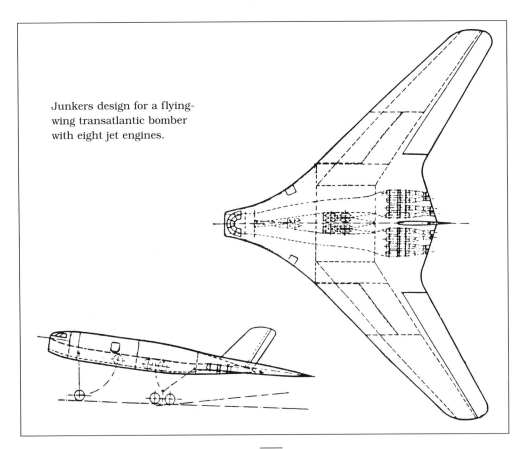

Junkers design for a flying-wing transatlantic bomber with eight jet engines.

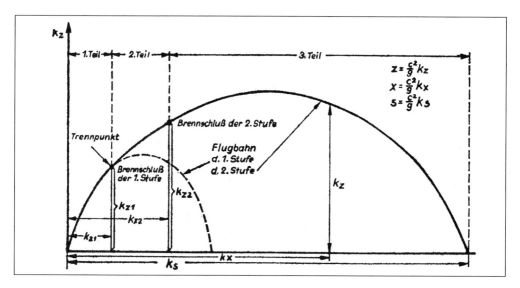

$$z = \frac{c^2}{g} k_z$$
$$x = \frac{c^2}{g} k_x$$
$$s = \frac{c^2}{g} k_s$$

Contemporary flight trajectory calculations: (*above*) of the two-stage A10 long-range rocket; (*below*) of a two-stage long-range rocket with a maximum range of 4,000 km.

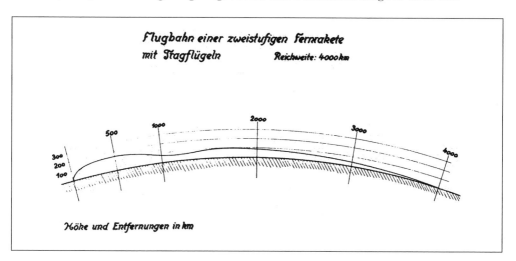

Flugbahn einer zweistufigen Fernrakete
mit Tragflügeln   Reichweite: 4000 km

Höhe und Entfernungen in km

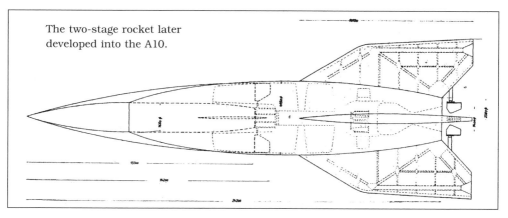

The two-stage rocket later developed into the A10.

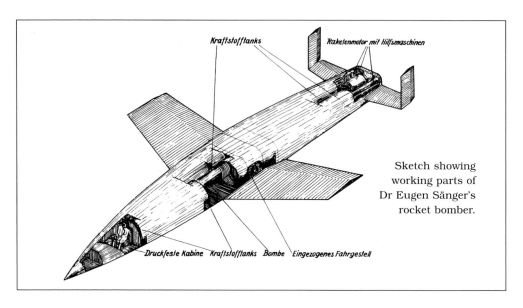

Sketch showing
working parts of
Dr Eugen Sänger's
rocket bomber.

Kraftstofftanks   Raketenmotor mit Hilfsmaschinen

Druckfeste Kabine   Kraftstofftanks   Bombe   Eingezogenes Fahrgestell

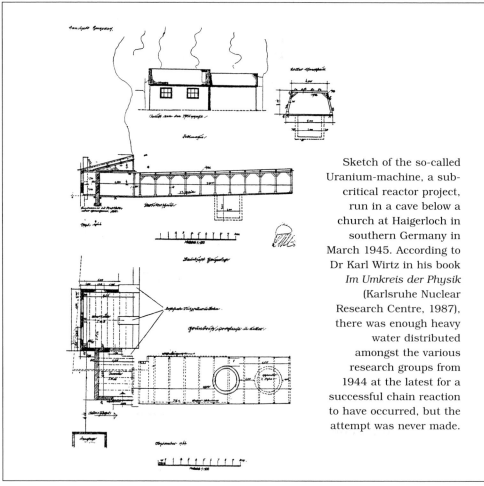

Sketch of the so-called
Uranium-machine, a sub-
critical reactor project,
run in a cave below a
church at Haigerloch in
southern Germany in
March 1945. According to
Dr Karl Wirtz in his book
Im Umkreis der Physik
(Karlsruhe Nuclear
Research Centre, 1987),
there was enough heavy
water distributed
amongst the various
research groups from
1944 at the latest for a
successful chain reaction
to have occurred, but the
attempt was never made.

Chapter 13

The Ordnance

Perhaps the United States came close to receiving a German attack in the Second World War. Certainly it was always a latent possibility and to the last could never be ruled out. On 28 January 1942 the Office of Civilian Defense in Washington DC issued a 'Handbook for Air Wardens' containing tips and instructions for the eventuality, should it ever come.

The military might of Hitler's Germany had been great enough to set half of Europe ablaze but whether it would extend to world mastery was another question. The unsuitable aircraft at the disposal of the *Luftwaffe* made a massive air bombardment of the US East Coast impossible but nuisance raids could have been flown in favourable weather conditions from the summer of 1943 onwards had the appropriate order come down from the highest level. With large flying boats or long-range bombers refuelled in mid-air, the *Luftwaffe* certainly had the capability to make an appearance along the Atlantic coast. By the outbreak of war with the United States, German manufacturers had developed the necessary aircraft but a short-sighted strategy, Hitler's constantly changing intentions, and limited industrial capability undermined any idea of putting the more ambitious plans, which included offensive action against America, into practice.

For their part, although Americans could never know how far advanced the German preparations for such an attack might be, having the Atlantic as their border afforded the best defence against enemy attack. Despite the occasional period of disquiet, the American population therefore endured, in relative security, to the war's end.

The typical *Luftwaffe* everyday bomb-load would have fitted comfortably into the spacious bomb-bays of the planned long-range and transatlantic bomber fleet. The stock inventory was the SC 50 to SC 1800 range. Neither these, nor other thin or thick-cased high-explosive or shrapnel bombs were ever in short supply. By the end of 1942, about 100 of the heavier SB 2500 A-1s and SC 2500 B-1s became available. A 5-tonner, SC 5000, had also been developed but lack of capacity frustrated output. This land-mine was over 5.2 metres long and intended for use against cities and industrial complexes. Another heavy land-mine was the SA 4000, of which only a few were produced and tested. Once the air offensive against Britain had been scaled down, the SC 2500, SC 5000 and SA 4000 bombs went into store. The SHL 6000 was designed for large naval targets, bridges and industrial zones and its hollow charge was greater than that carried by the un-piloted Ju 88 *Mistel.*

The largest planned conventional bombs of the time would have reached between 10 and 30 tonnes and were destined for the bomb-bay of Sänger's space glider project. The great weight and impact speed from 150 km altitude were expected to cause a massive explosion; studies forecast a crater 100 metres deep. Steel-reinforced concrete 10 metres thick was no defence against such a bomb. Each projectile would have been 11.2 metres long with a 1.4-metre diameter. This weapon, together with a 1-tonne land-mine for dropping from a great height, only ever existed on the drawing board.

Remote-controlled weapons systems for transatlantic bombers included the PD 1400X, PD 2500X and PD 2600X glider bombs as well as the television-image steered Hs 293 and Hs 294 for pinpoint accuracy.

Hitler ruled that Germany would not make a pre-emptive strike with chemical or bacteriological weapons even if it meant losing the war.

At the commencement of hostilities, the *Luftwaffe* had available phosgene, the nerve gases, several mustard gas types and so-called 'gas-mask removers'. All these gases came in cylindrical containers designated 'KC'. Standard payloads were KC 50, KC 250 and KC 500. The most lethal was KC 250 IIGr filled with 100 kg of nerve gas.

A total of between 61,000 and 64,000 tonnes of battlefield gases were produced in Germany, so much that only by the spring of 1943 were sufficient bomb cases on hand for all the material. By the autumn of 1944 the *Luftwaffe* had a stock of 1,160,340 chemical-type bombs, of which, according to the documentation, 1,600 contained nerve gas.

The fearful complications presented by bacteriological weapons were known to all major belligerents. The former head of Canadian military medical services stated that in his opinion 'compared with bacteriological warfare, atom bombs and hydrogen bombs are just child's play'. Whether any such substances were available in Germany outside the laboratory is not known.

An especially opaque chapter of weapons development is that of the German 'atom bomb'. Various research groups occupied themselves both before and during the war not only with the idea of 'atom-splitting' but also investigating the possibilities of using uranium to build nuclear weapons. The actual investigation does not necessarily imply that Germany intended to have a nuclear arsenal: the *Heereswaffenamt* wished to know expressly whether any potential enemy was likely to have a nuclear capability and the probable timescale for its development.

In October 1939, the so-called Uranium Club (*Uranverein*) composed of Germany's leading atom physicists met in Berlin to outline a broad programme of activity. The leading personality was the Nobel Prize winner Professor Werner Heisenberg. Scientific papers submitted by him to the *Heereswaffenamt* in December 1939 described the materials required for a pilot atomic reactor and pointed out that huge quantities of radioactive material would be bred in such a reactor. Heisenberg did not state that this would be useful as a weapon, although a researcher at Hamburg, Professor Paul Harteck, admitted after the war that in 1940 he had personally advocated building a nuclear reactor precisely for this purpose – for radioactive terror attacks on enemy cities. Heisenberg confirmed that an atom bomb was possible if substantial quantities of the fissile isotope U-235 could be isolated from uranium. The Uranium Club had centres at several universities as well as the Kaiser Wilhelm Institute for Physics in Berlin: another important centre of nuclear research was Baron Manfred von Ardenne's *Reichspost* Institute at Berlin-Lichterfelde which co-operated closely with the rocket specialists at Peenemünde.

In 1940 various research groups in Austria and Berlin reported that plutonium-239, another fissile isotope, would be bred in a working reactor, and this would also be bomb material. In August 1941, Professor Fritz Houtermans, a researcher at the *Reichspost* Institute, circulated a paper pointing out that the easiest method of building an atomic pile was to use uranium powder with methane at an extremely low temperature as the moderator instead of the so-called 'heavy water'. This would enable Germany to go atomic almost immediately, since all necessary materials were to hand. There is no evidence that any attempt was made to construct a zero-energy reactor of this kind, and since it would have been the obvious first step into the atomic age, the explanation may be that Hitler really was opposed to nuclear weapons and atomic reactors on doctrinal grounds.

By the beginning of 1942, Heisenberg's easy-paced research at Leipzig University had established the rate of neutron multiplication in an apparatus consisting of uranium powder and heavy water, and the precise quantities of materials required to build a working reactor of this type were now known.

On 4 June 1942, high-ranking representatives of the three services, including Field Marshal Milch, attended a meeting at Harnack Haus, the Berlin headquarters of the Kaiser Wilhelm Institute, to hear speeches on nuclear physics subjects delivered by theoretical physicists such as Otto Hahn and Werner Heisenberg. Afterwards when Armaments Minister Speer asked Heisenberg whether an atom bomb was possible, he was told that the problem had been solved in theory but that nothing could be expected in the short term.

Possibly Heisenberg had calculated that far more plutonium would be required for a bomb than it would be possible to procure in a mere couple of years. To be on the safe side he added that the United States might have something by 1944. Milch was told at this conference that the new bomb – or at least the fissile core – 'would be the size of a pineapple' and he therefore began to envisage that a large flying boat such as the BV 238, refuelling in mid-Atlantic, could reach New York with the weapon.

The unimpressive nuclear research programme progressed at Gottow in the autumn of 1942 with the G1 experiment in which cubes of uranium oxide – a retrograde step as regards materials purity – were tested with layers of paraffin. In the summer of 1943, G2 followed, the previous squarish configuration being replaced by a sphere containing alternate layers of heavy ice and uranium metal. In the winter of 1943, experiment G3 had more materials than the earlier two tests. Uranium cubes were suspended on thin wires into heavy water in a large sphere lined with paraffin.

Long after the war Heisenberg mentioned an attempt to achieve a chain reaction in an underground gallery in the Erzgebirge. The experiment was a failure because of an alleged mathematical error, and after Dr Diebner's idea of using uranium cubes in place of uranium plates had provided a better result, the *Heereswaffenamt* began to doubt Heisenberg's work. His remark that atomic energy would have great benefits for Germany's energy requirements after the war may also have upset the *Heereswaffenamt*. In view of the more immediate military requirements the reference to the civilian uses of nuclear technology may have cooled the authorities' enthusiasm. Certainly thereafter little further interest was shown in Diebner's ideas, and from late 1943 the uranium project was continued on a reduced scale. It is worth mentioning that a very comprehensive nuclear research facility existed near the Eulenberg in 1944 which may also have been geared up to the production of heavy water and developing a strange high-energy technology based on SS earth sciences. Siemens AG and IG Farben were particularly involved in these projects. The secret *Waffen*-SS underground factories at places such as Stechowitz in Czechoslovakia were satellites of the great subterranean weapons facility at Ohrdruf.

Whether Heisenberg's nuclear project was all part of a great charade to conceal what was really afoot, or if all these highly gifted atom physicists were really all confused and at cross-purposes is difficult to determine. Various German writers of recent years tend to the former explanation, relying on two or three reports of so-called 'atom-bomb' tests carried out in and over Germany.

The first of these declassified papers is to be found in NARA/RG 38, Box 9-13 Entry 98c, Top Secret Naval Attache Reports 1944–1947 of the US National Archives. It is an Intelligence Report issued by COMNAVEU London on 24 January 1946 by Captain R. F. Hickey, USN, and entitled 'Investigations, Research, Developments and Practical Use of the German Atomic Bomb'. A footnote to the enclosure states: 'Enclosure (A) is a discussion of the developments of the German atomic bomb. Listed are the principal scientists involved, plus what is known by them of similar developments in the United States. A short discussion of the materials required and the energy capable of being released is included.' The whereabouts of this enclosure is not known. The declassified portion of the report, signed by Captain Helenes T. Freiberger and circulated to various departments in 248 copies, reads as follows:

> A man named ZINSSER, a flak rocket expert, mentioned what he noticed one day. 'In the beginning of October 1944 I flew from Ludwigslust south of Lübeck, about 12 to 15 km from an atomic bomb test station, when I noticed a strong, bright illumination of the whole atmosphere, lasting about two seconds. The clearly visible pressure wave escaped the approaching and following cloud formed by the explosion. This wave had a diameter of about 1 km when it became visible and the colour of the cloud changed frequently. It became

dotted after a short period of darkness with all sorts of light spots which were, in contrast to normal explosions, of a pale blue colour. After about ten seconds the sharp outlines of the explosion cloud disappeared, then the cloud began to take on a lighter colour against the sky covered with a grey overcast. The diameter of the still-visible pressure wave was at least 9,000 metres while remaining visible for at least 15 seconds. Personal observations of the colours of the explosion cloud found an almost blue-violet shade. During this manifestation reddish-coloured rims were to be seen, changing to a dirty-like shade in very rapid succession. The combustion was lightly felt from my observation aircraft in the form of pulling and pushing. The appearance of atmospheric disturbance lasted about ten seconds without noticeable climax. About one hour later I took off in an He 111 from the aerodrome at Ludwigslust and flew in an easterly direction. Shortly after the start I passed through the almost complete overcast (between 3,000 and 4,000 metres altitude). A cloud shaped like a mushroom with turbulent, billowing sections stood, without any seeming connections, over the spot where the explosion took place. Strong electrical disturbances and the impossibility to continue radio communication as by lightning, turned up. Because of the P-38s operating in the area Wittenberg-Merseburg I had to turn to the north but observed a better visibility at the bottom of the cloud where the explosion occurred. Note: It does not seem very clear to me why these experiments took place in such crowded areas.'

This interrogation was evaluated B-1 on a reliability scale A-1 to E-0. The principal pointers to be drawn from the report are: a nuclear 'fireball' (if there was one) lasting about two seconds indicates an explosion with a force equal to 1,000 tons TNT; Zinsser gives no description of the 'fireball' itself, nor does he say whether he was looking at it or away from it; Zinsser has no qualms about radioactive fallout; and from his note neither did the municipal authorities of the communities near where these tests were made. This prompts the question: was there any radioactive fallout, and if not, why not? Furthermore it would seem that if this actually was fissile material, Germany had amassed so much of it as to carry out at least two, and probably more, tests.

Despite the aerial bombardment of Berlin, the nuclear research programme continued there until the end of 1944. In January 1945 a reactor experiment using an arrangement of 680 uranium cubes weighing 1,500 kg was tested after which the project was evacuated to Berlin-Kummersdorf and from there, on 7 February 1945, to Stadtilm in the Harz where a laboratory had been established in the cellars of the village school the previous year.

Exactly what stage the other research groups reached is not clear. A Dr Seuffert headed the principal SS project which had a laboratory between Ohrdruf and Arnstadt in a place code-named 'Burg'. This is believed to have been the secret gigantic underground *Führer* HQ below the military training ground at Ohrdruf. Seuffert's group received massive financial and material support from the *Reichverband* of German industry.

According to authors Edgar Mayer and Thomas Mehner, a 100-gram nuclear explosive was tested at the Ohrdruf military training ground at 2126 hours on 4 March 1945. The explosive charge was attached to a funicular device and detonated a few metres above ground level. German sources allege that about 680 prisoners and 20 SS guards were positioned too close to the explosion, as a result of which all suffered very serious burns. Those worst afflicted in both groups were put out of their misery, their bodies being removed to an open pyre at Gut Ringhofen near Wechmar in Thuringia, the ashes being scattered far and wide afterwards. The other survivors continued to complain of severe headaches and persistent nosebleeds, and many more succumbed to their untreatable burns over the next few days. On 12 March 1945, towards 2214 hours, a second 'atomic test' was made at Ohrdruf, this time without casualties.

The Ordnance

It is said that on 27 March 1945 Hitler arrived in Thuringia for a secret conference with Göring, Himmler, Field Marshal Kesselring, Kammler and Speer to discuss how best to use the new miracle weapons. Hitler is reported to have been in favour of using 'a radioactive explosive', although what form this would take is not explained. Both Speer and Himmler were vehemently opposed to the use of this particular weapon as the warhead for long-range rockets.

After this altercation, Hitler allegedly suffered a nervous breakdown, feeling himself betrayed. Whether the alleged meeting ever took place is an open question although it may have done, for according to his valet Linge, Hitler absented himself for short periods from the Berlin Chancellery bunkers on several occasions during March 1945. For his part, Field Marshal Kesselring (a *Luftwaffe* officer who was then Commander-in-Chief West) stated in his autobiography that his last meeting with Hitler was on 12 March 1945, when the *Führer* seemed buoyed up with great optimism and spoke of new weapons which would finally bring the turn of the tide for Germany's abysmal fortunes.

Some German authors seem convinced that Germany had a number of small atom bombs in store at the beginning of April 1945, but for various reasons these were not operational. What the Allied research groups uncovered in terms of nuclear-type technologies at Ohrdruf when the area was overrun in April 1945 remains unknown, since all documents have been classified for at least 100 years from 1945. Nevertheless, US scientific officers left broad hints that the German research was close to a successful conclusion. The reader is therefore left to draw his own conclusions. It is the conclusion of this author that Germany had an acute lack of resources for the manufacture of tactical nuclear weapons, and it is extremely difficult to take seriously the idea of 'tactical nuclear weapons' or *Siegeswaffen* thrown forth by certain areas of German publishing in recent years.

Acknowledgements

I owe a special debt of gratitude to Karl-Ernst Heinkel, son of the late Professor (Ing.) Ernst Heinkel, who supplied works files relating to the He 177, He 274 and He 277 bombers enabling fresh light to be thrown on the development history of these aircraft. Dr Sönke Neitzel provided comprehensive special knowledge regarding *Luftwaffe* operations over the sea. Dieter Herwig supplemented the material with many hitherto unpublished files, sketches and photos, those particularly important being the Focke-Wulf and Junkers planned long-range aircraft. For information on Dornier and Messerschmitt designs I am indebted to their respective archive staffs. Help also came from many aviation enthusiasts. I make special mention of Messrs Balss, Bekker, Borzutzki, Creek, Dabrowski, Grosz, Jarski, Jurleit, Dr Koos, Dip-Ing. Kössler, Krieg, Lang, Lutz jr, Morrn, Müller, Müller-Romminger, Nowarra, Radinger, Ransom, Ricco, Rohrbach, Schliephake, Schmitt, Schreiber, Selinger, Sengfelder and Walter who lent advice, photographs and unpublished files. Fraport AG Frankfurt, Deutsche Lufthansa Cologne, Airbus Industries Bremen and the former Messerschmitt-Bolköw-Blohm (EADS) archives co-operated selflessly in the provision of illustrations and documents.

I feel it right to emphasise that the development of aviation has been an integral part of European history and the record must be preserved for future generations. Research into the German *Luftwaffe* needs all pertinent photographs, books and documents to be put at the disposal of the historian. The setting up of aviation archives by groups of enthusiasts is another way in which our unique aviation-historical heritage can be maintained.

On a personal note I am always grateful to receive substantiated indications of error, fair criticism, encouragement and suggestions. Most important, however, is a very broad echo from the readership.

Manfred Griehl

Bibliography

UNPUBLISHED SOURCES – SELECTED LISTING
Files and reports of KdE Rechlin
Files and documents of Fighter and Armament Staffs
Ministry for Armament and War Production (RMfRuK) Documents
Correspondence and Reports of KG 76
Correspondence and files, Reich Air Ministry Technical Office
Technical and sales files, Arado, BMW, Dornier, Heinkel, Horten,
   Junkers/Jumo and Messerschmitt companies

A listing of the approximately 5,500 individual original
documents consulted has not been included for reasons of space.

PUBLISHED SOURCES – SELECTED LISTING
Absolon, R., *Rangliste der Generale der Deutschen Luftwaffe nach
   dem Stand vom 20 April 1945* (Podzun-Pallas Verlag: Friedberg,
   1984)
Baumbach, W., *Zu Spät: Aufstieg und Untergang der Deutschen
   Luftwaffe* (Richard Pflaum Verlag: Munich, 1949); trans. as *Broken
   Swastika: The Defeat of the Luftwaffe* (Robert Hale: London, 1960)
Bekker, C., *Angriffshöhe 4000: Ein Kriegstagebuch der Deutschen
   Luftwaffe* (Gerhard Stalling Verlag: Hamburg, 1964)
Benecke, T., K.-H. Hedwig and J. Hermann, *Flugkörper und
   Bordraketen* (Bernard & Graefe: Koblenz, 1987)
Bontrup, H.-J., and N. Zdrowomyslaw, *Die Deutsche
   Rüstungsindustrie: Ein Handbuch* (Distel Verlag: Heilbronn, 1988)
Boog, H., *Die Deutsche Luftwaffenführung, 1939–1945* (Deutsche
   Verlags Anstalt: Stuttgart, 1982)
Bower, Tom, *The Paperclip Conspiracy: The Battle for the Spoils and
   Secrets of Nazi Germany* (Michael Joseph: London, 1987)
Brandt, L. (ed.), *Bordfunkgeräte der Deutschen Luftwaffe, 1939–1945*
   (Ausschuß für Funkortung: Düsseldorf, 1958)
Brütting, G., *Das Buch der Deutschen Fluggeschichte* (Drei Brunnen
   Verlag: Stuttgart, 1979), vol. 3

Bibliography

Cescotti, R., *Kampfflugzeuge und Aufklärer* (Bernard & Graefe: Koblenz, 1989)

Dabrowski, H. P., *Deutsche Nurflügel bis 1945* (Podzun-Pallas Verlag: Wölfersheim-Berstadt, 1995)

Dierich, W., *Die Verbände der Luftwaffe, 1939–1945* (Motorbuch Verlag: Stuttgart, 1976)

Dornberger, W., *V2: Der Schuss ins Weltall* (Bechtle-Verlag: Esslingen, 1952); trans. as *V2* (Hurst & Blackett: London, 1954)

Feuchter, G. W., *Geschichte des Luftkriegs: Entwicklung und Zukunft* (Athenäum Verlag: Bonn, 1954)

Fleischer, W., *Heeresversuchsstelle Kummersdorf 1874 bis 1945* (Podzun-Pallas Verlag: Wölfersheim-Berstadt, 1999), vol. 2

Fliedl, G., and B. Perz, *Konzentrationslagen Melk* (Niederösterreichische Landesregierung: Vienna, 1992)

Freund, F., *KZ Ebensee* (Dokumentationsarchiv des Österreichischen Widerstandes: Vienna, 1990)

Georg, F., *Hitlers Siegeswaffen* (Amun Verlag: Schleusingen, 2000), vol. 1

Gersdorf, K. von, and K. Grasmann, *Flugmotoren und Strahltriebwerke* (Bernard & Graefe: Munich, 1981)

Green, W., *The Warplanes of the Third Reich* (Macdonald & Co.: London, 1970)

Griehl, M., *Jet Planes of the Third Reich* (Monogram Aviation Publications: Sturbridge, MA, 1998)

Griehl, M., and J. Dressel, *Bombers of the Luftwaffe*, trans. M. J. Shields (Arms & Armour Press: London, 1994)

—— *Deutsche Fernkampfflugzeuge der Luftwaffe* (Podzun-Pallas Verlag: Friedberg, 1993)

—— *Die Deutschen Kampfflugzeuge im Einsatz, 1936–1945* (Podzun-Pallas Verlag: Friedberg, 1990)

—— *Heinkel He 177-277-274* (Motorbuch Verlag: Stuttgart, 1993)

Hahn, F., *Deutsche Geheimwaffen, 1939–1945* (Erich Hoffmann Verlag: Heidenheim, 1963)

—— *Waffen und Geheimwaffen des Deutschen Heeres, 1933–1945* (Bernard & Graefe: Koblenz, 1987)

Hellmold, W., *Die V1* (Bechtle Verlag: Esslingen, 1988)

Henshall, P., *Vengeance: Hitler's Nuclear Weapon* (Alan Sutton: Stroud, 1995)

Bibliography

Hentschel, G., *Die Geheimen Konferenzen des General-luftzeugmeisters* (Bernard & Graefe: Koblenz, 1989)

Hildebrand, K. F., *Die Generale der Deutschen Luftwaffe, 1939–1945* (Biblio Verlag: Osnabrück, 1990), vols 1–3

Hillgruber, A., *Der 2. Weltkrieg: Kriegsziele und Strategie der Großen Mächte* (Kohlhammer Verlag: Stuttgart, 1982)

Hoffmann, D., *Operation Epsilon* (Rowalt Verlag: Berlin, 1993)

Hogg, I. V., *German Secret Weapons of the Second World War* (Greenhill Books: London, 1999)

Hölsken, D., *Missiles of the Third Reich* (Monogram Aviation Publications: Sturbridge, 1994)

Horten, R., and P. F. Selinger, *Nurflügel* (H. Weißhaupt Verlag: Graz, 1983)

Hubatsch, W., *Hitlers Weisungen für die Kriegsführung, 1939–1945* (Bernard & Graefe: Koblenz, 1983)

Irving, D., *Die Tragödie der Deutschen Luftwaffe* (Verlag Ullstein: Frankfurt, 1970); trans. rev. edn *The Rise and Fall of the Luftwaffe: The Life of Luftwaffe Marshal Edward Milch* (Weidenfeld & Nicolson: London, 1973)

Johnson, B., *Streng Geheim: Wissenschaft und Technik im 2. Weltkrieg* (Motorbuch Verlag: Stuttgart, 1983)

Klee, E., and O. Merk, *Damals in Peenemünde* (Gerhard Stalling Verlag: Hamburg, 1963)

Köberl, M., *Der Toplitzsee* (ÖBV Publikumsverlag/ Wissenschaftsverlag: Vienna, 1990)

Köhler, H. D., *Ernst Heinkel: Pionier der Schnellflugzeuge* (Bernard & Graefe: Bonn, 1999)

Kössler, K., and G. Ott, *Die Großen Dessauer* (Aviatik Verlag: Planegg, 1993)

Kranzhoff, J. A., *Arado-Flugzeuge: Vom Doppeldecker zum Strahlflugzeug* (Bernard & Graefe: Bonn, 2001)

Krausenberger, W. W. G. E., *Dokumentation zu Leben und Werk* (Deutsche Gesellschaft für Luft- und Raumfahrt e.V.: Bonn, n.d.)

Lange, B., *Typenbuch der Deutschen Luftfahrttechnik* (Bernard & Graefe: Koblenz, 1986)

Lusar, R., *Die Deutschen Waffen und Geheimwaffen des 2. Weltkriegs*, rev. edn (Lehmanns Verlag: Munich, 1971); 2nd edn trans. as *German Secret Weapons of the Second World War*

(Neville Spearman: London, 1959)

Mason, H. M., *Die Luftwaffe: Aufbau, Aufstieg und Scheitern im Sieg* (Paul Neff Verlag: Vienna and Berlin, 1973)

Mayer, E., and T. Mehner, *Die Atombombe und das Dritte Reich* (Jochen Kopp Verlag: Rottenburg, 2002)

Mehner, K., *Die Geheimen Tagesberichte der Deutschen Wehrmachtsführung im Zweiten Weltkrieg, 1939–1945* (Biblio Verlag: Osnabrück, 1984–95), vols 1–12

Mehner, K., and R. Teuber, *Die Deutsche Luftwaffe, 1939–1945: Führung und Truppe* (Militärverlag Klaus D. Patzwall: Norderstedt, 1993)

Myhra, D., *The Horton Brothers and Their All-Wing Aircraft* (Schiffer Military Aviation: Atglen, PA, 1998)

Naasner, W., *Neue Machtzentrum in der Deutschen Kriegswirtschaft, 1942 bis 1945* (Harald Boldt Verlag: Boppard am Rhein, 1994)

Nagel, G., *Atomversuche in Deutschland* (Heinrich Jung Verlags: Zella-Mehlis, 2002)

Neitzel, S., *Der Einsatz der Deutschen Luftwaffe über dem Atlantik und der Nordsee, 1939–1945* (Bernard & Graefe: Bonn, 1995)

Nowarra, H. J., *Trumpf oder Bluff? 12 Jahre Deutsche Luftwaffe* (Selbstverlag: Genf, 1947)

Powers, T., *Heisenbergs Krieg* (Hoffmann & Campe: Hamburg, 1993)

—— *The Rise and Fall of the German Air Force, 1939–1945* (Arms & Armour Press: London, 1983)

Roeder, Jean, *Bombenflugzeuge und Aufklärer* (Bernard & Graefe: Koblenz, 1990)

Rohwer, J., and G. Hümmelchen, *Chronik des Seekrieges, 1939–1945* (Gerhard Stalling Verlag: Oldenburg, 1968); 3rd trans. rev. edn *Chronology of the War at Sea, 1939–1945* (Greenhill Books: London, 2005)

Schaber, R., *Die Illusion der Wunderwaffen* (R. Oldenbourg Verlag: Munich, 1994)

Schliepharke, H., *Die Bordwaffen der Luftwaffe von den Anfängen bis zur Gegenwart* (Motorbuch Verlag: Stuttgart, 1977)

Schramm, P. E. (ed.), *Kriegstagebuch des Oberkommandos der Wehrmacht, 1940–1945* (Bernard & Graefe: Munich, 1982)

Schulze-Wegener, G., *Die Deutsche Kriegsmarine-Rüstung, 1942–1945* (Verlag E. S. Mittler & Sohn: Hamburg, Berlin and Bonn, 1997)

Bibliography

Simon, L. E., *Secret Weapons of the Third Reich* (WE: Old Greenwich, CT, 1971)

Smith, J. R., and E. Creek, *Jet Planes of the Third Reich* (Monogram Aviation Publications: Boylston, MA, 1982)

Stockhorst E., *Wer War Was im Dritten Reich* (VMA Verlag: Wiesbaden, n.d.)

Stubner, H., *Das Kampfflugzeug Heinkel He 177 'Greif' und Seine Weiterentwicklung* (Eurodoc Cooperation Verlagsgesellschaft: Zurich, 2003)

Stüwe, B., *Peenemünde West* (Bechtle Verlag: Esslingen/Munich 1995)

Tessin, G., *Verbände und Truppen der Deutschen Wehrmacht und Waffen-SS im Zweiten Weltkreig, 1939–1945* (Biblio Verlag: Osnabrück, 1980), vol. 14

Trenkle, F., *Die Deutschen Funkmeßverfahren bis 1945* (Motorbuch Verlag: Stuttgart, 1979)

—— *Vom Funkensender zum Bordradar* (Bernard & Graefe: Koblenz, 1986)

Wagner, J. C., *Produktion des Todes* (Wallstein Verlag: Göttingen, 2001)

Wagner, W., *Kurt Tank: Konstrukteur und Testpilot bei Focke-Wulf* (Bernard & Graefe: Munich, 1980); trans. as *Kurt Tank: Focke-Wulf's Designer and Test Pilot* (Schiffer Military Aviation: Atglen, PA, 1998)

Wolf, W., *Luftangriffe auf die Deutsche Industrie* (Universitas Verlag: Munich, 1985)

Zuerl, A., *Arado-Flugzeuge* (Luftfahrt Verlag A. Zuerl: Steineback, n.d.)

Index

Page numbers in *italics* refer to illustration captions.

Index

Index